Coaching Champions for Life

Coaching Champions for Life

Coaching the whole person, not just the athlete.

By *Adam Sarancik*

Foreword by Jamie Quirk

Coaching Champions for Life

To my wife, Karen, without your love and support I could not accomplish anything worthwhile in my life. And, to my girls, Corinne and Lauren, you are my heroes and my inspiration.

Charlie,

Thank you for being such a great student of the game. Please remember to always coach "Champions for life"!

Peace,

Coach Adam

What Champions are saying about *Coaching Champions For Life:*

"This is an excellent book for preparing coaches in all sports activities because it defines the process of teaching athlete's responsibility, confidence, respect and trust which ultimately leads to success in all areas of one's life."

Jerry Gatto, **Head Baseball Coach**
Lewis & Clark College 1980-2002
NAIA District II Hall of Fame
Oregon HS Coaches Hall of Fame

"Coaching Champions for Life is a unique look at coaching with baseball as the backdrop. It reminds coaches just how important a role we play in the lives of our players and challenges us to look closely at the core of what we are teaching our athletes and the values they will need to succeed in life. This inspirational, educational and thought-provoking book provides you with a 'how-to' formula for doing just that."

Donald E. Reynolds
MLB Scout
Arizona Diamondbacks

"This book is a great resource for sports organizations, individual coaches at all levels and colleges on the mental, physical and spiritual aspects of coaching philosophy, skills of the game and time management."

Randy Rutschman, **Assistant Coach**
George Fox College
2004 Division III National Champions

"I have been coaching baseball for over 30 years, and this book is outstanding. The baseball concepts are very good, but more importantly, the methods used to teach kids baseball and life skills are exceptional. If coaches really understand that our main job is to develop 'championship people' through baseball, then this book is a must read."

Steve Nicollerat, **Head Baseball Coach**
St. Louis University High School
Missouri High School Coaches Hall of Fame

"While the book inspires as well as outlines specific, detailed, non-negotiable team winning baseball fundamentals and strategies, *Coaching Champions for Life* also calls out coaches to recognize the benefits, responsibility and higher calling of mentoring athletes within the game, for beyond the game."

Alex Esquerra, Head Baseball Coach & Pastor
Horizon Christian High School
3A Oregon State Champions 2011

"This is a fabulous book that gives readers so much more than just coaching the mechanics of baseball. It gives them the methodology to teach life skills that will carry our youth well beyond their playing days. These life skills will help make our youth honorable and productive adults in the competitive world we live in. *Coaching Champions for Life* is a great tool for any coach, athlete or parent looking to become a True Champion."

Greg Cochran, Pitcher
Arizona State University
Career Record 18-1, era 2.41
3-time Conference Champions
2-time National Runners-Up

"Coach Adam's book has opened my coaching eyes to new philosophies, drills and coaching awareness for players that I have never used before in my day-to-day baseball practices. You will learn something new you didn't know about coaching baseball. This is a must read for all coaches on any level of baseball who try and teach the game of baseball the right way to kids and young adults."

Joe Melendez, Baseball Coach
High School & Youth Travel Teams
Southern California

"As a player, I appreciate the detail in which Coach Adam describes the teaching methodology to coaching baseball and more importantly, to building young athletes into people of character and integrity. In particular, I think the philosophies of 'Let Your Players Play' and avoiding 'Motivation by Intimidation' need to be more widely adopted. The chapter on preparing an athlete for playing a sport in college is spot on and is something every athlete should know and follow."

Ben Swinford, Infielder
Cornell University Baseball
2010 - Present

CONTENTS

Foreword   x

Preface   xiv

Chapter One   **Developing Championship Teams**   1
Chapter Two   **Developing Championship Athletes**   11
Chapter Three   **Championship Physical Conditioning**   25
Chapter Four   **Championship Mental Conditioning**   49
Chapter Five   **Developing Championship Leaders
                    & Team Chemistry**   71
Chapter Six   **Preparing For Championship Practices**   81
Chapter Seven   **Executing Championship Practices**   107
Chapter Eight   **Developing College-Bound Champions**   183
Chapter Nine   **Let Champions Play**   209
Chapter Ten   **Coaching Championship Games**   213
Epilogue   **Champions for Life**   227

Appendix A   **Coaching Philosophy**   229
Appendix B   **Top Ten Things Teams Need To Do
                    To Have A Championship Season**   231
Appendix C   **Team Rules**   233
Appendix D   **Running Form Warm Up**   234
Appendix E   **Running and Stretching Warm Up**   235
Appendix F   **Rules When Talking To The Media**   238
Appendix G   **Player and Family Contract**   239
Appendix H   **Sample Team Inventory**   242
Appendix I   **Sample Informed Consent Form**   244
Appendix J   **Sample Inherent Risks and
                    Participation Agreement Form**   246
Appendix K   **Sample Consent for Medical
                    Treatment and Facility Use Form**   248
Appendix L   **Sample Practice Plan**   250
Appendix M   **Multi-tasking Option List**   252
Appendix N   **Continuous 1st and 3rds Game**   255
Appendix O   **Throwing and Receiving Progression**   256
Appendix P   **General Pitching Strategy**   258

Appendix Q	**Pitch Sequence Rules and Drills**	259
Appendix R	**3 'n 1 Drills**	261
Appendix S	**Wall Ball Routine**	264
Appendix T	**On-Field Batting Practice Routine**	266
Appendix U	**SAQ/Conditioning Drills**	267
Appendix V	**Camp/Tryout/Showcase Guidelines**	275
Appendix W	**Sample Letter to College Coach**	277
Appendix X	**Questions College Coaches Ask**	279

Bibliography	280
Index	284
About the Author	294
Book Order Form	295

FOREWORD

I have been blessed to excel as an athlete and to play, teach and coach at the very highest levels of my chosen sport of baseball. I've played and coached for some 39 years in Major League Baseball. And before that, I participated in youth and high school baseball, which is where I first came to know Adam Sarancik as a player.

Adam's new book, _Champions for Life_, is an outstanding assemblage of teaching and coaching techniques developed by him during a lifetime of playing on and leading very successful athletic teams. In this book, Adam presents his tried and true methodologies for teaching readers how to move from "just coaching" to "developing future leaders".

These leaders will not only compete at the highest levels of their sport, but will be ready for life as confident, self-assured, contributors to their families, professions and communities.

Adam's approach as a coach is to impart to our youth (and some parents) lessons in character development -- "skills for life"-- how to deal with and learn from adversity and to trust in themselves and their teammates. His attention to modeling and teaching exemplary character behaviors, both on and off the field, is central to his book's goal of building personal and spiritual integrity in your players.

Winning is phenomenal and losing is inevitable. As I've seen over these many years, it is how you deal with both that makes a true champion. Humility in winning and learning from adversity.

Through the following pages, Adam will guide you step-by-step on a journey as a coach, teacher and leader that can not only alter your life, but can make all those involved with you, **_Champions for Life._**

- Jamie Quirk

Jamie Quirk was a three sport star and an All-State quarterback in high school in California. In 1972, he was offered a scholarship to play football at Notre Dame University, but chose to go directly into professional baseball.

For 18 years, he was an outstanding catcher and utility player for the Kansas City Royals, Milwaukie Brewers, St. Louis Cardinals, Chicago White Sox, Cleveland Indians, New York Yankees, Oakland Athletics and Baltimore Orioles. He won a world championship with the Royals in 1985 and American League Crowns with the Royals in 1980 and the Athletics in 1990.

Since 1994, he has been a pitching coach, bullpen coach or a bench coach for the Kansas City Royals, Texas Rangers, Colorado Rockies , the Houston Astros and currently the Chicago Cubs. In 2009, he was a professional scout for the Cincinnati Reds and a third base coach for Team USA in the World Cup competition in Europe. He also works with the MLB Cable Network.

Jamie and his wife Anna live in Kansas City, Missouri and have three children, daughter, Kindal, and sons, Kelly and Kemer.

Coaching Champions for Life

ACKNOWLEDGEMENTS

First, I want to acknowledge all of the boys and girls who have played for me in any sport. Your willingness to learn made all the hours worthwhile. Watching you play was a tremendous source of joy in my life. Seeing you continue to succeed at higher levels of the sport, hearing from you that you used what you learned on our teams to help you succeed in life and most importantly, hearing that you used what you learned to teach others how to live a life of high moral integrity gives me a feeling that my life had some significance.

I also want to thank all of my assistant coaches, the parents of my athletes and the coaches at the lower levels who taught sound fundamentals and instilled the joy of learning and of the sport into the hearts of my athletes. You are the unsung heroes of sports. Your efforts made everything I accomplished possible.

David Mays invested an enormous amount of time and passion into taking many of the photos in this book. They are awesome!

The cover of the book continues to have a profound impact on everyone who sees it. Thank you to Joe Valentine for his excellent work in its design.

Finally, I want to thank Jamie Quirk, Jim Paino, Doug Brewer and Alex Esquerra for your advice on the writing of the book, your friendship and your support of my coaching through the years.

You are great examples of *Champions for Life*.

PREFACE

I have been blessed to be a youth sports coach for both boys and girls ages 8 - 18 for many years. In reflecting upon how I could give back to the coaching profession through this book, I asked myself, "What is the most important part of coaching?"

The answer was easy.

It is not the "x's and o's", i.e., the mechanics of the sport, that are the most important part of coaching. The most important part of coaching is developing character in your players.

Therefore, I wrote this book to give others the benefit of my coaching experience so they can make a real difference in the lives of their players. "Experience", by the way, does not mean that I always did things right. Many times I did, but sometimes I learned what I should have done.

In the book, what I say applies equally to both men and women coaches and to both boy and girl athletes. For ease of reading, I have not always referred to both genders in a sentence.

When I do not, please understand that both genders are always implied unless I specifically state to the contrary.

There may be things in this book that those who read it do not know. There may be things in this book that those who read it already know, but they are in denial about admitting. And there may be things in this book that those who read it already know and acknowledge, but they are grateful I took the time to write them down so they can use them as an easy reference.

Most importantly, I want the persons who read this book to pass along the information to other coaches and athletes. As Jackie Robinson said, *"The measure of a life's significance is the impact it had on other lives"*.

Most of this book is not about the fundamentals and mechanics of coaching baseball. In short, this book is more about methodology than mechanics.

The methodology and lessons I recommend in this book apply to coaching all sports, not just baseball.

I will admit, however, that I'm amazed I could write an entire book without giving my opinion in great detail about how to properly throw, field or hit a baseball. After many years of coaching many successful baseball players and teams, I think I have sound advice on how to do these things, but many resources already exist describing these things. I have given you some great references for this in the Bibliography at the end of the book. What I've done instead is to give you tools and a process so that while you're coaching the "x's and o's", you can be sure your players are getting the most from your coaching, about your sport, but more importantly, about life.

What I am asking you to remember always is that *we coach people not sports.*

All successful coaching starts with understanding the individual players. You may coach a team sport, but until you understand the values, emotional make-up, hopes and dreams of each of your players, you cannot truly be a successful coach.

Your success as a coach is not defined by your wins and losses.

Your success is defined by how many of your players want to coach other players *using to teach what you taught them about life.*

You have also been successful as a coach if your players use what you taught them to be great parents, spouses and community leaders. You will be a successful coach when you stop coaching primarily to win championships. Although if you follow the advice I give to you in this book, you will win championships. You will be a successful coach when you are successful at developing players with high moral character and integrity - *Champions For Life.*

It is for you, for them, and for that purpose that I wrote this book.

Coaching Champions for Life

CHAPTER ONE

DEVELOPING CHAMPIONSHIP TEAMS

"Be strong and courageous, and He shall strengthen your heart, all of you who put your hope in the Lord." Psalm 31:25

The formula for winning championships is really no secret.

If the quality of the competition is high, winning championships is not easy, but how to do it is no secret.   In baseball, an age-old saying is that pitching and defense win championships.

Yes, okay, if everyone knows that, why are some coaches more successful at consistently winning than others?

Above Average Talent at the "Skill Positions"

True, you have to have talent to win consistently.

Players with great natural skills make good coaches look great.   But I do not think you need to have great players with great natural talent to win championships.   What I think you need are players *at the skill positions* with above average talent.

In baseball, for example, you need players with above average talent "up the middle" on defense (catcher, pitchers, shortstop, second base and center field) and fundamentally sound, unselfish hitters on offense.

I will discuss the specifics of how to develop individual talent in the next chapter.

Extraordinary Commitment

As a team, the second thing you need is extraordinary commitment by the coaches and the players to getting better every day.

What is "extraordinary" is somewhat relative to the level of commitment of your competition. The first year I was head coach of my last high school team, the team in prior years had become comfortable with being mediocre. They assumed they could never win league championships because other teams always had better talent and facilities than they did.

Of course, the first thing I did as the new coach was to eliminate this type of self-defeating thinking.

Next, I challenged my team to look closely as to why the school that typically won the league championship each year was so successful. During that first season, the traditional powerhouse team beat the second place team at home 9-2.

Instead of packing up and leaving to celebrate their victory, once the other team got on the bus, the *winning team* began a two-hour practice!

This type of "commitment" may not be appropriate for every team and game, but it was a key insight into the level of commitment we were going to have to exceed if we were going to win championships in that league.

That traditionally powerful team beat us easily both times we played them that first year with them using mostly second team pitchers and players. The following year we did not play them because the State rezoned the school districts and put them in a different league. However, the next two years we beat them in the State playoffs while going 31-1 in League and winning back-to-back League Championships.

We did not have extraordinarily talented players. We just had extraordinary commitment from our coaches and a core group of our players.

A "Get Better Every Day" Work Ethic

The next thing the team needs is a "get better every day" work ethic. This is not just a philosophy. It is an everyday work habit that never changes. The "Need To Get Better" list for *myself* and for the team is written every season the evening of the last game. The team cannot get better if I do not get better. And we both need to get better regardless of whether we won the Championship or not.

There are only two types of games from my perspective- well played or poorly coached.

If we lost, I did not do a good enough job of coaching. No other type of thinking will lead to winning consistently and being the best you can be as a coach. Losing does not mean that my players did not do many, many things well. They probably did and that's all they need to hear immediately after the game. But if we lost, I always think I was the difference maker and somewhere in my teaching the physical, mental or emotional components of the game I failed to make a winning difference.

I mentioned above that immediately after the game anything said to the players should be positive. I know many coaches will disagree with this. It is customary in baseball, for example, to take your team to the outfield after the game, have the players "take a knee" and have the coaches give them "feedback" about what they observed during the game. Some of this feedback is harshly negative at times.

I would challenge you as a coach to do things differently in the future if this is your habit up to now. Remember when you played the game? What was the time you were the least attentive and receptive to others giving you "constructive criticism" because you were deeply consumed with dealing with your own emotions? That's right, immediately after the game. Furthermore, would the content or tone of what you said after the game have changed if you had more time to process it?

Most importantly, you want your players to learn to think the game. Give them 24 hours to think about what they saw and felt during the game and let them tell you at the next practice about it.

An age old saying in sports is, *"No game was ever won by what the coach knows. It's what the players have learned that matters."*

The players will learn best when they talk first and have had more time to think about it. The primary responsibility for learning is on the players, but you must be a good facilitator for that learning. You, as their coach, will also learn more about how well you have taught them if they speak first.

And no, you should not have the "constructive criticism" conference right after the game because you think the details will be fresher in their mind. They will not forget the details about the game by the next day. On the contrary, you and they will think of more to say, be able to express it more clearly and in a more appropriate manner if you have taken some time to think about it.

It's similar to that old sage advice about the harshly negative letter you want to send to someone you are extremely upset with. They tell you to put the letter in a drawer for two days and if, after that time, you still want to send it, then it is probably okay to do so.

The same goes for harsh criticism of your team. If you still feel like being harsh with them by the next day or practice about how they performed during the game, then go right ahead and let them know how and why they need to do better.

Just be sure to let them know you're equally disappointed in the coaching staff. Remember, we are the first persons responsible for every poor performance.

If you suffer an intense, heart-breaking "walk-off home run" type of defeat in a big game, you definitely want to talk to your team immediately after it to be sure they remain positive and do not carry the emotion of the game home with them in any significant way. That type of conference, however, is not done with them "taking a knee". For that conference, they should all stand close to one another and to you. You look them all in the eye so that they can see into your heart to know you truly believe everything is okay. Whether they believe you or not, whether they walk away from the conference with their heads held high and whether they have a bounce in their step after the conference will be a big insight into whether you have a championship team in the making.

Talk to your team after each game, but keep the comments all positive and supportive. If you cannot say anything nice, don't say anything at all until the next day or practice. In that case, you need to take a good long look at your coaching before you say anything negative about the team.

So far we have looked at the first three components to developing championship teams: (1) developing above average individual talent at the skill positions; (2) having an extraordinary commitment from the players and the coaches to getting better every day; and (3) the development of an extraordinary time commitment into the practice of an extraordinary work ethic.

A Standard of Excellence

The next essential component to a championship program is *setting a standard of excellence, not just a goal to be excellent.* Everyone knows, *"Practice does not make perfect. Practice makes permanent, only perfect practice makes perfect".* However, few teams make this their standard every day, at every practice and in every way.

John Wooden, Hall of Fame basketball coach at UCLA and recognized as one of the greatest coaches of all time in any sport (but whose favorite sport was baseball, by the way), taught his players "the proper way to put on their socks and shoes". Hall of Fame pro football coach, Vince Lombardi said, "Perfection is not attainable, but if we chase perfection we can catch excellence". Championship teams understand that excellence must be their standard in every detail on and off the field.

> *There is no "light switch for excellence" for performing under pressure. You either live it day-to-day in every way or you watch the other team hoist the trophy.*

This standard of excellence must be enforced by the players themselves as well as by the coaches. *The link between preach and teach is player accountability.* And player accountability starts with players who know how to be leaders. I will discuss developing leaders in another chapter as well. But the fact remains, a team with no leaders or poor leadership is a team headed for dissension and disaster.

Adequate Time

The next component is the element of time. "Rome was not built in a day" and neither are championship programs.

How long it will take to build a championship program may be the biggest variable. The number of other high caliber programs you are competing with, the depth of their talent pool and the consistency of their "feeder" programs compared to your program will greatly influence how long it will take you to develop a program that consistently contends for the championship.

Effective and Efficient Practices

Some of these factors may be tough to control or to influence. However, one factor definitely in your control, which distinguishes most top programs I know of, is the efficiency of the practices. Good coaches know that *when it comes to teaching the fundamentals, 12 x 5 is greater than 60 x 1.* Your players will retain more of what you teach them if you do it over and over again day after day rather than, for example, bunting 500 balls in one day to "cover it".

However, to be able to teach the fundamentals frequently you must have well-planned, well-conceived and highly organized and efficient practices. You will see in Chapters Six and Seven that this requires adequate facilities and equipment, coaching talent and player accountability for the proper attitude, work ethic and development of their teammates.

Perfect practice will lead to perfect execution and great results in games. Make excellence your standard, not just your goal.

Model Feeder Programs

Whatever "feeder" program(s) you have to your program must teach the same fundamentals and systems that you teach.

Your practices will be much more efficient and your time table for achieving excellence will be much shorter if you do not have to re-teach your players when they enter your program.

Every top football and basketball program I know of has ALL of their youth programs run the same offensive and defensive schemes that they do at the high school program. By the time the players arrive at the high school program, the fundamentals and systems seem like second nature to them. The skills do not need to be taught or re-taught. They just need to be refined. This is a huge advantage to those programs that do this, compared to those programs that do not.

The same is true for baseball programs. As the head coach of the high school Varsity program, you need to spend as much time as possible doing coaches' clinics and attending practices and games at your youth feeder programs. When you spot coaching errors, both in teaching the fundamentals and in methodology, they must be corrected immediately. (Of course, the corrections must be done tactfully and at the appropriate time or

Coaching Champions for Life

else you're likely to lose hard-working coaches who, with proper guidance, may do an excellent job.)

The methodology errors may be even more significant than the others because if you take the fun out of the game you may motivate a player to try another district or try another sport altogether.

A strong, well-coached feeder program is a huge key to developing and maintaining the depth of your talent pool.

Player Participation

Once again, the purpose for your program is not primarily about winning games. It is about developing *Champions for Life*.

This requires player participation in every possible aspect of the program. So if you want strong feeder programs to your program, involve your current players in helping with events for the feeder programs. Your current players should take large responsibilities in helping to run the clinics and selected practices of the feeder programs.

This philosophy does not apply exclusively to a high school team. Junior players (11-12 year olds) should help with Midget level (9-10 year olds) events; Senior level (13-14 year olds) players should help at Junior events and high school players should help with Senior level/middle school events.

Sense of Community

Another key to developing a consistent player pipeline is developing a feeling of community for your sport. This should involve players at all levels for your sport in your area.

For example, your high school baseball team could host an annual pancake breakfast as a joint fundraiser for all of the baseball programs. Have the high school players wear their uniforms while serving the event. They should not only serve at the event, but they should make an active effort to socialize with players at the other levels. They should show a sincere interest in the lives of the other players, as well as, communicating how much they enjoy being a part of the high school program.

It is also a smart idea to have a local charitable group, like the Lions Club, to donate equipment and food supplies for the event. This will save you money thereby increasing your profit margin and the community impact of the event.

A fundraiser like a pancake breakfast is one idea, but there are many other good ideas, like service events. Any idea that brings the community together for a common purpose can be a good idea.

In fact, since we are in the business of teaching life lessons, events which are held purely for charitable purposes are much more valuable than those which merely raise money for your program. Gathering baseball equipment and clothing for less fortunate youth in Mexico had a huge impact on my last high school team.

Remember also that one of the biggest mistakes in fundraising comes from thinking that money must be raised directly from the event itself.

I have witnessed many times someone or a group doing something for free out of the goodness of their hearts, which resulted in someone sending in a check for an amount much larger than anything that could have been raised by a for-profit event.

When your players gather equipment and clothing for the less fortunate, you will be teaching them a much more valuable life lesson than when you hold events which merely raise money for your own program.

Becoming Accustomed to Performing Under Pressure

Winning championships requires that players perform at their best under pressure. In my opinion, this is the single biggest reason why "the best team does not always win the game". We all have seen many examples of teams who could beat anybody when it didn't really matter, but when it mattered the most they played poorly.

Obviously, having players who "have been there before" is one way of relieving the feeling of pressure during a championship game. This experience may have come from the players playing in championship games in that sport with that team in prior years or from playing in championship games in other sports that year or in prior years. The "culture of winning" usually spans the entire athletic department if the athletic director and administration are talented, dedicated leaders committed to the same standard of excellence that you are. Remember, *tradition never graduates.*

It bears repeating here again that *there is no light switch for excellence.*

You have either practiced perfectly repetition after repetition, day after day or, when you need it most, the pressure will cause you to perform at less than your best. Confidence is derived from knowing that you have worked harder and smarter, both individually and as a team, than your competition.

Gaining confidence for being able to perform under pressure can be built through your practice time as well. I will detail this more in the chapters on Championship Practices, but the basic message is your players must compete with each other as much as possible every day in practice. 1 v. 1, 2 v. 2, position v. position, "game sim" after "game sim" they must get comfortable with competition at game speed.

> *Any drill in practice that does not, as much as possible, simulate game conditions and game speed is of little value in developing championship players and teams.*

Let me just state one last note on a player's ability to perform under pressure. You will be assisted greatly in your training if the standard of excellence and the need to get better every day is the same at home and at school as it is in your program. Players who can "do no wrong" in other parts of their life are tough players to motivate to practice perfectly every day. This is just a fact, but it is largely out of your control.

> *Parents ask me all the time what they can do to improve their child's chances to be a better athlete. I tell them, "Have them pull more weeds and have them do it perfectly".*

Developing Championship Teams - 9 -

Summary

Championship teams do not just happen. They are built day-by-day through careful design. "Feeder programs" are developed so that high quality athletes, particularly at the skill positions, are consistently fed to your program.

Systems and fundamentals learned by those athletes in the "feeder programs" need to be the same as those you teach in your program. You and your current players will instill a spirit of pride in your program by holding clinics and assisting at practices at those "feeder programs". You and your players also need to host fundraising or charity events to cultivate a feeling of community for your sport in your area.

When players arrive at your school or in your league, they should be welcomed and enveloped by a standard of excellence and a "culture of winning". Championship programs do not tolerate excuses for anything less than an extraordinary commitment to getting better every day. This is accomplished through mastering the fundamentals by thousands of perfect reps performed day-after-day over a long period of time.

Championship practices are well-planned and designed, are highly efficient and emphasize game-speed and game-intensity competitions at every phase. (My general coaching philosophy is summarized in Appendices A-C at the end of the book.)

Finally, when you think you have done everything right to develop a team to win a championship and you do not, you must remember two things: First, the ultimate goal is to develop champions. This is a process and is not determined by whether you won the championship game. Amos Alonzo Stagg, the famous college sports (football, basketball and baseball) coach was asked once if his team had a successful season and he said, "I will not know that for another fifteen or twenty years".

It takes that long to see if the seeds of leadership that you planted have come to fruition by the service of your players to others.

Second, there is no such thing as luck, only the Lord's will. Your plan may be to win the championship. His plan may be for your team to demonstrate how to lose it with class.

There is only one score that counts...His.

CHAPTER TWO

DEVELOPING CHAMPIONSHIP ATHLETES

"A good name is more desirable than great riches, and high esteem, than gold and silver. The rich and the poor have this one thing in common: the Lord is the maker of them all." Proverbs 22:1-2

Unquestionably, you have to have good players, at least at the "skill positions", to win championships. The best coach in the world will not win many games against high caliber competition without good players to effectively implement the systems he has taught them.

As Hall of Fame catcher, Yogi Berra said (as only Yogi could) when asked what makes a good manager, "A good ball club". Many coaches understand the basic mechanics and fundamentals of what their players should do to play their sport well. I also think there are many books, clinics and on-line resources containing basic drills to help you teach the basic mechanics of the sport.

This chapter and book are more about methodology and some of the other areas essential to developing championship athletes, and more importantly, character in championship athletes. In other words, I will not discuss in detail how to throw, field and hit a baseball. It has been said many times, *"There is nothing mysterious about winning. It's a matter of executing the fundamentals"*. Instead, in this book, I will discuss these questions-- when two teams with players of relatively equal ability compete, why will one team prevail? When two players do the exact same mechanics to throw, field and hit, why does one of them do it better?

I will also discuss how to use drills which teach the fundamentals of the sport, in the most effective and efficient manner.

Characteristics of Championship Teams

First, while I will not spend a lot of time discussing them, a few coaching axioms need to be acknowledged. God has given some athletes more physical tools and potential than other athletes. However, if you spend enough time coaching, you will see many more instances of teams with lesser talent winning championships and players with lesser ability excelling at the highest levels than players and teams with exceptional talent maximizing their potential.

In the previous chapter, I discussed why this is true from a team perspective. Championship teams have an exceptional commitment to getting better every day through "perfect practice". This same standard carries over to other sports they play and to all other areas of their life. Championship teams spend more time on more days over a longer period of time mastering the fundamentals, particularly on defense.

Championship teams are mentally tougher, have more "heart" and have a better "team chemistry" than the rest. As a result, they are able to perform at their best even under great pressure because to them it feels like just another game. Much of this "mental toughness" is determined by how much adversity they have been required to overcome in other areas of their life, particularly by how high "the bar has been raised" by their parents, their teachers and by coaches in other sports. So what can you do to get the best out of the athletes you coach?

Why are some coaches able to get their athletes to perform at a higher level when those athletes are doing the same fundamentals as their competitors are doing?

You hear coaches comment all the time that some athletes are just "more coachable" than others. This is just another way of saying that the key to teaching is giving the right person, i.e., one with the requisite skill level, the right information, at the right time, by the right person and in the right way.

Let's break this down, component by component, so you are clear about what I am saying and why some coaches maximize the potential of their athletes while others do not.

The "Right People"

The first thing you need, as I discussed somewhat in the prior chapter, is a deep talent pool. You must develop and nurture your "feeder" leagues and systems.

You must also have a tradition of "success" (the definition of which is subjective, e.g., winning championships, players being successful at the next level after being involved in your program, players enjoying being on your team, players learning "life skills" from you which benefit them in other areas of their life, etc.) and a culture that entices players to want to be involved.

Once they arrive at your program, however, you must be able to recognize talent and potential when you see it.

My advice is to spend your time developing an athlete with average skills with an exceptional work ethic and commitment and a lesser amount of time on an athlete with exceptional skills with a marginal work ethic and commitment. The former will be better team players, will likely develop into better players in the long run and more importantly, will be happier and more of a strong advocate for your program. This will result in you having the opportunity to spend all of your time coaching athletes that have what you really want, i.e., those with exceptional skills, work habits and commitment. The "team player" will also last longer in your program.

Marginal work ethic and commitment players usually drop out when you ask more of them regardless of their talent. Remember, however, that your assessment of a player is only a "snapshot" in time. Regardless of what level you are coaching at, you need a system which encourages players to stick around or to come back to try again. I could have won championships with players that I saw "cut" from other teams. Players grow, mature and develop at different rates. Almost everyone knows that Michael Jordan was "cut" from the basketball team early in his high school career. While there are not many Michael Jordan's around, there are many "difference makers" waiting to be developed, but are never given the chance because they are prematurely "cut" and discarded.

Players with the "love of the game" in their heart and a willingness to work to get better every day just need enough time, good coaching and the opportunity to contribute. Even if time runs out for them to be a contributor to your program physically, you will be surprised how much motivation they will supply to your other players mentally. Re-evaluate often and keep as many players involved as possible.

> *Start with the premise that God has given everyone physical and mental gifts. We need to learn how to recognize them, utilize them, and get the player to fully appreciate them.*
>
> *When we do, we develop Champions for Life.*

The "Right Information"

Next, after you have enough of the "right players", you need to give them the right information. In other words, you need to be able to teach them the proper fundamentals of the game in a progressive, building-block manner that is fun for them to do every day.

I will discuss this at length in the chapters on developing Championship Practices. For now, I would like to address "staying current".

I think coaches who are successful over a long period of time are always learning. Two of my favorite quotes in this regard are: *"It's what you learn after you think you know it all that counts"* and *"Although he has coached for seventeen years, he really does not have 17 years of experience. He has one year of experience 17 times"*.

As I said before, the need to get better for our team *starts with me* every day.

Rod Dedeaux was the head baseball coach at the University of Southern California from 1942 - 1986. He won eleven Division I National Championships, more than any other college baseball coach. He was voted the best college baseball coach of the twentieth century. He had many great sayings which I will refer to in this book one of which was, *"Never make the same mistake once"*. He wanted his players to learn from the mistakes of others so that they could avoid making the same mistakes themselves.

The same is true for you as a coach.

Be insatiable when it comes to gathering information about your sport. Read books constantly, scour the internet for favorite sites you can keep and refer to often. Attend coaches' clinics and visit practices at the next level as often as you can.

Take thorough notes from all of these sources and have a quick, organized system to incorporate the information into your coaching notebook. Yes, every serious coach has a "notebook" of some kind, on-line or otherwise.

When you are learning by attending games and practices, get out of the habit of watching players and *learn to watch coaches*. Pay as much attention to *how* they teach as to *what* they teach. You can learn from watching good coaches coach any sport, not just your sport.

> *Even when you do not learn a new mechanic, you can learn a new way of teaching it.*

When you are studying the fundamentals of your sport, say hitting a baseball for example, study all of the historical references, not just the latest book or resource. Ted Williams' advice on the most important thing in hitting a baseball (i.e., getting a good pitch to hit) is still as valid today as it ever was.

Whatever John Wooden thought was a good idea to help his basketball teams is probably a good idea for your team too regardless of whether you are a basketball coach. Josè Mourinho is currently the head coach for the powerful Spanish soccer club, Real Madrid. He is regarded by many as the best soccer coach in the world, and quite possibly, the best coach *in any sport* in the world. Recently, he very adroitly stated the value of learning from coaches in other sports when he said, "A football coach who only understands football is not a great coach."

The "Right Time"

Okay, we have talked about giving the "right players" the "right information". Next, this information has to be given *at the right time*. The player must be able to understand and assimilate what you are telling him.

I remember coaching one of my first youth soccer teams and being frustrated that I could not get them during the game to break up the "bumble bee hive" around the ball. I attended a coaching clinic given by a very successful high school coach in our area. I asked him what the best teaching method was to get my players to spread out and not congregate around the ball.

He simply asked, "How old are they?" I said, "Second graders".

He said, "Much too early, too young. In practice, focus on the basics of dribbling and passing with both feet, but in games, stay positive and keep it fun".

It was great advice and advice I have applied to all of my coaching ever since. Start with teaching your athletes the most basic building-blocks, have your players master them, keep it fun and don't push for too much too soon.

Furthermore, the "right time" can also mean that today is not the right day. You must stay connected to what is going on in your player's life at that time. A player who is having serious problems at home or at school, with his studies or socially, is not going to be receptive to new concepts or to "constructive criticism" during that time. "Finals week" or prom weekend are also examples of "back off" times.

The "Right Person"

The "right players", must be given the" right information", at the "right time" *by the "right person"*. As a general rule, a coach's son should be given "need to do better" advice from another coach not his father. Fathers and mothers who coach their sons or daughters, after the sons or daughters reach about sixth grade, should only give praise to their children.

While there are definitely exceptions to the rule, most high school age athletes do better being coached by someone other than their father or mother.

The next *right person* issue is a tough one. When are personal coaches helpful and necessary? Personal coaches are very common today in most sports. They are usually very qualified former college or pro players who want to own their own business and may not want to deal with the other challenges that go along with coaching at a school or in a formal league. However, coaching is about relationships. Relationships are about trust. Trust is built delicately day-to-day.

Personal coaches can teach the same mechanics, but in a different way and the player can become confused if he is receiving help from his in-season team coaches and from his personal coach at the same time.

Multiple coaches on one team can be successful coaching the same thing at the same time because they have a day-to-day relationship with the player and if they are delivering the same information in the same way. However, the trend today in some areas is to have every parent who knows anything about the sport participate in some way in coaching the team.

Prior to high school, having more than two or three coaches for a single team is too many.   In this instance, conflicts in coaching style and information are inevitable.   Confusion from receiving information in different ways can lead to frustration. This frustration can be detrimental to the athlete and to the team.

As for the "team coach vs. personal coach during the season" issue, the players' team coach can be working through some "emotional growth issues" with the player and the timing for "tweaking" mechanics by that coach is not right. But to have another "personal coach" intervene is usually not appropriate.

The relationship between the player and his team coach most likely just needs time to work through some necessary maturity issues, but that is no reason to have a personal coach step in.

Generally, during the season, the team coaches should coach the players and the personal coaches should back off. In the off-season, however, the players should be free to get whatever coaching they think will help them maximize their potential.

This assumes, of course, that the team coaches are willing to spend enough time during the season coaching individual skills. Many times, they are not willing to do so because they are consumed with winning and they feel the need to focus primarily on team-building skills during the season.

However, even when the team coaches are willing to spend a significant amount of time coaching individual skills, there are exceptions to the general rule that personal coaches should stay away during the season. If the need of the player for "life issue" and maturity coaching is so great that it is predominant at the time and will last most or all of the season, the team coaches should focus on that and should allow the personal coach to continue coaching the mechanics.

This is a rare exception and definitely not preferable, but sometimes a coach has to realize the priority should be on keeping the athlete moving forward in life and keeping him in a positive frame of mind. This is what will be best for the athlete and for the team.

I know what many of you are thinking. If he is that big of a "head case," he is a cancer to the team and should be required to leave the team.

Yes, there may be circumstances where this is true, but I think coaches jump to the "cut" alternative way too soon. If the commitment and work ethic are there, don't give up on the athlete because your life skills coaching needs improvement. Remember, those are the most important skills we teach.

If we give up easily on our players, will they give up on their "special needs" children if our Lord asks them to raise one?

Furthermore, which of us do not have "special needs" especially during our youth?

The "Right Way"

The final component to effective teaching is that the information must be delivered *in the right way*. Long time Major League baseball player and coach, Lou Piniella, was asked by a reporter, "Are you worried that your style of coaching will not be accepted by your new team". He replied, *"It is not the concern of the players to adapt to the coach. It is the responsibility of the coach to adapt to his players".*

It is true that a coach's "standard of excellence bar" is never lowered from team to team. The standard of excellence never changes. Practice is always perfect practice. However, the method of delivery and the style may change depending on the age, maturity and personality of the athletes.

> *Expecting athletes to adjust to a coach's style is one of the most common, detrimental mistakes made in coaching sports.*

I am not one to generalize principles by gender, but at least one very successful coach thinks gender should be accounted for in considering how to motivate your players. Anson Dorrance, one of the most successful college soccer coaches of all time, started his career at the University of North Carolina, coaching both the men and women's teams.

He tells the story of a group of his women players came to him one day and asked, "What to do about a certain player?"

He knew the player was one of his best and although a bit confused by the inquiry, he replied, "Clone her?" The players responded, "No, we were thinking more of like getting rid of her". Coach Dorrance said, "Get rid of her! Why? I would love to have ten more like her!" They said, "Sorry, we don't like her".

He realized then that he needed to have a "girls weekend out" event so they could "bond". He has had one every season since that time.

On the other hand, Coach Dorrance says his men players are much different. They could care less about liking one another.

"Just make sure the ball is at my feet when I need it there and we're cool" is what they would likely say. However, now I'm sure Coach Dorrance would agree that "bonding events" are a great idea for all teams every season.

One other constant that applies to both genders unquestionably is that you have to be able to make them smile and laugh.

> *A day without seeing smiles on the faces of your players is a day wasted in coaching.*

Vince Lombardi is credited with saying, *"Coaches who can outline plays on a blackboard are a dime a dozen. The ones who win get inside their players and motivate".* I think laughter is the key to this. Make it fun, make them laugh and motivating your athletes will be much easier.

Practices v. Games Balance

The next issue I would like to discuss is one of the most common mistakes I see in coaching today, particularly baseball.

I watch so many players who do not improve significantly from year-to-year. In high school, they are not really much better as a senior than they were as a freshman. If you are going to impress a college scout, you had better show him something significantly new every time he sees you.

Old news is usually not good news in the world of recruiting athletes.

In my opinion, the primary reason for this lack of improvement is an imbalance in the number of practices compared to games played. In youth sports, "trophy hunting" coaches are a huge problem. Fathers who have a "flame throwing", home-run hitting son want to relive their youth by show-casing their son throughout the land. This does nothing more than lead to "burnout" of the son's love for the sport and builds a false sense of worth and entitlement in his mind and maybe in the mind of his parents too.

In youth soccer, for example, games are played all year around.

Players who "want to keep up" with their peers are guilt-tripped or threatened (with not staying on the team) into playing year around. What starts out as great fun wearing fancy uniforms, traveling to different States and winning huge trophies and medals ends up, after several years, feeling to the players like a way too serious job.

It is very common for a soccer player who has played high level Club Soccer from the age of 10 to not even want to play in high school. And if they do, their love of the game is usually nowhere near as great as when they were younger.

Many times they play out of a sense of obligation. "Well, I've done this for so long now and me and my parents have invested so much into it, I think I *need* to keep going". In this case, their development will obviously suffer and has probably suffered for a long time for many reasons.

In baseball, my experience is that way too many games are played in the Summer. Youth teams play games during the week and play in tournaments almost every weekend. High school teams rarely practice in the Summer because they play league or tournament games almost every day. Often, when they *do* practice, they spend an insufficient amount of time working on individual skills. Winning teams and coaches have a ton of fun, but player development suffers greatly if individual practice time is diminished.

This lack of individual improvement costs players an opportunity to play college ball and costs teams championships.

I understand the necessity of playing enough games. It is almost impossible to duplicate game speed and intensity on a regular basis in practice. You need to see a variety of different offenses, defenses and game situations in most sports. In baseball, for example, you need to see many different types of pitchers with different velocities, arm angles and approaches.

You need to get experience with playing different positions in game situations. In short, there is no substitute for playing real games.

However, at a young age, players playing too many games can lead to a number of problems as I discussed previously. At an older age, what I have seen is that the players' individual skills are not improving much year-after-year because they are not spending enough time working on them in a different way.

> *It is very difficult to make significant changes in individual skills without starting at a very basic level and retooling.*
>
> *In baseball, it takes a minimum of 30 consecutive sessions of mechanically perfect repetitions to make a permanent change.*
>
> *Less than that may get some immediate temporary change, but eventually the player will revert back to old habits, particularly under pressure.*

For example, if a player is going to significantly improve his hitting, assuming his swing mechanics are not already close to perfect, he would need to start his learning progression over with repetitions off of the tee, then soft toss, short toss, hitting off of a machine and then live pitching in practice before he could expect to see the change be consistent and permanent in games.

Improved results could only be expected permanently if the retooling progression happened in 30 or more consecutive practice sessions of about an hour each over about an eight-to-ten week period, assuming again that the player's repetitions in the practice sessions were near perfect.

This rule does not apply to the player whose mechanics are already exceptional and the need for improvement is purely mental. In baseball, for example, a hitter may just need to change his approach at the plate, e.g., start trying to hit the ball up the middle or to the opposite field. He may need to get his confidence back by being placed further down in the lineup so he can see more fastballs and less "off speed" pitches.

He may need to just follow the most important rule, which is getting a good pitch to hit. This will be discussed more in a later chapter.

For now, my point is significant individual improvement takes a whole lot of individual work which most players are not getting because the coach is demanding too much team time.

In basketball, maybe more than any other sport, I have been amazed how many players cannot do the most basic fundamental in their sport, i.e., shoot the basketball.

Their shot as a senior in high school is basically the same as it was in elementary school! In addition, it is nowhere near what it needs to be for them to play college ball. It is so sad because the mechanics of the shot in basketball are some of the easiest to change in all of sport. However, basketball players, while they spend a ton of time shooting the ball, spend very little time perfecting *how* they shoot the ball. Maybe if they spent more time shooting the ball while being guarded by someone who is a great defender they would be more motivated to change how they shoot the ball.

This is actually true in many sports. Coaches can get off the hook of having to spend a lot of time teaching individual skills because wins can be achieved by maximizing team efficiency and synergy. Wins can also happen because a team has one or two dominating players at the skill positions, like baseball or softball pitchers. Unfortunately, a coach's job security usually has a direct correlation to his win/loss record, not by whether the individual players have significantly improved or, more importantly, if they have been taught important life skills.

I am not advocating eliminating games, of course.

I have already said that here is no real substitute for playing games. However, a team can win a lot of games and still fall short of winning *Championships*. I think that championship players and teams should practice twice for every game they play and that a significant amount of time in the practices, particularly in the off-season, should focus primarily on individual skills. In baseball, the ratio of practices to games is sadly just the opposite, when you consider both the Spring and Summer seasons, i.e., there are two games played for every practice.

Also, it is not reasonable to ask the players to practice on their own time when they are already spending 3-5 hours a day traveling to and attending games and team practices.

In that case, something will definitely suffer, i.e., school work, family relationships, time for community service, and their ability to get and hold jobs. How many great high school athletes have a significant amount of work experience to put on their resume by the time they graduate?

Of course, as I discussed above, all of this assumes you have enough coaches and facilities to accommodate the individual needs of your players. If not, you cannot blame a player for using a qualified personal coach. In that case, you had better be sure the personal coach and you are on the same page about what is being taught and how it is being taught.

Playing Multiple Sports in High School

Playing multiple sports in high school while having aspirations to play college sports in one of them is an even tougher balance issue. Unquestionably, playing multiple sports has many benefits. Players get huge benefits from adapting to different coaching styles and schemes in different sports. Muscles grow and are strengthened by the "cross-training" from the different ways they are used in different sports. An athlete's mind is sharpened by the different mental challenges each sport brings.

Baseball and basketball coaches welcome as many football players, wrestlers and water polo players as they can get on their teams because of their mental and physical toughness.

These are just a few of the many benefits a player derives from playing multiple sports.

However, if a player wants to play a sport in college, he must realize a few critical things in his freshman year of high school.

Very, very few players have the exceptional talent to get by on the amount of individual training afforded by the coach during the high school season of that sport. Many, many hours of individual time will be required in the "off season" if they are going to develop into a college level player. Those off-season hours will be difficult to fit into the schedule of other sports, school, church service, a job, etc. Here is the most over-looked fact: Very, very few players will develop naturally into an elite athlete in a given sport without specialized training in that sport to make him or her bigger, stronger and faster. Yes, the bigger, stronger and faster hours will need to be *in addition* to the hours spent in the off-season getting better at the individual skills. Also, a player will not get bigger, stronger and faster while maintaining good health without an equal amount of rest!

It is very rare for a player to remain happy and motivated without a good deal of "down time" simply to rest and be a kid. Furthermore, the bigger, stronger and faster work done in one sport, like football for example, may not be the most effective for other sports like baseball. Sport-specific development is essential.

You can see why this balance issue is so difficult. For the player with merely above average skills to play college sports, he or she will have to have an exceptional amount of planning and commitment for four years to develop properly. That planning and commitment will have to be done and supported by the player's entire family!

Summary

Athletes, even those with exceptional God-given talent, must be properly developed in order for teams to win *championships* and for athletes to be the best they can be, both as athletes and as people.

Athletes must be given the right information in a progressive, building-block manner, at the right time, by the right person and in the right way. They must have a proper balance between practices and games and between individual skill development time and team development time. In the off-season, they must balance time for other sports, time to get better, bigger, stronger and faster in their chosen sport, with time to have a normal life, i.e., time for school study, friends, a job, time with their family and time for service.

Most importantly, they need time simply to be a kid and to rest.

With this balance, sufficient guidance by you and support from their family they will become *Champions for Life*.

Coaching Champions for Life

CHAPTER THREE

CHAMPIONSHIP PHYSICAL CONDITIONING

"You need endurance, so that after you have done the will of God, you may receive what He has promised." Hebrews 10:36

"The son who gathers during the summer is prudent; the son who sleeps during harvest is disgraceful. " Proverbs 10:5

The single biggest reason high school athletes do not develop into the best athlete they can be is they do not dedicate four to six months of the year exclusively to getting bigger, stronger and faster *in ways designed specifically for their chosen sport.*

Let me be clear here.

This is not necessarily a bad thing. If the athlete's goal is simply to be the best team player he or she can be and to derive as much as they can from playing multiple sports, there is no need to dedicate a significant portion of the year to maximizing their individual development. Following closely the advice of good coaching during each sport season and taking appropriate care of themselves health-wise and in school will lead to very rewarding results.

However, if playing a sport in college at the highest possible level is the goal or if consistently winning championships in a particular sport is the goal, then exceptional commitment beyond the season to maximizing individual development will usually be necessary.

Some "old school" parents and sports commentators frequently opine that high school athletes should not have to train year around for a single sport. They correctly point out that in the past, multi-sport athletes could still play multiple sports in high school without having to train for any single sport year around and still have a good chance of being able to play their best sport in college.

However, very few athletes "back in the day" trained year around for a single sport in the intense, systematic ways elite athletes train today . Times have changed.

It is now the norm for elite athletes in almost all sports to train year around in their favorite sport. It is now necessary for almost every athlete who wants to compete at the elite level to do the same. Furthermore, the extraordinary cost of college today makes the drive for an athletic scholarship almost mandatory for many families.

"Training" year around does not mean avoiding time off.

On the contrary, taking a month off from sports and training every year is healthy for an athlete's mind and body. Sports must, above all, remain fun for the athlete. As soon as sports and training feel like a job, "burn out" will occur and the athlete will soon start looking for other ways to occupy their time or, at a minimum, will no longer give maximum effort to their training.

Furthermore, prolonged periods of rest are sometimes necessary for proper recovery of the athlete's body.

Pitchers in baseball, for example, need to avoid pitching for 2-4 months every year to allow their arm to recover or they risk serious injury according to Dr. James Andrews, the orthopedic surgeon who has performed thousands of "Tommy John (*i.e., tendon replacement*) surgeries" on professional and college pitchers.

However, this "down time" each year may include one month of complete rest and three months of "active rest," i.e., training in other ways to improve their conditioning and athleticism.

I must also emphasize that getting bigger, stronger and faster is also not, by itself, sufficient. The athlete must also dedicate considerable time in the off-season to developing and mastering the fundamental skills of the sport.

Furthermore, there are also many more athletes with the physical tools to play college sports, but who come up short in their grades in high school, their college entrance exam test scores or their study habits, which will allow them to stay in college once they are admitted.

There are many coaches at all levels who do an excellent job of teaching the fundamentals of their sport.

Those excellent coaches at the lowest levels working with the youngest athletes are the primary reason for the success of the teams and coaches at the higher levels. They are owed a huge debt of gratitude and do not receive the appreciation they deserve. At the high school level, more often than not, team development supersedes individual development because the coaches do not educate their players about how much and what kind of off-season work is needed. Very little planning help is given to athletes by their coaches to allow them to understand how they can coordinate the demands of the various aspects of their lives.

However, the athletes themselves and their families must also bear some accountability for the athlete not reaching his potential. Athletes, many times, fail to seek out appropriate role models for their life and choose the "exceptions" to the rule to set the standard for their conduct.

In other words, if the athlete is tall, instead of improving his strength, speed and quickness to be the best it can be, he relies on his natural abilities which are already better than his teammates in hopes of being the next "big man" to make it to the "big time".

This inevitably turns a contender into a pretender and real promise into false hope once the athlete discovers he was just a "big fish in a small pond" when his skills are compared to athletes on a regional or national level.

> *Probably the most common mistake made by high school athletes is expecting maximum results from only partial compliance and commitment to the development program.*

An athlete cannot have great workouts one week and average effort workouts the next and expect optimum results. The same is true for all other parts of the program, e.g., nutrition, rest, schoolwork, etc. You are either a full-time, fully committed student-athlete or disappointment will likely be the result. Similarly, athletes today expect exceptional results and improvement far too quickly. Elite athletes train consistently for years to achieve their results and status. They understand it is not a point and click operation.

Long-term commitment and dedication are the keys to success.

Stretching

Stretching is an essential component to maintaining good health and to maximizing the potential of an athlete. Many athletes treat it as a nuisance and it is the first thing to be cut short or eliminated when training time is limited. This is a huge mistake. Stretching should be done by all athletes and by all teams at every age. All coaches should stress it as an essential part of exercise and of their sport.

> **TIP** - Without proper stretching, flexibility and elasticity of the muscles will be reduced or not properly developed leading eventually to diminished results of the athlete and possibly to injury. Proper warm up and stretching sets the foundation for maximum strength gains, muscle development and kinetic power.

Prior to stretching, the core body temperature must be raised by doing a light cardio exercise like a five-minute jog, a walk on the treadmill or a ride on a stationary bike. For my baseball teams, I prefer to do a series of running and footwork patterns for our core warm-up routine. (See Appendix D)

The trend today is to do traditional "static" stretching *after* the game or practice and a functional or "dynamic" stretching routine *prior* to the game.

Dynamic stretching means that the stretching is done while the athlete is in motion rather than the stretch position being held statically while the player is still. My mind is open to this new trend, but static or dynamic, the problem I see is the same.

Athletes do not take enough time and do not commit enough effort and concentration to do the stretching routine properly. And from a coaching perspective, this is the area where the "perfect practice" bar is lowered most often.

Many coaches ignore the lackadaisical attitude of their athletes when they are doing their stretching routine. The "get better every day" standard must be enforced regarding stretching as well.

Also, I am a big proponent that all routines in training should be done in a progressive, building-block manner. Many of the "dynamic stretching" routines that I observe being done by teams are done randomly without any logical progression to gradually build the stretch, body part to body part, in a logical kinetic manner.

In defense of the "old school" static stretching system, everyone should remember that decades of world-class, professional and Olympic athletes performed at elite levels without ever doing "dynamic" stretching. Specifically, pick an athlete *in any sport* prior to the year 2000 that you think was the best in that sport and almost none of them did dynamic stretching or even knew what the term meant.

They did almost exclusively static stretching prior to their competition and did so safely and with optimum results.

Problems occur in the static stretching system when the core warm up is skipped prior to the stretching being done and when blood is not pumped into the muscle group prior to the muscles being stretched. Problems may also arise because the athlete does not hold still while doing the stretch, i.e., he bounces or jerks while doing it. These things cause "micro-tears" in the muscles to occur.

For example, prior to the shoulder muscles being stretched, an athlete's hands should be placed on his shoulders and *large* circles with the elbows should be done *slowly* in a front and backward motion. With arms extended and palms facing first down and then up, small, medium and large arm circles should be done.

Both of these exercises will pump blood into the shoulder muscles so they can then be safely stretched.

Rarely does an injury begin on the same day as the athlete feels the first significant pain. Most often, the injury and the "micro tears" began weeks prior to the day of the athlete feeling the significant pain due to the lack of a proper warm-up and stretching routine on a daily basis.

Another common mistake made by athletes when they stretch is failing to breathe deeply during the stretch. Breathing pumps oxygen into the blood and it is *oxygenated blood* that is required for muscles to be properly stretched avoiding micro-tears to them. Breathing deeply and properly is also essential for muscle relaxation and for optimum mental concentration in sports in general. Symmetrical development of an athlete is essential if the athlete is going to maximize his or her potential and if they are going to avoid injury. This is as true for stretching as it is for strength training. The range of motion or elasticity of the muscles must be equal from left to right and from top to bottom.

For example, in baseball, if a pitcher has more flexibility and elasticity in one leg compared to the other, he will lose velocity and control of his pitches. Coaches must monitor this very carefully. Many athletes today are taking Yoga classes to help them with improving their flexibility and their breathing while doing their stretching. Some pitchers in baseball, for example, are discovering that dedication to Yoga classes is a key factor in improving the velocity of their fastball.

> *Asymmetrical muscle flexibility and elasticity are some of the most common undetected causes of injuries to athletes.*

Every practice and game should include a combination of static and dynamic stretching monitored very closely by the coaches.

A left hamstring, for example, that is tighter and less flexible than the right is trouble waiting to happen. It is probably only a matter of time before a significant injury will occur. In the interim, the athlete will not perform at peak capacity.

Again, dynamic or static, the stretching routine should begin every game-day routine and every training session.

It should begin with the core body temperature being raised and by blood being pumped into the muscle group before it is stretched. The entire routine should never take less than 15 to 20 minutes and should be done in a kinetically logical building-block progression with particular attention being paid to both proper form and symmetrical development. The stronger and more muscular an athlete is, the more time he needs to spend on stretching and the more proficient he needs to be in his technique and methodology.

Strength Training

While all athletes at almost any age can benefit from strength training, not all athletes need to spend a great deal of time lifting weights. Strength training needs to be designed for the specific sport of the athlete.

Successful football programs are usually one of the few profitable sports at a high school or a college. Therefore, what the football coaches want usually gets priority.

If the football coach wants his players to "max bench" or "max squat" during P.E. class on the day of a high school baseball pitcher's game, the baseball coach usually has no chance of talking the football coach out of it. This can obviously lead to disastrous results for the baseball player. At a minimum, his pitching performance that day may be subpar because his legs will not be at 100%.

At worst, he could eventually sustain a serious injury from using tired muscles repetitively in a very explosive manner.

Coaches of the various sports need to work cooperatively for the benefit of the athletes. Athletes must educate themselves that weight lifting for football may not yield maximum benefits for them in other sports. Even in football, a paradigm shift may be necessary about how much and what kind of weight lifting is most beneficial.

A friend of mine who coaches high school football and played football for years in the NFL told me, "The only time a football player uses his legs at 90 degrees or greater (i.e., a squat rep in weight lifting) is when he is being knocked down. The only time he uses a bench press motion is to push the guy off of him that just knocked him down".

This might be a slight exaggeration, but the point is are we really using the most effective weight lifting methods and exercises for football players by putting so much time and emphasis on max bench presses and squats?

Weight lifting with moderate-to-heavy weight should not be done by athletes younger than about fifteen years of age (and should not be done by athletes of any age without a thorough physical exam) because their bones are not strong enough yet to handle the severe stress being put upon them. I say "about" fifteen years of age because an athlete's physical age may differ from his chronological age.

In short, people's physical development occurs at a different rate for different people. An arbitrary chronological age should not determine when an athlete is ready to begin lifting moderate-to-heavy weights.

Only a thorough physical exam by a qualified sports physician should determine when the athlete is ready to do so.

However, using very light weights, whether in the form of hand weights, weighted balls or the like, can be used safely at almost any age if the routine is designed and supervised by a qualified trainer. This type of training is primarily for the development of muscle strength not for muscle development or growth.

The goal of strength training for athletes in most sports is to develop *functional strength*, not *absolute strength*. *Functional strength training* is the development of strength, endurance, power and flexibility while incorporating the entire kinetic chain of the body to help the athlete perform the mechanics of his sport better.

Absolute strength training is merely training to lift more weight which many times can lead to an imbalance in muscle function, reduced performance and injury.

Proper strength training at any age can give an athlete a definite advantage over athletes who do not do it or do it improperly.

A "qualified" trainer is someone who understands the functional strength demands of the sport and who understands kinetically what needs to be done to perform at the highest level of the sport.

Here are the most common mistakes in strength training and weightlifting:

Athletes fail to warm up and stretch properly before, during and after the workout

Most athletes, if they warm up at all, do it only in a token manner and only *before* the strength training session. Each body part should be re-stretched *after* it is trained during a weight training session. In other words, once the sets are completed working out the "quads", the athlete should *carefully* stretch them again immediately to maintain the flexibility and elasticity in them. This should be done for each muscle group that is trained and should be done again at the end of the workout as well.

This *before, during and after* stretching routine is almost never done by athletes and is a significant reason why they eventually sustain injuries and why they underachieve in their results.

Athletes do not train their body symmetrically

The front of their body (the "mirror parts") is much stronger than the back of their body. Pectoral muscles are much stronger than the scapular muscles, anterior shoulder muscles (the "accelerator muscles" when throwing a ball) are much stronger than posterior ("decelerator") shoulder muscles, quadriceps muscles are much stronger than hamstring muscles, abdominal muscles are much stronger than lower back muscles or vice versa, etc.

Sometimes it is a top/bottom asymmetry problem. The top abdominal muscles are much stronger than the lower, the top quad muscles are much stronger than the lower quad muscles, the trap and scapular upper back muscles are much stronger than the latisimus dorsi muscles (the "lats"), the erector muscles (middle) and lower back muscles, etc.

And finally, it can be a left/right, inner/outer asymmetry problem. The abdominal muscles are much stronger than the oblique and serratus muscles, the strength of the inner biceps muscle is out of proportion to the outer biceps muscle, the forearm muscles are much stronger than the triceps muscles or the triceps and biceps muscles are not developed proportionately, etc.

There is a huge emphasis by athletes on developing the "core muscles", and rightfully so, but these symmetry mistakes are why you are hearing so many abdominal and oblique strains, in baseball players in particular.

The motion when weightlifting is not initiated by the body part the athlete is primarily trying to work

For example, how many weight lifters do you see with huge shoulders or huge "trap" muscles that look out of proportion to the adjoining body parts?

This is because they initiate every lift with these body parts, and as a result, they get most of the work. *An athlete must learn to isolate the muscle group he or she is training.* This is done first by learning to initiate the movement with the body part you are training.

For example, when doing exercises for the "lats", the athlete should initiate the pulling movement with the last three fingers of each hand. This will cause the "lats" to initiate the movement rather than the shoulder and trap muscles.

Athletes do not do full-length repetitions

Athletes try to increase their bench press "max" by doing short partial "reps".

Some say full reps for bench press are dangerous. This is not true. What is dangerous is doing bench press without a proper shoulder warm up and *lifting too much weight for the sport you are training for.* Baseball players, for example, do not need to bench press 300 lbs. This is simply an ego trip to compete with their football player classmates. The upper, middle and lower portions of the "pec" muscles need to be conditioned and strengthened, but not over-developed like a bodybuilder.

When doing bench presses, baseball players should use light-to-moderate weight dumbbells from all three angles, middle, incline and decline. Be very careful to go very slowly on the negative/downward part of the rep so you do not strain or tear something. Use only very light weights for any kind of "fly" motion for the same reason. Be careful not to build much "bulk" in the chest area if you are a baseball player. This will restrict your throwing motion and possibly lead to an injury.

Another reason for so many abdominal strains occurring in baseball players is they do partial rep "crunches" to train the muscle group. It is no wonder pitchers who train this way strain their abdominal muscles so often. The pitching motion explosively and fully expands and contracts the abdominal and oblique muscles. If the muscle group has been extensively trained with partial rep crunches, a strain or tear is almost certain to occur.

All abdominal "reps", including "crunches," should feel the full expansion and contraction of the muscle group for the training to translate into optimum and safe performance.

The same is true for the other muscle groups as well.

Poor Posture

Good posture is essential to optimum performance when performing the fundamentals of all sports. Poor posture when strength training will lead to poor posture and poor performance by the athlete when they are competing in their sport. Unfortunately, poor posture is very common when athletes train and is one of the most over-looked components by coaches and trainers.

Failing to breathe properly

Most athletes hold their breath when they exert maximum effort in their training and when they compete, particularly when they are running. This habit depletes their muscles of much-needed oxygen, which leads to muscle fatigue, under-performance and possibly injury. Athletes must learn to relax and to breathe properly when they train and when they compete.

> *Healthy breathing habits have the benefits of muscle relaxation, lower blood pressure, improved circulation, optimum mental concentration, and clarity of mind.*

When performing weightlifting "reps", the motion should be a little slower on the "negative" (decelerating) portion of the "rep" and should be a little faster on the "positive" (accelerating) portion. The athlete should inhale on the "negative" part of the "rep" and exhale on the "positive" portion.

This breathing needs to be monitored very closely by the trainer because the athlete very rarely does it properly and consistently.

Failing to perform a sufficient number of repetitions per set and failing to perform each rep perfectly

The sport of most athletes requires that the athlete perform many repetitions of the mechanics and fundamentals in an explosive manner. Athletes should generally train in the same way.

Ten to fifteen "reps" should be done in each set of their strength training routine for most body parts. Maximum muscle development when lifting heavy weight may require 4-8 reps per set in some of the workouts, but this is an exception for most athletes in most sports. In fact, even in sports demanding maximum muscle development, the current thinking is the best results are achieved by varying maximum weight, low rep workouts with lighter weight, high rep workouts, sometimes even in the same week.

Rest intervals are too long and are inconsistent in length

Rest intervals should be limited to 1 to 1-1/2 minutes between sets and to no more than 2 to 3 minutes between body parts. Athletes' recovery times while they are competing in most sports are very short and so their training recovery times should be short as well.

Talking should be done between the training of different muscle groups or before and after the workout.

Otherwise, talking should be kept to a minimum.

Workouts are not designed and supervised by a qualified trainer

Workouts should be designed and supervised by a qualified trainer. Components, results and progress should be recorded in a *daily* journal.

All athletes, particularly older ones, love measurable results and progress. Keeping a daily record will motivate the athlete to keep training hard and, more importantly, will educate them about how to train others in the future. Maximum results, effort and safety will only be achieved if the training sessions are supervised by a qualified trainer or training partner.

Failing to get proper nutrition and rest

The best strength training methods without proper nutrition and rest are a waste of time and may lead to illness or injury.

In fact, once the athlete has done a properly designed sport-specific strength training session, the keys to maximizing an athlete's results from it are:

(1) consumption of the right quantity and quality of calories to match the level of exercise of the athlete and

(2) getting the exact amount of rest between training sessions to maximize recovery (called the "recovery cycle") while maintaining the benefit of the training.

Nutrition

If you ask most parents about their son or daughter's eating habits, they will respond, "He actually eats pretty good. He rarely eats junk food and he really does not drink much soda pop at all".

This type of response illustrates that most parents do not understand that the key to nutrition for a young athlete is not avoiding too much junk food. The key challenge is eating enough good food!

As odd as it may sound, young athletes do not eat enough; i.e., enough good food to maximize muscle growth and strength. In addition, when they do eat enough good food, they eat too much of it at one time.

Athletes should think of it this way: Your body is like the finest sports car you can think of which you have spent years designing and engineering. All of the finest parts possible are worthless without the best possible fuel. One great tank of premium fuel will only last a short time in the race before it needs to be replaced by another tank of premium fuel.

A tank of premium fuel to start the race followed by low-grade fuel in the next tank will lead to disastrous results.

Ditto for your body.

A great breakfast followed by skipping the mid-morning snack and a poor lunch will cause your "sports car" to run and develop poorly. Sleeping in until 11:00 am or noon so that you miss your first two meals of the day (breakfast and a mid-morning snack) will deprive your body of energy and the essentials of maximum development.

Skipping breakfast or a meal regularly will also shut down your metabolism because your body thinks you are starving it by going too many hours without food.

Carbonated drinks can make you feel full and lessen your appetite for real food. Foods and drinks with too much sugar in them decrease muscle performance, increase fat production and create the need for a "sweet tooth" in your food.

An athlete training to get bigger, stronger and faster should eat three main meals plus three in-between healthy "snacks" each day. Each meal and each snack should be carefully planned at the beginning of each week along with the other things on the athlete's schedule. An athlete and his or her parents will have to work closely together to become educated about what the nutritional requirements are for the athlete, when the food needs to be eaten and in what proportion.

Healthy "back up" meals and snacks need to be kept in the refrigerator and in the trunk of the car when the inevitable changes to the schedule occur.

A case of water and sport drinks should also be kept in the trunk of the car and in the garage so it is easily visible and accessible to the athlete.

Inadequate hydration is one of the biggest mistakes made by athletes.

> *Hydration in preparation for a game or intense workout must start the day prior to the event, not the day of or during the event. If an athlete is thirsty, dehydration is already present.*

Water should be consumed before athletic contests and low sugar, high-quality sports drinks should be consumed during and after them to replace essential electrolytes in the body.

48 to 64 ounces of water and/or sports drinks should be consumed, at a minimum, *every day* by an athlete in training.

Be careful about sport drinks, however. Most of them are very high in sugar and are therefore not a "healthy" drink at all.

In fact, some studies have shown them to be worse for the enamel on your teeth than cola drinks especially when they are sipped over an extended period of time.

Another popular, but potentially troublesome trend among athletes, and teenagers in general, is the consumption of "energy drinks". They contain several ingredients which are un-researched, especially in combination with one another. One 16 ounce can of energy drink may contain as much as 13 teaspoons of sugar and as much caffeine as four cola drinks.

Research has shown that certain susceptible people risk dangerous, even life-threatening, effects on blood pressure, heart rate, and brain function. Furthermore, caffeine supplements are banned in some sports and, therefore, consumption of "energy drinks" too close to a competition may disqualify an athlete.

Athletes should buy a calorie and nutrition guide at a bookstore. They should educate themselves about nutrition and keep a detailed daily journal about what they eat.

Athletes must be diligent label readers.

Athletes will be amazed how much improvement will occur in their development and performance when they do these things!

Caloric Intake Guidelines

Here are some general guidelines for *elite* athletes (not the average person) to follow *during the "bigger, stronger, faster" months of intense training:*

Body Weight	Main Meals (3)	Snacks (3)
120-150 lbs.	600 calories per meal	200 calories per snack
150-180 lbs.	700 calories per meal	200 calories per snack
180 + lbs.	750 calories per meal	250 calories per snack

Carbohydrates, primarily complex carbohydrates (potatoes, whole grain pasta, whole grains, etc.) should make up 50-60% of an athlete's calories and should be the primary component of an athlete's pre-workout meal or snack.

Protein should come primarily from lean sources of *complete protein* (i.e., chicken, turkey or fish) as much as possible, should be 20-30% of your total daily calorie intake and should not be consumed in greater quantities than 27-30 grams (about two medium chicken breasts) in a three hour period.

I'm also not a fan of protein shakes because they become an expedient substitute for real food. Many of them are of poor quality and do not contain complete protein. The can contain many potentially harmful additives, sugars, flavorings and artificial sweeteners. Most concerning is that the athlete can lose count of how many grams of protein he is consuming at a time or in a day. Too many grams in a meal and the protein will just be turned into fat because the body cannot process all of it. Too many grams of protein a day over an extended period of time can cause kidney problems and can cause calcium to be leeched from the bones, increasing the risk of osteoporosis.

As soon after the workout as possible, the athlete should consume a meal of complex carbohydrates to replace the glycogen used for fuel in the workout and of lean protein to help with muscle repair.

The percentage of protein consumption should decrease to about 15-20% of the total calories when the athlete is not in a muscle-building, intense strength training phase.

Fat should be 15-20% of the athlete's calories in the muscle-building phase and 20 –30% when they are not. Furthermore, athletes should not obsess about avoiding it because fat is an excellent source of energy for long-term aerobic activity. However, there are obvious differences in the types and sources of fat which are more or less healthy that the athlete will need to educate himself about. The words *hydrogenated oil* or *partially hydrogenated oil* on food labels signal the presence of bad *trans fats*.

Here's some good news for young athletes. They do not need to worry about, within reason, what they put on or in high quality food to make it taste good. They just need to get it down! Every meal, every day!

Briefly, I want to give you the benefit of my experience as a nutritionist and a personal trainer when it comes to losing weight. Please keep in mind, however, that asking a young athlete to lose weight would be a *very rare* occurrence. In almost all cases, the athlete should just adopt a permanent healthy eating and training lifestyle and whatever weight they maintain is just fine.

> *There is no such thing as a "diet," there are only good eating habits or bad eating habits.*

Here is my six-step weight loss program:

1. Change your eating habits permanently to a program that is a well-balanced consumption of fresh, healthy foods six times a day as outlined above.

2. The total calories for the day and the total milligrams of salt consumed in a day should be ten times the desired body weight (e.g., if the desired body weight is 120lbs., 1200 calories should be consumed each day divided into 3 - 300 calorie main meals and 3 - 100 calorie snacks with a total daily salt consumption of 1200 milligrams. In no event should the total calories consumed in a day drop below 1100 or the body will go

into shut down mode and will not lose weight because it's in starvation mode.

3. Eliminate all drinks except 8 - 8 ounce glasses of water a day.

4. Eliminate or keep pasteurized dairy and gluten-rich (gluten is a protein found in wheat, barley and rye) products to a minimum.

    I have found that many women are allergic to, or have low tolerances for these products. Be careful to calculate your calcium intake carefully if dairy products are eliminated.

    Calcium and vitamin D may need to be supplemented if dairy products are eliminated to avoid problems with the heart, blood pressure and colon. Start by consuming lactose-free milk, low-fat yogurt and goat or sheep cheese.

5. Do some form of cardio exercise for 30 minutes every other day at a pace that works up a good sweat. Rest days in between are very important and the time period for the cardio exercise should be worked up to gradually if the person is not already accustomed to doing this amount of exercise.

6. Get a minimum of eight hours of sleep a night, going to bed and getting up the *same time each day*. Remember, overstressing the body through extreme changes in exercise or sleep habits will cause the body to go into a protective holding pattern regarding weight loss. Do not expect to lose weight while nursing an injury. A body will naturally protect itself by holding on to weight while healing.

Patience and persistence are the keys to this program.

Permanent, healthy change takes time, but every person that adhered to this program was very happy with the results within a few months. I had to be very careful to remind the women, however, that physical beauty is not a function of weight. If you look in the mirror and like what *you* see (it should not matter what anyone else thinks or what society says you should look like), then the weight is irrelevant if you are strictly adhering to this program.

There are many people who are *not* overweight according to some medical chart, but are very unhealthy people. Conversely, there are many large-boned, strongly muscled people who are "overweight" according to the chart, but are actually in perfect health and should not lose more weight if they like how they look.

> *The stress of worrying about the weight will kill you faster than the weight itself.*

Lastly, once the desired weight and look are achieved, occasional treats to the person's eating habits are just fine. Life is too short to deny yourself those pleasures. Once the goals have been achieved, the daily salt parameter can be relaxed by 50% or so and fresh, healthy fruit or vegetable drinks can be added to the plan.

Be careful to strictly limit coffee and soft drinks, however.

I have found that consuming these drinks prevents significant weight loss originally in many people and can cause them to put back on unwanted pounds again after the goals have been achieved.

Any strictly weight loss program should be done prior to the season and not during a time when the athlete is doing a muscle development program.

An intense strength training and SAQ (Speed, Agility & Quickness) program and competing in a sport require more calories and more salt intake than the strictly weight loss program outlined above.

Furthermore, dieting without exercise is a waste of time because the body will just naturally slow its metabolism down as a reaction to the sudden restriction of calories.

The other eating program that I outlined above for elite athletes should be followed when an intense strength training and SAQ program is being done or when they are competing in their sport.

Healthy eating, sleeping and training habits are the keys in this case and weight is irrelevant.

In summary, the biggest deficiencies in the eating habits of high school athletes are:

- ❖ Not consuming enough high-quality calories;
- ❖ Eating too many calories at one time;
- ❖ Skipping meals and not eating healthy snacks;
- ❖ Not eating enough fruits and vegetables throughout the day every day;
- ❖ Inconsistent habits day-to-day, week-to- week;
- ❖ Not drinking enough water and drinking too many "Soft drinks" ("soft drink" = soft body).

Supplements

I always get a lot of questions from athletes and parents about supplements. Be cautioned, however, that coaches in some States are forbidden from giving specific information or advice about supplements to the athletes they coach.

Here are the basics about supplementation that athletes and coaches need to know:

1. Supplements are just that--supplements. They do not take the place of eating real healthy *fresh* food.

2. Supplements should not be taken without the approval of an athlete's parents and qualified physician.

3. High-quality multi-vitamin, multi-mineral tablets are usually necessary because most people's diets are deficient in more than one area the majority of the time. People are creatures of habit and well-balanced meals on a daily basis are a rare habit indeed. Furthermore, food is rarely fresh when you eat it. From the time it is harvested in the field until it reaches your mouth, it loses a significant amount of its nutritional value during shipping, sitting in storage and on the store shelves, in your refrigerator and during cooking (most people overcook their food).

   Additionally, many people obtain a significant portion of their daily calories eating at places other than home in food establishments that have low nutritional standards in the quality of their food and the way they prepare it. However, vitamins should not be taken on weekends.

   The body needs a couple of days each week to cleanse itself from this type of supplementation.

4. Many athletes obtain significant gains in development and in recovery time by taking *natural* (not drug) supplements.

   However, most athletes get little or no gain or actually do damage to their bodies by doing this because they did not get competent professional advice on what to take, when to take it and how to much to take. Athletes, high school age and older, should consider supplementing:

   ❖ A multi-vitamin, multi-mineral tablet to ensure the consumption of essential nutrients due to the lack of proper variety and quality of fresh foods in the athlete's normal eating habits.

   ❖ A B-complex tablet to help the cells burn energy and to help the body handle stress. (Consider reducing or eliminating this if the athlete is having trouble sleeping. Recent research indicates that an excess of B vitamins may cause sleep problems.)

❖ Creatine for increased power and speed in short durations - it should be taken in small dosages (20 -30 grams per day) spread throughout the day (5 grams with each meal and snack for example) and taken in strict adherence to the directions on the container.

This supplement should be stopped once the athlete no longer competes in sports because the long-term effects of it are unknown.

Its benefits to women are also not documented.

❖ Omega 3 fatty acid anti-inflammatory tablet(s) of 1200 mg/day (follow directions on the container carefully)

❖ Glucosamine sulfate of 1500-2500mg/day to help recovery and repair of cartilage, ligaments and tendons.

More is definitely not better when it comes to supplementation.

Over-consumption of supplements can be a waste of time and money at a minimum (e.g., overconsumption of vitamin C, i.e., more than 200mg at a time unless taken in a time-release form, can lead to very expensive urine) or to toxicity issues in the worst-case scenario.

Furthermore, combining the right supplements is also essential to maximum results. For example, vitamin C needs B-6 for proper absorption.

---

5. Drugs of any kind (e.g., steroids, human growth hormone, etc.) are illegal and dangerous to an athlete's body for any purpose, i.e., performance enhancement, body development or recovery time.   Avoid them period!

Rest

Muscle fibers are "broken down" during training and are built back up, i.e., strengthened and developed, when the athlete gives his or her body proper nutrition and rest. Poor nutrition and insufficient rest will lead to poor development, poor performance and possibly to injury.

Failure to get proper rest and sleep is the single biggest deficiency in a young athlete's training regimen.

A young athlete needs nine to ten hours of sleep every night with few, if any, exceptions for optimum development.

Furthermore, and this is where most athletes make their mistake, *the time during which the athlete gets the sleep must be the same each night.* An athlete will not get optimum results if they sleep from 10:00 p.m. to 7:00 a.m. on school nights and midnight to 9:00a.m. (or later) on weekends.

The body's *natural growth hormone* regulator will not distribute it in maximum amounts if it is not convinced that the body is going to get sufficient sleep every night. And the only way it will be convinced of this is if a person *gets the same amount of sleep at the same time every night.*

This is the "body clock" you have probably heard so much about. It is the same as the body slowing its metabolism down when a person skips meals. It is the body's natural defense mechanism to the perception that it's being deprived of nutrition so it is going to conserve everything it gets.

I have known several aerobics instructors who had their first meal of most days at lunch and they could not lose that last ten pounds they needed to lose even though they taught three or four one hour aerobics classes every day five days a week!

When an athlete does too many reps or sets for his level of development and training or when the athlete fails to take regular rest days in their training regimen, *over training* occurs. Over training, like poor nutrition and insufficient rest, will also lead to a plateau in muscle growth and strength.

Eventually, over training will also lead to injury because the athlete is over-stressing fatigued muscles.

Moderation, moderation, and moderation – more is usually not better when it comes to training.

Athletes should perform their reps perfectly, do them under the best supervision they can afford and be committed to their workouts week-after week, month-after-month, year-after-year and they will maximize their potential.

Athletes must be as disciplined in planning their rest time as they are with their workout time. They are equally important.

Muscle soreness is also best treated with rest and ice/heat therapy, i.e., 20 minutes of ice followed by 20 minutes of heat - repeated twice.

Soreness that lasts more than 24 hours may be best treated with heat only and a very careful, technically correct stretching program. An athlete that experiences sharp pain, as opposed to just general soreness, should see a qualified sports physician immediately.

Speed, Agility and Quickness ("SAQ")

The value of an athlete who has exceptional speed, agility and quickness has always been highly prized, but today it is being scrutinized more closely than ever.

In the past, we heard it said often that, "speed cannot be taught, you either have it or you do not". We now know that this is not true. Almost every major city in the country has training facilities that are able to make dramatic improvements in an athlete's speed, agility and quickness. In fact, the single biggest athletic deficiency that most athletes have is poor running form. With long-term training and commitment, an athlete's running form can be perfected and his or her speed improved dramatically. Training to be the best you can be from a SAQ perspective will, most of the time, yield many more athletic benefits than time in the weight room trying to compete with classmates in max bench and squat contests. Athletes need to be educated about what a SPARQ (*Speed, Power, Agility, Reaction and Quickness*) score is and where they can train locally to get those scores to an elite level.

Let me add a couple of cautionary notes, however.

While training to be the best you can be from a SAQ perspective is an admirable goal, elite SPARQ scores will not guarantee your success in sports nor will not having elite scores mean that your chances are irreparably damaged.

SAQ factors are only a few of the many indicators of an athlete's potential, but they are things that an athlete needs to spend a significant amount of time each year trying to improve. A sub-seven second sixty-yard dash time is not that essential for a high school baseball catcher, for example, but a sub-4.30 second SPARQ shuttle time is very desirable. SAQ drills and apparatus need also to be an integral part of most practices in almost all sports. I use SAQ ladders, cones, discs and balls in almost all of my baseball practices. SAQ drills are useful tools for athletes any time and can be very advantageous for team and individual competitions during the conditioning part of practices.

Let me state very clearly, however, that there is no substitute for running most of the time when you are training athletes.

Implementing SAQ drills into your practice plan every day will make your players more athletic and versatile.

You can do certain drills to improve running form and to improve leg or core strength, but to be a good athlete you have to run a lot of sprints to be fast ("anaerobic" training) and do a lot of distance running to have endurance ("aerobic" training) when you are competing in your sport.

It's just a fact, running for conditioning is essential for most sports.

Here is another cautionary note about "qualified" trainers at these SAQ facilities.

Some trainers are very qualified to teach SAQ drills and techniques, but still do not have the training and experience to know how to kinetically maximize the results in the chosen sport of your athletes.

Be sure you, as the athlete's sport coach, have thorough conversations with the athlete's SAQ coach and that you monitor the content and the results of the athlete's workouts.

The SAQ workouts at these training facilities may not be specifically designed for maximum results for athlete's sport of choice. The SAQ workout will either need to be modified in this regard or may need to be supplemented by training on different days at a different facility. In that case, *the athlete's rest and energy level will need to be monitored closely so that over*

Coaching Champions for Life

training does not occur. Women athletes seem to incur a significant number of knee injuries.

Women who play sports like soccer, basketball, field hockey, lacrosse, etc. that require sharp changes in direction while running at or near top speed should spend a significant portion of their training doing exercises and drills to strengthen their knees. Be sure the athlete's trainer is very knowledgeable and qualified to condition women athletes to prevent knee injuries. A torn ACL is a very common injury for a woman to sustain and can undo a whole lot of hard work on the part of the athlete. Exercises to train the athlete's core will be a significant and essential part of their SAQ training and should be a part of their everyday practice regimen during their sport's season.

Let me emphasize again the basic core training principles: The front and back muscles must be of equal strength. The muscles must be trained symmetrically and proportionately. The lower abdominal muscles must be as strong as the upper abdominal muscles. The side oblique and serratus muscles must be as strong as the abdominal muscles, etc. The muscles must be trained in a full expansion and contraction manner and not using partial reps. Proper breathing technique is essential and will greatly assist this process. Good posture is just as essential when training the core as it is in training other body parts. Most of these muscles are "fast twitch" muscles and require higher rep sets (20 – 50), but the rest intervals between sets should still be short, in the 1 to 1 ½ minute range.

Summary

You can now see why so many athletes with great potential fail to realize their potential. It takes an extraordinary amount of education, planning and discipline by an athlete and his or her family to achieve optimum results. A *four-year* commitment to these principles, not exceptional talent, is the big difference-maker for a high school athlete. Partial compliance and commitment to the program and principles will not yield the desired results. You are either "all in" or you are just another "could have been". While much of the advice I have given in this chapter applies to persons who desire to be an elite athlete, a coach at every level should emphasize that good exercise, nutrition and rest habits are healthy habits for an athlete's entire life not just during the time the athlete is competing in sports. As usual, the best way to send this message to the athletes is for the coach to model the lifestyle for them every day in every way.

You need to be a *Champion for Life* to coach *Champions for Life.*

Coaching Champions for Life

CHAPTER FOUR

CHAMPIONSHIP MENTAL CONDITIONING

"Humble yourselves under the mighty hand of God, that he may lift you up in due time, casting all your care upon Him, for he cares for you." 1 Peter 5:6-7

Every good coach's goal is the same for his or her athletes. Good coaches want their athletes to teach others what they have taught them about how to help others.

Coaches are teaching their athletes the fundamentals of their sport and about competition as a vehicle to teaching them how to be successful in life. When coaching young athletes, a coach's primary goal should be to maintain the athlete's enthusiasm for the sport so the athlete will stick with it long enough to learn the life lessons he needs to learn. Older athletes need to be pushed out of their comfort zone to achieve things individually and as a team that they did not think were possible.

In sports, as in life, this is done by being able to handle adversity appropriately and about being unselfish, always thinking of others first. When you do these things you "win".

When you do not do them, you "lose," regardless of the score of the game. Good coaches teach this by patiently helping their athletes learn the fundamentals of the sport, using the occurrences in their sport to illustrate how to overcome adversity and by being good role models themselves.

Proper Perspective

If we define "winning" as handling adversity appropriately and by being unselfish, we need to educate our athletes about perspective. Specifically, we need to teach them to be thankful and appreciative for what they have and for what they have accomplished already in their lives.

This "glass half-full" philosophy must be a constant theme in our daily interaction with them.

Baseball coaches have an easier time teaching this philosophy because baseball is a game where failure is the norm.

Reaching base as a hitter 3 or 4 times out of 10 is considered successful in baseball. I'm not sure this success rate translates very well to some other parts of life, but it does provide a useful medium to educate athletes about appreciating the good times when they are present. This need for perspective applies to coaches too.

Sometimes I think it is beneficial for a coach who has been blessed with having the opportunity to coach gifted athletes year-after-year to take a year or two to coach young athletes who have little or no natural talent. When coaches do that, they are not only so much more appreciative of the athletes they normally have the privilege to coach, but they also are much better coaches after discovering ways to teach physically challenged athletes.

Being Proactive

The first step in teaching the mental aspects of a sport is to be proactive. Prior to every season, we all know the lessons that will need to be taught. We all know the mistakes the players will make. They are the same lessons we needed to be taught and the same mistakes we made in our youth.

They are the same for every year and for every generation.

In baseball, for example, players will strike out, make errors, give up game winning home runs, umpires will make bad calls, the game will be played on a rough field in very bad weather, players will say disrespectful things to other players, to coaches and to umpires for any reason or for no reason, etc., etc. Some coaches make a huge mistake by waiting until the event occurs before they educate the athlete how to deal with them. Proactive role-playing should be a scheduled part of most practices. Let me give you some examples from my experience.

On my baseball teams, we do not just talk about how we are going to act when we make an error or give up a home run.

We actually practice it. When my shortstop makes an error in practice, he does the same things he will do in a game. He calmly turns toward the outfield, takes a deep breath, brushes his foot along the ground (signifying his wiping away of the memory of the error), fills his mind with a positive thought *and says something positive to a teammate.* The last part, saying something positive to a teammate, is a critical life lesson.

When facing adversity, you need to stay positive and not wallow in your own "pity pot" and you need to reach out to others. We all know that you make yourself feel better when you make others feel better.

In baseball, we have a mental pre-routine for almost everything. We have a pre-pitch mental routine for pitchers, catchers, the defense in general, hitters, base runners, coaches, etc. We have pre-game routines and post-game routines. All of these routines have a purpose and all of them must be practiced over and over again prior to game day. These "pre-routines" are some of the ways we act proactively to teach how to handle adversity and to prepare for success.

Another example has to do with media relations. Not all high school athletes have to deal with being interviewed by the media.

However, I knew that eventually my last high school team would win championships and would be asked to give interviews to members of the media. Therefore, I not only developed a list of rules when talking to the media (See Appendix F), we role-played how to deal with being interviewed.

When traveling on the team bus to away games, I designated one player to be the interviewer and I had prepared a list of tough questions for him to ask each of the players on the team.

One-by-one each player took their turn answering questions and after each one, his teammates would evaluate how well he did in following the rules. It took some practice, but after a while all members of our team did a very good job of handling a situation with which not many high school athletes are comfortable.

Meeting Expectations

Keeping perspective is largely about meeting expectations.

When expectations are not met, trouble happens. What the expectations are is a matter of education of the athletes, their parents and the coaches. There are expectations at every level – the expectation for wins and losses for the season, for a player's attendance at practice, for conduct during practices and games, for playing time, for balancing schoolwork, home life, social life and the sport, for following team rules and the consequences for not meeting all of these expectations.

> *When a coach's expectations differ from those of his players' and/or the players' parents, trouble and conflict are inevitable.*

A "meeting of the minds" of all interested parties is essential.

Without this "meeting of the minds", mental conditioning to handle adversity appropriately and for being unselfish is very difficult if not impossible.

At your pre-season meeting between coaches, players and families you need to address each of these issues directly and invite comment and discussion about them.

The rules, expectations and consequences must be clearly set forth and any dissension proactively eliminated at the beginning of the season.

Be sure that the information is a two-way information sharing process. You must hear from each player and each family what their expectations are. You must encourage the parents to "release their child to the experience of playing for the team and to the coaches as the sole navigators of the players' experience playing for that team".

Remind the parents of the many valuable lessons that players learn from participating in a team sport without their parents' involvement. This is how players learn to advocate for themselves, learn how to respect authority, how to manage relationships between themselves and an adult and with peers.

The extent to which parents interject themselves into that environment (the current phrase describing over-protective parents who cannot stop hovering over their children is "helicopter parents") is the extent to which the player's learning experience is diminished. *(Player and family conduct contracts are a great idea for many teams and can be a helpful tool for documenting this necessary "meeting of the minds". See Appendix G)*

Madeline Levine, wrote an extremely insightful book entitled, "The Price of Privilege" wherein she details how well-meaning, yet over-involved and over-protective parents can do great harm to the development of their children by greatly inhibiting the child's discovery of their sense of self.

In that book she states, *"No matter how worried we are about our child's future we must always emphasize integrity over prerogative".*

Boy, how much stronger our youth and our teams would be if parents would take that saying to heart!

My teams also have a separate pre-season meeting for just the coaches and players. We go into great detail at this meeting about the rules, expectations and consequences for the season and our program. More importantly, we role play how we will handle situations that are common like communicating when a player will miss or be late to practice. We brainstorm ideas about how not to miss practice as a result of extra homework, tests, dental appointments, driver's license exams, etc.

We clearly set forth the consequences for a player not meeting the expectations of the team. Yes, we make sure the players understand that the rules benefit *the team* and are *team rules*, not just the coaches' rules.

Players must be clear that they must take accountability, individually and as a team, for following the rules and for supporting the consequences to a teammate for not abiding by them.

Players criticizing coaches behind their backs during the season for implementing such consequences is a common cancer that will ultimately sabotage the success of the team.

Community Service

The next step in educating athletes about perspective is to involve them in community service, i.e., charitable acts outside the sport. The goal here again is to get them to appreciate what they have and what the true purpose of life is all about.

In baseball, in addition to gathering equipment and clothing for the less fortunate, one of my favorite events is The Miracle Baseball League for children with "disabilities". Children with physical and mental challenges are placed on baseball teams and are assisted by other athletes, like our team, in playing their games.

Needless to say, my athletes receive one hundred times more benefit from these games than the athletes who are thought of as having the physical and mental challenges. We not only participate in these games, we have a team meeting at the next practice specifically to hear each player witness to us about how his life was touched and changed by the experience. It is easily the most powerful, beneficial and meaningful event or "game" of the year. Teaching how to handle adversity and how to be unselfish is much easier after events like that.

Empathy Training

Young athletes, in particular, can be predominantly focused on themselves and their families. Empathy is a very slow developing life skill and must be taught on a daily basis by coaches. Unfortunately, we see many examples of professional athletes who never learned empathy as a youth and as a result of great wealth and fame later in life are still only concerned with "more for me".

Empathy for a youth is difficult because they are trying to develop a self-image and trying to survive a home-life in a very complicated world.

We must educate our athletes about who they represent by their actions. When they do something good or bad, athletes affect the lives and reputations of their immediate family, their extended family, their teammates and coaches, their classmates, teachers and administrators at their school, the teams in their league, their sport in general, the people and groups at their church and possibly their city, State and country.

Their ability to accomplish great things in their lives was also made possible by these people. Coaches must remind their athletes constantly of this by talking about examples from the daily lives of the athletes and from the news in general about other athletes who do good things, inappropriate things and the people who are impacted by them. Coaches need to be careful that when educating athletes about *who they are responsible to* that the athlete does not feel *responsible for* those people. Being responsible *to others* requires an athlete to take accountability for his own actions to be the best he can be. This is very healthy. Feeling responsible *for others* puts undue pressure on an athlete to accomplish things to please others. This is unhealthy and will cause an athlete's performance to suffer.

> *Reasonable goals set by the athlete are healthy. Playing sports primarily to meet the expectations of others is not.*

The most important games you play every year are not the ones in your League. They're the ones that matter to Him.

On days like these, your boys will become young men.

Prayer

I am a baseball coach and God's favorite sport is baseball.

He made this very clear by the first few words of the Bible, "In the 'big inning'...".

Seriously, prayer is an important part of my team's practices and games. We pray out loud together sometimes as a team, sometimes as a small group or in pairs. In any case, I require that my athletes and coaches pray for people, places and causes outside of our team and outside the athlete's family in addition to the usual people and causes. Our athletes must learn to widen their awareness of the needs of others.

As the athlete gets older, the scope of that awareness must be global.

On my high school teams, for example, freshmen are required to pray first for members of their immediate and extended families and then their friends and teammates before praying for themselves.

Sophomores do the same, but must also pray for people they do not know at school including their teachers and administrators and for people and groups at their church before praying for themselves.

Juniors must expand their awareness to the community at large and to the State. Seniors' awareness and concern must be nationwide and global.

On my youth teams, we will have competitions outside of prayer to name all of the people responsible for allowing the players to be able to play baseball on a given day. The youngest players may recognize their mom who drove them to practice and their teammates who play with them.

Older players will acknowledge people like the League and City officials who provide and maintain the field.

Whether you think prayer is appropriate for your team or not, the point is if we want our athletes to become *Champions for Life* and to play unselfishly to win championships, we must train their minds to think of others first every day.

To do that, we must raise their awareness at a very early age about who they represent, the many people who support them and the many people who are impacted by their actions.

Discipline

Despite our best efforts as coaches to educate our players and their families to be proactive and to come to a meeting of the minds, players will make mistakes and will need to be disciplined. Many times, however, the need for a player to be disciplined can be avoided by staying in touch with what is happening with the player at home and at school.

It is common knowledge that athletes act inappropriately many times when playing their sport because they are simply "acting out" their anger and frustration about what is happening at home or at school.

A coach may not be able to resolve the issue at home or at school himself, but he may be able to help others resolve it by:

(1) asking questions of the player, his teammates, teachers, parents, etc. at the first sign of unrest to learn the nature of the problem.

(2) by confidentially making others aware of the problem; and

(3) acting jointly to come up with a way to tactfully help the player resolve it.

Don't add to the players' stress in practice by only commenting publicly when a player does something incorrect. Motivate players by catching them doing something right!

> *At all times and in all ways, obtain motivation by inspiration, not intimidation.*

Coaches, when it comes to individuals, should get in the habit of praising them publicly, but giving "constructive criticism" privately.

When your team is doing a drill, for example, only "call out" the players who are doing things the way you want them done. If a player is not doing it the way you want, state the correction quietly and privately in a 1v.1 manner. What you will discover is that when you are in the habit of only commenting publicly on the positive, the players not doing it the way you want will try their best to change their ways to earn your praise.

Some people call this the "honey before vinegar approach".

Furthermore, many coaches negate the effect of public praise both to the players individually and as a team, by stating something negative immediately after stating something positive.

Do not give qualified praise…

"That was a great hit Eric, if only you could have done it during the prior at-bat, so you could have helped the team with an RBI". Eric will not hear the compliment about the hit. He will only hear that he is not a clutch hitter.

The comment, "You girls played very well today except for a few minutes at the end of each half," may be intended by the coach to mean that she was really proud of the way the team played for most of the game.

However, the team will only hear that the coach thinks, "We are too weak to finish strong". Keep the comments immediately after the game positive.

Save the corrections for the next practice.

One of my daughters attended a school once that had a policy of teachers only putting comments on essay papers in blue or green ink and only positive comments were allowed.

No red ink.

No negative comments.

The need for improvement was a given to be worked on by both the teacher and the student prior to the *next* essay assignment. The result was that students at that school maintained a very high enthusiasm for their work, a very high self-esteem and a very high opinion of their teachers.

Not surprisingly, the school turns out very successful students who make their parents very proud. What a great business model for everyone!

Discipline or the consequences for inappropriate actions must be, for the most part, pre-determined by a "meeting of the minds" in a pre-season meeting as I stated earlier. This can be difficult at times because it has been my experience that in recent years many players are not held accountable in other parts of their lives for inappropriate behavior. They are frequently "let of the hook" with a warning or a slap on the wrist.

I am amazed at how many times an athlete will get caught doing something clearly wrong and the athlete's parents will defend him by stating that in prior cases similar (in their minds) to the one at issue, the institution did not punish the offender by the "letter of the law" so their son or daughter should get off the hook too.

This is the same argument put forth by many members of the media and the public in general when talking about criminal and inappropriate behavior of professional athletes.

Whatever happened to living by the saying "two wrongs do not make a right"? Have athletes, particularly elite athletes, risen in social status to such a level that they are allowed by institutions to play by a different set of rules or by no rules at all?

Are parents in our post 9/11, fear-based world so defensive of their children that they cannot see the self-destructive sense of entitlement they are instilling into them by jumping in to defend them at every instance?

Madeline Levine's "integrity over prerogative" advice comes to mind again here as well.

When discipline is necessary, it must be fair, consistent and proportionate to the offense at issue. Many coaches erroneously have a "fix all" remedy for any infraction - the player does extra running. If a player is lazy, will not hustle or is caught sitting down when he should be working, extra running is an appropriate consequence.

However, if a baseball player is late to practice for example, the more appropriate consequence is that the player should have to stay after practice and do field "dress down" duties for other players for the next week or so.

If the player throws a piece of equipment in anger (in addition to probably being removed from the game), the player should have to carry all of the team's gear to the storage facility or to the team bus after the game and after practice for the next week and place the gear in the storage facility in a very neat and orderly manner.

The consequence should be tailored to fit the infraction. Sometimes the consequence may also have to be tailored to fit the player as well. I am not talking about one set of consequences for the elite athletes and another set for the others. This is wrong too. Everyone who does the same type of infraction gets the same general consequence regardless of his or her ability or their status on the team. When I say, "tailored to the individual player," I mean the severity of the consequence may be harsher for a Senior than a Freshman and for a repeat offender versus a first-time infraction.

Furthermore, if a baseball player who is also a star cross-country runner is caught being lazy and not hustling, having him run extra "poles" (running the fence line from one foul pole to another and back) is not usually the same consequence to him as having your 215 lb. catcher do it. In the case of the cross-country runner, I would have him carry a full bucket of baseballs while he is doing his extra running.

If the 215 lb. catcher were also a star runner, he would run his poles with all of his catcher's gear on.

On the other hand, young athletes must be forewarned repeatedly that the same exact infraction done at the wrong time and in front of the wrong people requires much different consequences. If you are a football player and you punch a teammate or an opposing player in a scrimmage after being taunted and pushed by that player, you would probably get suspended for a game or two. If you are a college football senior and you punch an opposing player on National television in the year the NCAA is making an active effort to stress sportsmanship, your college football career may be over. Two different players did the exact same thing, but at different times and in front of different people and the results were much different.

This occurrence is very common and very difficult for a young person to understand.

> **The rules regarding discipline and feedback are so important, I want to summarize them:**
>
> 1. By far, the most important rule is that if your team is not playing or behaving the way you want, look at yourself and your coaches first. The players may not be getting the modeling or coaching from you they need.
>
> 2. Give positive feedback about the team or about a player in front of the team.
>
> 3. Give negative feedback about the team in front of the team, but at an emotionally neutral time like the next practice and not immediately after the game.
>
> 4. Give negative feedback about a player privately and when doing so, only comment on the behavior, not the player. Do not make it personal.
>
>   Players must be clear that failure reflects only on the performance, never on the performer.
>
>   Furthermore, even if true, do not generalize the behavior by saying things like, "You've got to stop always doing that!".
>
>   The player will only hear that you always think he or she plays poorly and makes mistakes and they will not hear your praises again.
>
> 5. Never breach a player or a team confidence. What is said between you and the player stays between you and the player.
>
>   Once this confidence has been breached, the player's trust in you and respect for you is lost forever;

6. Never make a promise you cannot keep. Coaches are known for wanting to "push the envelope" in every way possible and sometimes they overreach in their promises in both rewards and discipline.

   If you threaten a consequence, for example, for poor performance or breach of a rule and you do not follow through with it, your credibility will be undermined and your ability to motivate will be greatly diminished.

7. Have your assistant coach give the "constructive criticism" to your child. You stick to "praise only" comments.

8. Do not immediately follow a praise with a negative or "constructive" comment of any kind. It will nullify the praise.

9. Make sure the positive comments outweigh the negative comments 99 to 1.

10. Keep the consequences for the inappropriate behavior reasonable and consistent with the infraction.

Non-verbal Communication

Please remember that 70% of your communication is *non-verbal* . Be very aware of it and receive constant feedback about it from your assistant coaches. Non-verbal communication includes:

Body Motion - Gestures and movements of the hands, head, feet and entire body. A tilt of the head, a furrow of the brow or a shift of the eyes can communicate a great deal.

Physical Characteristics - A person's physique and own physical condition, for example, communicates the importance you give to physical fitness. This is true not only for young people, but for people of all ages.

Touching Behavior - Pats on the back, putting an arm around a player's shoulders, and so forth. These are appropriate touching behaviors that communicate positive reinforcement. However, in today's litigious society, keep your "touching behaviors" very limited and very conservative;

Voice Characteristics - Voice quality - its pitch, resonance, inflections, and so on. Often it is not what we say, but how we say it that conveys our real message.

Championship Mental Conditioning   - 61 -

Body position - The personal space between you and others and the position of your body with respect to theirs. Be slightly closer than usual when giving positive feedback and slightly farther away than normal when giving negative feedback.

Rewards

How you handle rewards is obviously just as important as how you handle discipline. Here is what you need to do when rewarding your players:

- ❖ Reward the performance, not the outcome.
- ❖ Reward the effort and the process more than the actual success.
- ❖ Reward the little things on the way to the larger goals.
- ❖ Reward the learning and the performance of "life skills" more often and with greater rewards than the sport-specific skills.

I think it is crucial for you to realize that they reason you should handle discipline and rewards the way I have outlined above has much less to do with winning games than it has to do with teaching your players how to be good spouses, parents, business managers and community leaders. The rules are the same in all of these areas!

So far in this chapter, my discussion of "mental conditioning" is probably not what you expected. If you are a baseball coach, for example, you probably expected a discussion of pre-pitch and pre-swing routines, visualization drills for pitchers and for hitters etc. My point in this chapter is, while those things are important, they are not going to be done or will be sabotaged by a player who does not have his "mind right" to begin with.

Players must have their self-image, self-worth and self-esteem in proper perspective and in balance or they will not bother with the sport-specific mental things because the player thinks they are beneath him or are unnecessary. They will think what's best for me is best for the team instead of putting the "we before the me" (or me, TEAM). Furthermore, we as coaches must constantly make the connection between our sport and life in general.

That is how we do more than train champions in our sport; that is how we train *Champions for Life*.

Preparing your Team To Be Mentally Tough

Since this is not primarily an x's and o's book , I will not go into detail about specific drills in a specific sport to get your athletes to be mentally focused and mentally tough. I have given you some fantastic resources for this in the Bibliography.

However, I will tell you generally how I prepare them to do so. In other words, once you have educated them about perspective, handling adversity and expectations, what do coaches need to do to get their athletes to be mentally sharp and avoid the critical mental errors that are the deciding factor in key contests?

Be a Role Model

First, and by far the most important factor, is that *you cannot get your players to do what you do not do yourself.* They will model your behavior. If you are constantly bickering about the officials, you cannot expect your players to be unaffected by bad calls. If you are an emotional roller coaster during every practice and during every game, your efforts at preaching being on an emotional even keel to your players are a waste of time.

> *Your players will be who you are. "Do as I say and not as I do" does not work in coaching. Live it yourself or lose the respect of your players.*

Let Them Play

Second, players cannot be expected to make split-second, instinctive decisions that champions make if they are not in the habit of thinking for themselves.

They cannot play at their best if they are operating out of a mode of fear. Fear that they cannot do the right thing on their own without you directing their every thought during the game and their every step on the field or court. Fear that if they make even the slightest mistake, you will come emotionally unglued and/or take them out of the game.

> **TIP** - If you want to develop mentally sharp and tough competitors, you need to let them play. Step aside, be quiet, stay positive and be supportive of your players no matter what happens. They will make mistakes and you will lose games.
>
> Be brave enough to lose. In the long run, you will win championships in your sport because they will want to listen to you and will want to play hard for you. This will be so because in good times and in bad you "have their back".

Train Them Under Pressure

Next, young athletes need to learn how to perform under pressure. Some coaches make the mistake of filling their practices with drill after drill with little or no opportunity for their players to compete. On the other end of the spectrum, some coaches minimize practice time and emphasize scrimmages or games to teach their players how to compete.

This A-to-Z thinking is not correct to me either.

Time, weather, player numbers or other practical factors may prevent a team from being able to play games. However, as I will discuss in detail in Chapters 6 & 7, almost every part of practice can be designed to have a competition between players.

> *No matter what the competition is, it must have two things for it to be worthwhile:*
>
> *(1) it must be done at game speed and with game-like intensity, and*
>
> *(2) it must have a consequence for losing that the players want desperately to avoid or a reward that is highly prized by them.*
>
> *Without the first factor, it is really not a "game sim" at all. Without the second factor, there is no pressure.*
>
> *Both factors are essential.*

Set a "Perfect Practice" Bar

I also discussed earlier about the need to "set the bar high" for your expectations in their approach to the game as well as their performance. Only "perfect practice" is acceptable.

When "perfect practice" is the standard and competitions with game speed, game intensity and dreaded consequences are the daily norm; games feel like just another "day at the office".

They are no big deal even if they are championship games. Mentally, a "big game" does not feel that much different from a practice or any other game. Of course, prior experience in championship games can be very beneficial. However, many first-time teams overcome the lack of championship game experience by the way they go about their business day-in and day-out.

I do not have a different mental bar for my younger teams than for my older, high school teams. I teach the same mental approach concepts to all of my teams. Yes, the time it takes for the teams to learn the skills and the level of performance *physically* differs from team-to-team depending on their skill level and their maturity. **However, the mental approach I teach and the "perfect practice" bar is the standard for every team.**

I must emphasize again that it is not whether the players do it perfectly that matters to me; it is whether they try their best to do it perfectly, every rep of every day.

Use Process or Execution-Oriented Thinking

One thing that I train on a daily basis with all of my teams regardless of the age of the players is learning to be *process-oriented* or *execution-oriented* and *not result-oriented.*

Young players are usually in the habit of thinking about results first, e.g., getting high college entrance exam scores, getting a college scholarship, impressing parents, fans and college scouts, hitting a home run or a game-winning hit, striking out a batter, etc.

In baseball, we talk about "trusting your swing or throwing mechanics" and not worrying about getting a hit or striking out a batter. The stress reduction of not worrying about the result usually pays off by the player accomplishing the result.

> *Players need to be taught to be concerned only with the process because that is the only thing they can control. The result is out of their control, but the proper process will achieve the desired result.*

The first step in getting your players to be process or execution-oriented and not result oriented is to teach them the difference between *internal and external controls.* *Internal controls* (e.g., a person's thoughts and emotions) can be learned to be controlled.

External controls (e.g., the umpire's strike zone, the weather, family, friends and scouts in the crowd) cannot be controlled. They are distractions which will hurt concentration and diminish performance if they are not eliminated from an athlete's thoughts.

Some external controls, like an umpire's strike zone and the weather, must be compensated for, but once that is done, they are no longer part of a player's thought pattern or "stream of consciousness".

Push Them Out of Their Comfort Zone

Another critical factor in preparing your team to be mentally tough and mentally sharp is pushing them out of their comfort zone *physically.*

All elite athletes know that the first step in overcoming a physical challenge is *mentally believing* you can do it.

Elite athletes agree that *concentration is easiest when self-confidence is the greatest. Athletes who are the best prepared have the greatest self-confidence.*

Athletes need to be gradually, progressively and carefully pushed out of their comfort zone in their physical conditioning and in their skill development so they are constantly challenging their minds to help them overcome their feelings of self-doubt.

Self- doubt is the main performance inhibitor. An athlete that is physically exhausted and spent during an athletic contest will have a very difficult time staying mentally sharp and tough.

All other things being equal, the team that has a decided edge in their physical conditioning will have an edge in the contest.

If both teams are exhausted and physically spent, the team who has been pushed out of their comfort zone the most often in practice will be mentally tougher and will usually prevail.

Confidence is what comes from knowing that you and your teammates have worked harder and are better prepared than your competitors.

Pushing a team out of their comfort zone physically can be done in small ways too. I force my baseball teams to practice outside in all types of weather. We need to remove the bad weather excuse right from the beginning.

Coach Dedeaux used to say "It's a great day in Omaha. Just the way we like it!" This was his way of training his teams to stay positive and to be ready to play in any type of weather condition or any *external control* that they may face in the future, particularly those extremely hot, humid weather conditions in Omaha, Nebraska where the Division I College World Series is played.

When I coached my last high school baseball team, I required them to wear an extra under garment layer in warm weather as well as in cooler weather. In warm weather, this made them sweat a little more than they were accustomed to, but they needed to be pushed out of their physical comfort zone in every way when I first started with them.

I remember the turning point for that team and for that program like it was yesterday:

I was the head coach of the team for four years. The first year the players struggled to not use Oregon's cold, wet and windy springtime weather as an excuse for their sub-par play and attitude. We played and practiced in it a lot, but they didn't like it and were vocal about it.

I, of course, was unsympathetic because playing baseball in Oregon in very bad weather is just a fact. Either you adapt to it, or you will never have a winning program. This is just another reason why it's so great to coach baseball in Oregon.

What an easy way to teach the great life lesson experience of over-coming adversity!

In any case, during the pre-season in our second year we traveled to play a team that was a traditional baseball powerhouse in our State. Year-after-year they are ranked in the top ten in the State in their division. Our team had improved dramatically in the past year and we were just starting to "get on the radar" of the State's better teams.

It rained on and off the entire bus trip to our opponent's school, and it was cold and raining lightly, but steadily when we arrived. When our bus arrived at their school and stopped in the parking lot, I stood up from my seat in the front of the bus, turned to my team and said, "Let me go check with the other team's coach to see if we are going to play this game today". I barely got the words out of my mouth and I had just turned around before the line of players behind me basically forced me out of the bus. There was no way they were not going to play that game.

Despite the field being a muddy mess, we played a great game and were leading 16-9 when the umpires finally stopped the game with two outs in the bottom of the 4th inning due to the constant rain and eventual darkness. It did not count as a "win" on our record because the 4th inning was not completed, but it was a landmark event and the turning point for our program.

We were lucky enough to "finish our unfinished business" two years later when we traveled to their school again and beat them 10-2, this time in a complete game, seven innings. After our "landmark event", the players never again used bad weather as an excuse. During the next three years, we played and won in every possible weather condition even snow.

Use Visualization Drills

Let me finish by stating the obvious as well…

To compete with the best today in most sports, in addition to the factors discussed above, you must also have your athletes do visualization drills as a part of their training and practice routines. Visualization drills are useful for many things, including relaxation, focus, clarity of mind, discipline and confidence. Athletes, to maximize their performance, must visualize and actualize successful outcomes in their thoughts and their feelings.

> *To be successful, an athlete must visualize handling the adversity prior to the game to be able to handle it appropriately during the game.*

In baseball, visualization drills are a critical component to teaching pre-pitch and pre-swing routines for successful players. Mental training drills must be a regular "station drill" and a regular part of most practices. Pitchers, for example, should have already pitched to a batter mentally before he faces him in a game.

In baseball, we have visualization drills for hitters and pitchers, some involving equipment (like smaller size balls), some involving objects (like focusing on a small pebble before you step on the pitching rubber or on the smallest letter on your bat before you step into the batter's box) and some purely mental imagery (like sitting in the family room of your home, closing your eyes and visualizing your pitches or your swing without hearing the TV or the other people talking in the room).

Visualization is just as important for coaches as it is for players. My players know that I take all of their swings and their throwing mechanics to bed with me every night. They get replayed in mind over and over again until I have a clear picture of how I am going to make them better the next day. Therefore, the visualization drills I give to my players I do myself. I am, in all things, their role model.

My step-by-step teaching approach to a player's thought process in a game can be summarized as follows:

- ❖ Focus on the positive, not the negative.

- ❖ Focus on the present, not the past. "This pitch, this moment".

- ❖ Focus on the process and the execution, not the results.

- ❖ Focus on your internal controls and eliminate the external controls from your mind once they have been compensated for.

- ❖ Focus on your target (e.g., the ball, glove, etc.)

Summary

Visualization drills, process-oriented thinking, pushing them out of their comfort zone, requiring them to compete under the pressure of avoiding dreaded consequences, never lowering the bar of perfect practice and letting them play and think on their own are all necessary steps in the mental conditioning process for training champions.

However, to train *Champions for Life*, coaches must first proactively teach athletes about the proper perspective of life by teaching them to appreciate who they are as people, their gifts, the people who support them and by getting them to appreciate what they have already accomplished in life.

Coaches do this primarily by being good role models themselves. They also do it through the players participating in community service, empathy drills, education about group membership, handling discipline and rewards appropriately, coming to a meeting of the minds about expectations and through team prayer. When coaches coach "mental conditioning" by emphasizing character and integrity first, success in what matters most will follow.

As will other things - like winning games and championships.

Coaching Champions for Life

CHAPTER FIVE

DEVELOPING CHAMPIONSHIP LEADERS AND TEAM CHEMISTRY

"God has not given us a spirit of fear, but a spirit of power and of love and of self-discipline." 2 Timothy 1:7

The goal of coaching is not to just develop leaders for your championship team. The goal of coaching is to develop leaders for life. Therefore, every player on the team must develop leadership skills. Yes, some players may be more vocal than others, some may display their leadership in different ways, but every player must develop leadership skills.

Leadership skills can be taught at any age and on any team.

I think there are two general ways of showing leadership.

The first is by being an example of what to do and what to say.

This is being a role model: *Leaders are thermostats not thermometers. They set the tone and the mood. They do not just react to them.*

The second is by reaching out to others and helping them to do better. These things are true in sports and they are true in life.

Once again, the coach's first obligation is to be a role model himself.

Do not ask your players to do something that you do not live out every day.

Second, the coach must educate the players about what a leader is and the different ways a player can demonstrate leadership. Next, the coach must devise ways for the players to practice leadership skills.

Finally, the coach must acknowledge frequently and publicly the many ways every day that the players are demonstrating good leadership.

Again, the key to motivation is catching your players doing something right.

Praise them!

All of these steps are essential. Not only are they essential, they must be done every day. Not just every day of the season.

They must be done every time a coach sees a player on or off the field. I teach my players to always recognize the positive in others and in life. You should do the same when you see your players. Always say something positive first about them that makes them feel good about themselves and acknowledges a way they are setting a good example for others.

It does not always have to be said explicitly, but the message is always clear. "I'm proud of you because..."

How and Why Should I Be A leader?

When a player is learning to be a good role model himself, the first step is figuring out "Who am I?"

Obviously, in one sense, this discernment is a very complicated life-long process and journey.

However, a coach can help a player greatly in this process by educating the player about the many groups the player represents. Young people go through life day-to-day interacting with many different people in many different places. Yet, they have no idea the impact their actions and words have on those people. They have no idea how many people watch and care about them. Players obviously know and would acknowledge that their parents, guardians and siblings care about what they do and say.

Yet, they really don't know or understand the depth of the impact. They probably rarely think about the impact they have on their extended family – the pride their grandparents, aunts, uncles, etc. have in them and the inspiration they are to nieces, nephews and cousins. The same can be said for their impact on school classmates, teachers, administrators, friends, church members, youth group members, teammates and coaches.

In fact, an elite athlete may draw attention and represent an entire city, State or country! The ripple effect of one great play, game or deed or one inappropriate incident can be vast depending on who did it and the "stage" on which it was done.

Young players must be educated and reminded about this constantly.

Leadership Roles On and Off The Field

Once a player has a general idea of who they are and whom they represent, they must be educated about the many ways a person can demonstrate leadership. They must clearly understand the many ways of being a role model. Coaches always talk about sports imitating life and about sports being such a good forum for teaching life skills.

However, coaches do not affirmatively and specifically make the connection between the two often enough. Most of the time they just leave the connection for the athletes to figure out on their own. This may happen or it may not happen, but if it happens, it will probably happen much too late to benefit the team.

Leadership Off The Field

I think a coach should first educate and acknowledge the ways his players can be leaders and role models off the field.

These can be obvious things like getting good grades in school, helping classmates with their schoolwork, being a member of student government or initiating volunteer and community service activities.

The most difficult way to demonstrate leadership off the field, of course, is to avoid the temptation to do or say the wrong thing to draw attention to yourself. Athletes at any age are in the spotlight constantly. Avoiding peer pressure that tempts them to take dangerous risks, or to escape law enforcement is very difficult for athletes. This must be a constant topic of conversation and education between athletes and coaches.

> **TIP** - If you learn of an athlete who ignores peer pressure and does the right thing, you must make a huge deal of it in front of the team!
>
> They must recognize and feel the pride you and the other "groups" the athlete represents have when someone shows such strength of character.
>
> Never pass on the opportunity to reward such conduct!

However, athletes can also do more subtle things to demonstrate leadership like showing pride in the way he dresses and grooms himself or by demonstrating good self-discipline by continuing to work on good study habits in an "easy class" that probably does not require an extraordinary effort to get a good grade.

Furthermore, many young people do not realize the impact that common courtesy has on others. "Please" and "thank you" are still some of most powerful words in the English language. Subtle, but very powerful. Coach, encourage and praise such subtleties!

There were a few players on my last high school team that always thanked the coaches after every game for coaching the team and for their efforts in the game whether we won or not. One of those players would smile, give me a good firm handshake and say, "You called a good game coach". I let him know that those words and actions were more impactful and impressive to me than anything he could have done on the field.

Not because he said it to me, but because when he does it to others for the rest of his life the impact he will have on them will be huge!

Making people feel appreciated is powerful.

Leadership Roles On The Team

If a player is a good student in school and the Lord has put the love of your sport in his heart, then he can be a huge contributor to the team by being a student of the game. Most coaches overlook this fact and do not nourish it.

Coaches always talk about how every player can hustle because hustle requires no talent, only your best effort. Few coaches, however, recognize the same thing is true about being a student of the game. Coaches should reward players for doing homework about the history of the game and about the great coaches and players, past and present, of the game.

Have frequent team discussions about how your sport has changed in the equipment that is used, the strategies employed to coach the games, the changes in mechanics for executing the fundamentals and what the former players took from their sport to be successful in life.

Reward your players for helping you keep the statistics of the team and of your opponents. All of these things make the game more interesting and can expand the fertile ground for learning life lessons. It is also another opportunity for demonstrating leadership.

Most coaches have similar general rules about being a member of a team. Players must wear the appropriate attire to practices and games, they must run from the locker room or parking lot to the practice field and they must volunteer to help or they have set duties to prepare for practices and games or to "dress down" the field after the game. However, many coaches just have these rules and they make no connection to life as to *why* they have these rules.

Yes, there is some value in teaching players to respect authority, but developing *Champions for Life* requires more than this.

It requires enlightening them about how these traits will lead them to success in their other endeavors in life. When you are making your points, don't overlook the obvious.

We run to the field to show our enthusiasm for the opportunity to play our sport and for our team and to get ready to practice with our best effort.

Yet, let us not forget to also be thankful for having two healthy legs to run on.

Players are required to run to the field and to be on time, but who is regularly the first player to arrive and the last one to leave?

Players are required to work hard and use their best effort to "practice perfectly", but who takes the most quality reps at game speed during drills and on their own time?

Everyone is required to compete, but who is the most tenacious competitor and who refuses to let down despite the adversity he faces? Who is the first one to take accountability for making himself and the team better when things don't go well? Who is constantly looking for ways to help his teammates get better?

Who are the vocal leaders and who are the ones who are quick to put an arm around a teammate when care, concern or forgiveness is needed?

Most importantly, how will doing these things on the baseball team make them better employees, managers, husbands, fathers, and community leaders, later in life?

Educate them. Make the connection!

Developing Leaders and Team Chemistry During Practice

The leadership roles both on and off the field that I have discussed so far are very valuable for your team and for the players later in life.

However, they should not be taught by inference. A coach must design his program and his day-to-day practices so that these skills are taught and rewarded explicitly *by design*.

> When we review at the end of *every* practice and the day following *every* game, we always start with the positive.
>
> Also, we always start by asking two questions:
>
> > (1) How did we get better today individually and as a team? and
> >
> > (2) When people watched us play today, how did we inspire them to do better in their own lives?
>
> These questions are discussed and analyzed *every* day. Players and coaches are recognized and praised by their teammates *every* day. This is a constant educational and self-esteem building process.

Team Cheers

The way a practice starts sets the tone for the practice. The way it ends sets the tone for the next practice. Traditionally, teams start a practice or a game with a cheer. That cheer is frequently the name of their school mascot. I think cheers are great, but they need to reflect something deeper.

Teams need to be families. Teammates must become brothers and sisters.

When my teams of boys break the huddle with a cheer we say, "Brothers!"

Team Handshake

I have always believed in teaching my players how to give a proper handshake, i.e., confident posture, firm handshake, eye contact and a smile. People of my generation were taught that how a person, man or woman, gives a handshake says a lot about that person. I still believe that today.

However, currently, I think we live in a very impersonal world. Email, texting, Twitter…all have caused many people to withdraw into a world of technology and away from real personal relationships.

Many people avoid human contact at all cost.

Championship teams are a family of "brothers"!

The Heartfelt Handshake

I've developed another way to take my players "out of their comfort zone". It's called the heart-felt handshake.

End every practice and game with this handshake and not with simply a team cheer. This is how it works:

If two people each take one of their hands and press them together firmly for ten seconds or more and then very slowly pull them apart, they will still feel like their hands are together.

The Lord made us that way.

When two people love each other, as friends or otherwise, no distance can separate them.

At the end of each practice and game, have the team, including coaches of course, divide into pairs. Have each person in the pair take one of their hands and press them together firmly and have them hold them together until each person has said something from his heart to the other person. Time will only allow for one pairing each day, but be sure you change the pairings every day and that coaches are paired with players as well as other coaches.

After each person has said something to the other from his heart, have the two people slowly pull their hands apart, then each person takes his hand and makes a fist with it (symbolizing that he will hold on to what the other person said) and then he puts his fist over his own heart (symbolizing that he will put what was said into his own heart to nurture himself and to be used to help others).

Try it. It's powerful!

Developing Vocal Leaders

All coaches love vocal leaders, but I am amazed how many coaches do not try to develop more of them.

Almost all players have the ability to be vocal leaders. They just need self-confidence and lots of practice. One way we develop vocal leaders is to have competitions during practice between two players who are usually too quiet.

Once per week we have a competition where only two players are allowed to give vocal praise to the other players on the team during the practice.

At the end of the practice, the coaches vote on which player was the best vocal leader. The loser not only is punished for losing the competition, but he also is one of the two players who will be in the competition again the following week. As I recommended in an earlier chapter in the book, the "punishment should fit the crime".

Therefore, for example, the loser of the vocal competition would have to do the morning announcements to the whole student body the next morning as school starts.

A few experiences like that and you will have a new vocal leader in no time!

Equal Opportunities For Leadership

Team captains are great as long as the team chooses them. *(With guidance by and approval of the coaches, of course.)*

Still, I think it is a mistake to limit leadership opportunities to these few individuals. On my teams, we require all players to take turns leading everything we do. At the high school level, it does not matter if the player is a Freshman or a Senior, he will lead prayer, stretching, drill demonstration and he will Captain a team during one of our many daily competitions.

The Freshman may not lead as well as the Senior, but he will lead. And he will lead frequently. By the time he is a Senior, he will be a great leader.

Partnerships

As you will see in the chapters on Championship Practices, I am big on partnerships during practice. My players know that we are only as strong as our weakest link and we are all responsible for there being no weak links.

Players "partner up" frequently during our practices and are mirrors for one another. They know what each other is working on and they are accountable for each other getting better that day. Partnerships are changed frequently and players learn that they can be comfortable communicating with and helping anyone on the team.

I teach them. The players teach each other. We develop a team full of leaders ready to lead the world.

Team Competition

Another great way to build your team chemistry is to have a team competition involving the practice of keeping a positive attitude at all times. Divide your players into two teams and have each player listen for negative comments during practice being made by players on the other team.

The negative comments may be about the weather, the difficulty of a drill, about the performance of another player, about his own performance, about school, teachers, teammates in general or whatever. Coaches should listen for and keep track of "glass half-full" comments where a player could have said something negative, but chose to see adversity as an opportunity for growth. At the end of practice, it is very important for the coaches to discuss how the negative comments should have not been made at all or how the situation could have been looked at in a positive manner.

Staying positive does not just happen, it takes discipline and practice.

Summary

Be a great role model yourself. Educate your players about what a leader is and the many ways for a player to demonstrate being a leader. Leave nothing to chance or inference.

Design your practices and your systems to develop leadership skills and for ways to have your players practice staying positive, and most importantly, frequently and publicly praise your players and assistant coaches for demonstrating good leadership.

Championship leaders and team chemistry are built this way.

More importantly, so are *Champions for Life*.

There will be definite signs to you if your efforts toward building team chemistry are working.

CHAPTER SIX

PREPARING FOR CHAMPIONSHIP PRACTICES

"Therefore, brothers, be steadfast and immovable. Always abound in the work of the Lord, knowing that your labor in the Lord is not in vain." 1 Corinthians 15:58

When developing the optimum practice for your team you must remember why you are coaching them. You are not coaching your players to simply help them learn the fundamentals of your sport.

You are coaching them to be *Champions for Life.*

Therefore, you must plan and design your practices to specifically instruct your players on all of the components of being a well-balanced, healthy person of high moral character and integrity, not just to be a good player in your sport.

Do not leave anything to chance or inference.

Although the specifics of the next two chapters will involve baseball practices, the basic concepts and philosophies will be generally applicable to all sports and to players of all ages.

This discussion on practices is divided into two main parts. This chapter discusses how to prepare for an effective and efficient practice.

The next chapter breaks down a sample practice plan so you can see how the components are implemented into executing a championship practice.

> *Jim Calhoun, the soon to be Hall of Fame University of Connecticut basketball coach says, "One of the best measures of a great coach is the ability of that coach to imprint his or her will on their team and then have the team impose that will on their opponent in every contest they play".*
>
> *Other coaches simply say that the task is to take a collection of individuals with different minds, bodies and talents and to mold them to think as one and to get them to have a single beating heart.*
>
> *Practice is your time to accomplish this mission.*

The Path To Success

To be successful in sport and in life, all athletes and coaches must do the following three things:

    (1 Set short-term, realistic, behavior-oriented (not result-oriented) goals (short-term good behaviors will lead to long-term good results);

    (2) Develop routines and practice plans that allow the desired behaviors to become instinctive habits; and

    (3) Have the discipline, commitment and perseverance to always do the routines and practice plans regardless of how you are feeling on a particular day or at a particular moment.

In other words, you must help your team and your assistant coaches to set appropriate goals for themselves physically and mentally. You must do the same for yourself. You must teach them how to practice the desired skills until they become instinctive habits. Finally, you must model for them and hold them accountable for doing the practice routines every day.

All of this requires a tremendous amount of preparation. *"Failing to prepare is preparing to fail".* For the past season, our first day of "official practice" was on February 23rd. Our first coaches' meeting to prepare for this practice was on July 7th of the previous year!

We met every other week in July, August and September and we met every week in October through January. Obviously, we met much more frequently in February prior to the first day of practice.

> *"Championships are won in the off-season when the also-rans are at rest".*

This begins with the coaches' preparation. Every component of the previous season must be torn apart, reevaluated and reassembled so that the next season is much better. *To do better you have to do different.* This is true whether you won the championship or not .

Or, as Coach Wooden said, "*Failure is not failure unless it is failure to change".*

Get to Know Your Coaches and Players on a Close, Personal Level

One of the keys to the off-season is to learn as much information about the *social personality* and the *stress personality* of your coaches and players. How a coach and a player handle adversity is a key component to your championship run and, more importantly, preparing the player for life in general. Legendary college baseball coach Augie Garrido says, "*Life's real trophies are the relationships we establish with others.*"

The more information you have on how your players and coaches currently handle stress and what it takes to make them laugh will make your practices much more effective.

Your research should include visits with the players' parents and your assistant coaches' life partners. In fact, getting to know the social and stress personalities of your players' parents may also be important information which will make your life easier during the season.

If the player is new to your program, talks with former coaches of the player will also be fruitful for these purposes.

 If you as the head coach are new to the team and program, it is very important that you take a "team inventory". The players' answers to these questions will give you valuable information about what they think are the strengths and weaknesses of the program, the players that you can build the team around and the players that are holding you back. (A sample Team Inventory is set forth in Appendix H.) This inventory, or one very similar to it, should also be given to any assistant coaches who have been with the program for as long as the current players.

Make Your Facilities & Equipment the Best They Can Be

I must upgrade my equipment and our facilities every year, no exceptions. In fact, everything about my program must be better every year. Not having the funds to do so is a given and is an obstacle to be overcome every year.

No worries.

Communicate your needs and your vision to your network of players, families, friends and school administration and see what help is available. You will be amazed at what you can accomplish if you start early enough and are persistent enough.

Dream big. Think outside the box. Be practical, but do not settle for the usual excuses: "I'm sorry, but we do not have funds for that this year". "We've never needed to do that before". "We don't do things that way at this school or in this League".

Let me give you an example. When I started coaching at my last high school, we shared the baseball field with six other teams, had very little equipment of our own and had no support facilities whatsoever (no batting cages, no bullpens, no indoor facilities, etc.).

More often than not, it rains almost every day the first two months of our season, so an indoor batting facility is essential. Actually, such a facility is needed for several months leading up to the season as well.

Little or no funds were available from the school for this need.

Therefore, I let everyone know in my sphere; i.e., the players, coaches and families of our team and in the local Little Leagues, Junior Baseball of Oregon leagues and softball teams in our area, the high school student body and local commercial real estate agents, what we needed. Through persistent networking in this sphere, we were able to get all the equipment for the indoor facility donated and the facility shared with three softball teams at a very affordable rate in a well-lit and heated facility suitable for hitting *and* pitching. It even had an auxiliary room we used for classroom and ab/core work.

> *One of the most common mistakes young coaches make is not having enough equipment to run an efficient practice.*

You cannot run an efficient practice with just a home plate and three bases. Ideally, you need enough high quality home plates so when you are running catchers' drills, each catcher has their own home plate and enough lesser quality home plates so that when you are doing hitting drills you have one for each station you are running at the same time.

You need enough regular bases so that when you are teaching base running you do not need to divide the team into more than two or three groups. For example, when I teach leads and extensions from first base and I have 14 players on the team, I will use the anchored first base plus six more "throw down" bases lined up vertically about 3 feet apart behind the anchored base.

Thus, while half of the team is doing the drill, the other half is watching, learning *and coaching their partner on how to get better* in their base running technique.

The same is true for the number and types of baseballs (my baseball practice can use as many as ten different types of balls), batting tees, pitching machines, etc. This is a key part of your pre-season planning and fundraising. You need to think about how you are going to teach the different fundamentals in both a building-block progression and in an efficient time management manner.

You will also need to factor in poor weather conditions and practicing both outdoors and indoors.

All of these factors (and a few years of experience) will help you plan properly for the type and quantity of equipment you will need to run an effective and efficient practice.

Schedule Pre-Season Meetings With Your Players and Their Families

Next, I want to emphasize again how important a well-planned comprehensive pre-season meeting with your players and their parents is to making your season a successful one.

Practices cannot be effective and efficient if the players and their parents are not clear on all of the rules and expectations that I discussed on this topic in Chapter Four.

Begin Planning for the Week's Practices on Sunday

Coaches "meet"(if only by conference call) to "break down," evaluate and discuss what went well the previous week and what needs to be improved. Then a vision is created where the team needs to be developed as the week progresses.

In other words, each practice has a progression and every week has a progression. Of course, the progression is frequently modified based on various factors that occur each day, but every day and every week have a definite plan nonetheless. *Failing to plan is planning to fail.*

The plan for the week is developed by thinking where do I want the team to be developmentally by the end of the week?

I work from that point backward. The same is true for planning a particular day's practice. I think about what game simulation drill or scrimmage I want to do at the end of the practice and I work backward from there.

For example, if I want to do a bunt defense game simulation drill or scrimmage at the end of practice, my base running drills will involve bunt reads and leads. My oral communication drills, verbal and non-verbal, will involve bunts, my sign review will involve bunt signs, my position fundamental drills will involve fielding bunts and bunt defense, and my hitting drills will consist of bunt mechanics, etc.

Everything will be designed in progressions building one upon the other all leading toward the scrimmage at the end of practice involving bunts and bunt defense. *(Please see Appendix L for a sample practice plan of this type.)*

And if I am not satisfied with how we looked in that practice, we will do virtually the same practice the next day until we get it right, i.e., perfectly.

Type Your Practice Plan and Divide It Into Specific, Timed Segments Which Build One Upon the Other

Each coach is given a copy of the plan well ahead of the practice. I email my practice plan to the coaches no later than the morning of the day of practice. (Practice usually started at 3:15p.m.) Coaches are required to arrive at practice 45 minutes to an hour before the players to do field prep and to review the practice plan for the day.

The practice plans are posted for my experienced older teams, but not for my younger teams.

Younger teams are distracted too easily by "FI", i.e., future information.

All practice plans for the year should be saved for review, evaluation and improvement in the following year.

While I recommend that the practice plan be divided up into timed segments so that the practice has a flow and continuity to it, strict adherence to the time table should not always be followed. When you reach the part of the season when the players should know how to perform certain mechanics

Coaching Champions for Life

and execute certain drills, you do not move on to the next part of practice until the drill is done perfectly.

Legendary UConn women's basketball coach Geno Auriemma may spend an hour of practice time on one half-court set and he will not move on to something else in practice "until the eight possessions in that half-court set are the kind of possessions that I would want with the game on the line - each ending up with a bucket or an offensive rebound".

I email my practice plans at the end of each day to the parents of my high school players.

I do this for two reasons:

First, I want them to know what we are teaching the players and how much effort we are putting into *educating the whole person not just the athlete.*

Second, I want a record of when the players were dismissed from practice. High school players who drive themselves home or share rides with teammates, do not always go directly home.

I want the parents to know when the players were dismissed so they can determine if the players are coming directly home or are making other stops. For my teams of younger players, I and at least one assistant coach stay after practice until the very last player is picked up by a pre-authorized person. For obvious legal reasons, two adults should always be present when supervising young children in this situation.

Furthermore, no player goes home with another parent or person without the prior express written consent of the player's legal guardian. Actually, the parents are informed at the pre-season meeting that I have a "fifteen minute rule", i.e., after fifteen minutes, any player who has not been picked up, will be taken by me or by an assistant coach to our home where the parent can pick the player up there.

We do not leave the player to wait in the dark, cold weather for a parent to arrive at some unknown time later. No exceptions are made even if the parent telephones me or the player and says, "I'm on my way and I'm almost there". If the last player has been picked up, I can leave. If not, I stay or take the player home with me. As a result of this rule, I rarely have a problem with a parent picking up a child late from practice. I also include in the email to the parents after practice the daily attendance report. This includes who missed practice and whether it was excused or unexcused, whether he arrived late, left early, was sick or injured and could not fully participate. I am always amazed at how poor a parent's memory is regarding their child's attendance or how often one parent is not informed of attendance or lack of participation issues.

You will need an accurate record of this to avoid problems as the season progresses.

Have Players Arrive 15 minutes before Practice "Officially" Starts

If they are not fifteen minutes early, they are late. (Coaches of my generation know this as the "Lombardi Rule". I don't know if Vince Lombardi started it, but most coaches since his time use the rule and attribute it to him.)

The rule gets players to understand that people who are successful in life are the first ones to arrive and are the last ones to leave in a sport, in the workplace or wherever.

The Joy Of Running!

The players must run from the locker room, the parking lot or wherever they're starting from to the field. It does not matter what they are carrying to the field, e.g., a huge baseball bag with catcher's gear in it or whatever, they must run to the field.

There are several reasons for this. The Lord gives different crosses of different weight to different people and yet He gives the same reward to everyone. *We all need to pick up our cross and run with it in service to Him regardless of how heavy it is.*

Second, we need to be thankful and praise Him for our blessings in life. Every day that we have two healthy legs to run with is a day to give thanks. We show our joy for this blessing and for the opportunity to play a sport by running to the field.

Of course, there is the obvious reason that running to the field reminds the players that *it takes no talent to hustle* and maximum effort will be required of everyone at every practice.

So, the players will hustle from the moment they are heading toward the field until their work is done. All of these lessons are in preparation for service to Him for the rest of their life.

Coaching Champions for Life

Require Players To Check The Posted Practice Plan

When the players arrive at the field, they must check the posted practice plan to begin mentally preparing for the "lessons" of the day.

Those "lessons" include not only fundamentals and mechanics of the sport, but quotes having to do with things like athletic principles, life skills, inspirational quotes, etc. like the ones you have read so far in this book. The players will be chosen during practice by their teammates to repeat the quote from memory and to give an example of its application to the team or to their life to be sure they have learned something from the quote.

Having the players read the posted practice plan before practice also gets them ready to be efficient during practice moving quickly from station-to-station, drill-to-drill, progression-to-progression.

A player needs to "warm-up" physically and mentally to be prepared to play his best. The mental preparation always comes first, in sport and in life.

Require Players to Ask If They Can Do Anything to Help Prepare for Practice

Helping to prepare for practice is a particularly useful life lesson to teach in baseball where there is a lot of field prep and station prep to be done prior to practice. Players need to learn that nothing in life should be taken for granted.

"If it is meant to be, it is up to me". We are a team and we are all accountable for making everything possible. It is not someone else's job. It is *our* job.

We are all responsible for making sure it gets done, before practice, at practice, in a game and in life.

Be A Role Model

The final pre-practice preparation has to do with you. I prepare every day from the last out of our last game in the prior season to prepare for the first day of practice in the next season.

As said in an earlier chapter, I prepare my "need to get better list" the evening of the last game of the prior season. The reason for this is my work in preparing for the next season begins the following morning. Your ability to prepare well for practices and games is also a key modeling characteristic for your players. You must also stay in good physical condition so that you not only look the part in your uniform, but so you can demonstrate the principles that you are teaching to your players.

> *Remember, the word coach is a verb, an action word.*

You must not only be able to explain it, you must be able to demonstrate it as well. As you get older, it may take some practice on your part prior to the season to be able to *consistently* hit all of the types of ground balls and fly balls to your players.

If you cannot do it, you need to find someone who can, or, in the case of fly balls, there are machines that can assist you in doing it, but they are expensive. If you want your players to stay hydrated during practice drinking the proper fluids in the proper quantities, you need to do the same. If you want your players to stay calm and poised in the face of adversity during practice and games, you need to model this behavior for them as well.

Ditto for being patient while they are learning what you are trying to teach them, being organized, knowing the rules of the game and all the other intangibles you are trying to have them learn.

The old saying, *"more is caught than taught"* is definitely true about coaching.

Look the Part Every Day

Whether at practice or at games, buy the best baseball gear and clothes you can afford. *And uniform means uniform* when it comes to the team's game day dress. Everyone dresses the same in their uniform if you are going to get the team to play unselfishly and with a "single beating heart".

How to wear baseball pants, e.g., pulled up to the knee or pulled down to the shoe top, is a frequent source of debate among players today. Reward someone on the team for exceptional effort in practice during the days leading up to the game by allowing them to choose how the players will wear their pants during the next game, but everyone wears them the same in that game.

When it comes to wearing your team hat, on the field or off, respect for the game and the team is vital. The hat must be worn by everyone in the traditional manner, fully on with the bill straight forward. No exceptions, ever (well, okay, one exception, during the game of "flip," to be explained later).

Also, there are no bangs in baseball, i.e., no hair hanging over the forehead under the bill of the cap. The player gets one warning and then I cut the bangs off or the team gives the player a proper haircut. Player's choice.

It is tradition in many sports like football and basketball that the players wear dress shirts and ties or some more formal form of clothing on game day. Be sure this is also true for your team regardless of your sport and regardless of whether you coach boys or girls.

Our baseball team wore polo shirts and pullover fleece jackets embroidered with our team name on them on every game day. Failure to do so should cost a player playing time. Be sure your youth teams do this as well. Let the world know what great pride you have in your program.

It is a great recruiting tool for you that is frequently overlooked!

Do Your Homework

You must not only be fundamentally sound on how to teach the mechanics of your sport, but you must know how you are going to teach them in a progressive, building-block manner.

In the off season, you must have broken down the mechanics of every player offensively, defensively *and mentally*. You should work with every player, even the new players, in the off- season to improve their skills in all of these areas so that when the first day of practice arrives, the players are already miles ahead of where they were the prior season.

Be Prepared to be Flexible

Despite your best efforts to be organized and efficient there are some things like the weather, illness and injury that are largely out of your control. You must have alternate plans every day of how you will modify your practice plan if the weather is bad or if a certain number of players do not attend for whatever reason.

Practices get modified, *never* cancelled. It is imperative in baseball that you *pre-plan* an indoor alternative, even in a classroom or a "bonus room" at a house, to move the practice indoors if the weather makes the practice impossible or dangerous outdoors. The operative word there is *impossible*.

Baseball, in most areas, is played in bad weather and tough conditions. You and the players need to get used to it and eliminate complaining about it forever. Whining about the weather is simply not tolerated, period. The first time I hear my team complain about the cold weather, for example, we stop practice immediately and they start a long distance run or sprints until they are not only very, very warm, but they also are so tired they will never, ever complain about the weather again! *"It's a great day in Omaha. Just the way we like it!"*

If the ground is too wet and muddy to hit real baseballs on the ground you either use a type of rubber coated ball that can tolerate being wet, you work on fly balls and pop-ups, you do "dry mechanics"(i.e., no ball involved) drills, ball-in-hand drills, base running drills, oral communication drills, mental imagery drills or you take rubber coated balls and hit ground balls on the asphalt in the parking lot.

There are hundreds of possibilities, but you must have them pre-planned to be effective and efficient.

Allow Enough Time for Practice

I agree that the younger the player is the less time they can be expected to give maximum concentration and effort. There is definitely a point of diminishing returns in practice time. Furthermore, you must be respectful to the other obligations of your players like school work and family time.

However, baseball practices need to be longer than the practices of most other sports. Baseball fields need extensive care before and after every use that other playing venues do not. This is not exclusively your job. It is everyone's job and a crucial one at that. A whole lot of life lessons and team pride are learned as a result of the hard work it takes to maintain a baseball field to be the best it can be.

Furthermore, baseball practices need to be longer because baseball is a game of thousands of details and the progressive, building-block manner in which they are taught require stations to be set up and torn down for every practice. As a result of field maintenance and set up requirements, my practices are never shorter than two hours and can be as long as three hours for my high school teams.

Parents and players need to be educated about these things which require longer practices at the pre-season introductory meeting. They also need to be reminded of them occasionally throughout the season. If you do not, you will hear a lot of whining and complaining from them.

"My son's basketball and soccer practices were not this long!"

How much "field prep" does a basketball court take?

Use the "ARC" Method

When designing your practices, remember "ARC" - Action, Repetitions and Competitions. Keep them fun! Keep as many of your players as possible active at all times. Active does not mean shagging balls in the outfield during batting practice.

Build in many, many repetitions of perfectly practicing the fundamentals *every* day. Again, *12 x 5 is > 60 x 1.*

Twelve repetitions every day for five days will lead to greater results than sixty repetitions in one day, and, as I said in an earlier chapter, it generally takes 30 consecutive mechanically correct sessions to make a *permanent* change to a player's mechanics.

Furthermore, the players must compete with each other in almost every phase of the practice every day. The competitions, to be effective, must be done at game speed, in game-like conditions and under the pressure of a avoiding a dreaded consequence or the incentive of obtaining a sought-after reward.

Speaking of rewards, one of my favorite things to motivate my U12 teams is to keep track of "points" every day. I cannot over-emphasize how much young players LOVE to compete for points! I start out by giving points for the obvious character things, like arriving early, volunteering to help prepare for practice, hustle during practice, good listening skills and knowing answers to questions about concepts we are learning in practice, etc., etc.

As the season progresses, points get tougher to earn.

Mid-season, a player gets points for a good job teaching a teammate how to do better in a skill we are learning, winning a competition, volunteering to be a leader or demonstrating good leadership skills, etc.

Give out points freely for all of the things you are trying to teach them about being a good teammate and a person of high moral character and integrity.

The players keep track of their points on the honor system and they tell me their point total *at the end of practice* when I take roll. I give out minor prizes to the top point earners at the end of each week, e.g., coupons to yogurt shops, and larger prizes at the end of each month, e.g., programs or t-shirts signed by major league players at Spring Training.

As for your older players, I think the key is convincing them that what NFL player Ricky Williams says is true, "One thing I've learned in my old age is the more you approach it as a job, it puts you in a position to have fun.

If you do not put in the work, you're not going to have success, and that's not going to be fun". "Fun is the great feeling of knowing that you just played well."

Choose The Right Coaching Style

Choose the right coaching style to fit the particular players you are coaching. No question you are there to teach, but more importantly, you are there to teach them how to teach others. This will make them a better team and will make them better leaders in life. As I said in a previous chapter, coaches must adapt to their players each season, not vice versa.

> **TIP** - Younger, less experienced and less mature players may need more of a *command style* of teaching, i.e., more direction by you and less freedom for the players to teach each other, at least in the beginning. However, on all teams, this style must be only temporary and must give way to a more *cooperative style* of coaching where the players are separated frequently into pairs or small groups and are allowed to coach each other without frequent intervention by the coaches. This accountability builds leadership skills, self-confidence and self-esteem.

One example of this in baseball is called a "catcher's bullpen" where during the time a pitcher is doing his bullpen work, only the catcher is allowed to talk and give instructions and encouragement to the pitcher.

All teachers know that people have **different learning styles (called "primary modalities")**. People learn primarily through visual cues, auditory cues or kinesthetic sensitivities.

It is imperative that coaches keep this in mind as well when attempting to teach their players the fundamentals of their sport.

The sports industry is now developing primary modality tests which will help coaches determine what is the best sense through which to teach a player.

The player's teachers at school may also have some valuable insight for you in this regard.

A visual learner should be shown a lot of photos, and video tapes of himself, and other athletes performing the fundamentals.

Doing drills in front of a mirror will also be quite useful for this type of learner. When giving instructions to this type of learner, using words with visual images will be the most effective.

You might say to a pitcher, "When you reach your balance point, make sure your ship is not tilting backward or that you don't dump the bucket of water on your head".

If the player is primarily an auditory learner, you will need to take more time to talk to him about the process involved and reasoning with him about why he should be doing what you want him to do.

On the other hand, if the athlete's primary learning style is one of the other methods, having long talks with him is largely a waste of time.

In particular, a kinesthetic learner wants to minimize the talking and wants to spend his time doing and feeling the mechanics.

Lots of "dry mechanics" drills and training aids are the keys to successful teaching for this type of athlete.

When you are talking to this type of athlete, make sure you use physical cues like touching the ball of his foot or grabbing his hips or shoulders so he can feel what you are talking about.

With a pitcher, for example, you may want to put your glove on his head to be sure he is not tilting at his balance point.

Having a kinesthetic pitcher do a bullpen blind folded or throw in the dark are also great training methods for him. If you want to use visual images with a kinesthetic learner, make sure they have a physical component to the words.

"When you hold a baseball, hold it the same way you would a baby bird".

You may not need a formal test to determine an athlete's primary learning style. Just be cognizant of the attention span and retention ability when you are coaching him. When you talk to him, if he asks questions back to you and wants you to explain to him the process and why he should be doing it your way, he is probably an auditory learner.

If he has little tolerance for discussion and his attention is easily diverted, he probably learns best by simply doing things over, and over again. When doing things, if he is not progressing by simply performing the drills with you using physical cues, he may need visual feedback in the form of work in front of a mirror or video tape.

It's not really rocket science. Just be aware of the three learning styles and be sure to identify the one each athlete needs for success.

Build Structure and Predictability Into Your Practice Plans

You should build in a certain amount of structure and predictability to your practices. You also need variety and flexibility in your practice plans to keep them fun and adaptable to the inevitable changes that will occur in your week.

However, a certain amount of predictability and familiar structure will give the players a sense of security that they know what to expect and the confidence that they can handle it. This will important if you need to miss all or part of a practice. Your players and assistant coaches will know that they can "step up" to be productive in your absence without missing a beat.

However, I believe in constantly pushing my players outside their comfort level in all aspects of their training. Therefore, as the season progresses, I am constantly adding new variations to familiar drills and training progressions and adding new things completely. However, early in the season, I establish certain "default" routines that can be implemented for a variety of reasons if they are needed.

I might need to talk to a player at the beginning of practice and the team may need to warm up and stretch out on their own. We both need to be confident that they can do this effectively in my absence.

Design Leadership, Ownership and Multi-Tasking Into Your Practices

The big difference makers in championship practices are leadership, ownership and multi-tasking. The team may have voted on "captains" who will lead the team at certain times during games and practices, but as I discussed in Chapter Five, everyone on the team needs to develop leadership skills and be given the chance to set the tone and the example.

This must be done in every part of the practice every day!

Secondly, the players must take ownership of and be accountable for the "get better every day" and "perfect practice" standards you have set. When they are grouped in pairs or small groups they must know what each other is working on and must hold each other accountable for getting better every drill of every day. Maybe the biggest deficiency I notice in ineffective and inefficient practices on other teams is the lack of multi-tasking.

As you will see when I discuss the sample practice plan in the next chapter, you can and should build in multi-tasking to almost every part of the practice. Even the multi-tasking is a progression.

For example, a combo base running, and oral communication running warm-up routine will later be incorporated into a batting practice progression which will be incorporated into the final game simulation drill at the end of practice. *(Please see Appendix M for some suggestions for how to multi-task during various parts of the practice.)*

Have Adequate Help

Hall of Fame college baseball coach, John Scolinos used to say that one of the keys to being a successful coach is "to surround yourself with good people and those 'good people' need to start with Him".

Your players need to see that you walk with the Lord every step of every day. He needs to be your manager to guide, enlighten and strengthen everything you do.

In addition, having adequate help at the high school level means hiring assistant coaches who are as committed as you are to developing the whole person, not just the athlete.

Your assistant coaches must be as committed as you are to the principles set forth in Appendix A.

They must be willing to accept the extraordinary time commitment that will be expected of them. Like you, they must be willing to be the first ones to arrive and the last ones to leave (but, as the Head Coach, you will always do both), and they must model being a Christian leader in every way.

When coaching younger teams, you may not be able to find the help you need to the same extent you can at the high school level. You may have to compromise on your assistant coaches making the same time commitment to the team as you do.

Their jobs and family responsibilities may make such a commitment impractical. However, *never* compromise on using assistant coaches who are willing to do the other things.

Using qualified volunteer help can be a valuable asset to your program.

It is better not to have them at all than to have coaches who will not be able to teach the same fundamentals as you do or who are not good role models for the athletes.

When coaching teams of younger players, use all the help you can get when it comes to pre-practice and post-practice set up and dress down tasks. Ditto for field maintenance. Just be aware that some parent help comes with strings attached in their mind. Some parents believe that their extra help to you physically and/or financially requires extra playing time or "star" treatment for their child. The moment you suspect that this may be the case for a particular parent, you must "clear the air" about the issue or find a way to decline their help.

As Hall of Fame college football coach Joe Paterno said to the parents of his players, "I want your money, but not your two cents".

At the high school level, be sure that your assistant coaches are just as willing as you are to discipline players and to hold the players accountable for the standards of excellence and integrity that you expect. High School athletes can sometimes go to extraordinary lengths to manipulate and "split" the coaches when it comes to these things. Be very careful that you are not always forced into being the "bad cop".

You and your assistant coaches should share the "good cop, bad cop" duties equally.

This is critically important if discipline and respect are to be instilled into the team!

Manage Risk Carefully

Obviously, from a practical point of view, the most important thing you must do is to keep your players and assistant coaches safe. One serious injury and the resulting lawsuit can really put a halt to an otherwise promising and successful program.

Here are the keys to managing your risk properly:

Properly plan the activities in your practice

Yes, multi-tasking in your drills and progressions is important, but you must always consider safety first when designing your practice plan. Protective screens and back-up players are a must in establishing a safe environment in baseball practices, for example. You must be vigilant at all times that your players are taking their roles as safety monitors as seriously as they are their roles as players.

Provide Proper Instruction

The teaching of improper mechanics can lead to serious sports injuries. Poor throwing mechanics in baseball, poor tackling technique in football, etc. can obviously lead to serious injuries.

Carefully monitor your assistant coaches that they are teaching sound principles in this regard. Actually, this is an essential part of your pre-season meetings, i.e., to be sure that you and your assistant coaches are on the same page regarding how you will teach the fundamentals and mechanics of your sport.

Warn Players and Families of Inherent Risks of Your Sport

Part of this needs to occur prior to the season and should require the players and their legal guardians signing Informed Consent, Inherent Risk and Medical Release Forms. *(See examples of these in Appendices I, J & K.)* However, some of this management occurs during the season as well.

In baseball, for example, players need to be constantly reminded that the netting on batting cages expands several feet every time a ball is hit into it and anyone standing too close to the net can be seriously injured. In fact, I usually mark a permanent line on the ground which serves as a constant reminder of where the players must stand. Still, I do not rely on this exclusively. My assistant coaches and I are very vigilant that the players are paying attention to the boundary and what is going on at all times.

Provide a Safe Physical Environment

Never test fate and never "push the envelope" when it comes to this. In some sports, extreme weather and field conditions are just too dangerous to practice in or on. Ditto for poor lighting. We have all read many sad stories of players who have died or were seriously injured because a coach tried to teach "toughness" in extreme weather or poor field conditions.

> *You need to push your players out of their comfort zone physically to get them to be the best they can be, but do so gradually and wisely.*

Provide Adequate and Proper Equipment

I find that many of the injuries in this category come from the players' own equipment. Monitor very closely the quality and state of repair of the players' shoes and equipment they use in your sport. Gloves and catcher's equipment that are in poor condition or that do not fit properly are frequent causes of injuries in baseball. Improper shoes for the playing surface or the weather conditions are common causes of injuries to players in other sports. Never try to "stretch the budget" by seeing if you can get another season out of worn equipment. Repair it like new or buy it new. It is not worth the risk to do otherwise.

Assume that a batted ball will sooner or later find that one small hole in the batting cage netting and that someone will be standing in the line of flight. Murphy's Law (*"anything that can go wrong, will go wrong"*) applies at all times in this regard.

Match Your Athletes Appropriately

This is a tough one for me because I *love* mismatches!

Obviously, if a ball is thrown to or hit at a player and the speed of the ball is quicker than the player's reaction time, then a dangerous situation could arise and this must be avoided at all costs. In general, players of relative equal ability must play together on a team, in a league and paired together in practice where reaction time is a safety factor. However, I do look for opportunities to push players out of their comfort zone by creating mismatches. For example, I want my younger, less skilled and less experienced hitters to face my best pitchers. I want the best players on the team to be partners with the least-skilled players in team competitions so that they are challenged to "coach them up" and to handle losing graciously if that is the outcome.

Coach Auriemma frequently requires his starting basketball players to play 4 v. 6 because such a drill is as challenging mentally as it is physically. "But when it's 5 v. 5 against another team in a normal game" says a current player, "it's easy". Life is, at times, a theoretical mismatch for us. Sports are a great opportunity to learn how to deal with failure and overcoming adversity.

Evaluate Your Athletes for Injury and Incapacity

This is another tough one for me. I make it clear to my players that I will not tolerate whining. You need to go to work when you don't feel like it. You need to be a patient spouse and father when you are exhausted or not feeling well.

I am responsible for my actions whether I feel well or not.

Bumps, bruises and pain are a part of life. You need to learn to deal with it graciously and to get your work done well despite the challenges you face.

However, I try to carefully educate my athletes about what is tolerable pain and discomfort and what is dangerous to them and to the team. But, frankly, even though I ask them at the beginning of every practice if anyone is sick or injured, they rarely tell me.

Therefore, I have to keep a close eye on every one of them during practice to see if I can see any irregularities in the way they go about their business, physically *and* emotionally. Yes, emotional troubles can lead to injuries just as easily as physical ones because the player will not be as focused as they should be. In either case, once I detect even the slightest problem, I talk privately with the player about it as soon as possible.

Supervise Activity Closely

One time, when I was an assistant to the Head Coach at a high school, on the *first day* of practice the Head Coach sent the freshman players to the indoor hitting facility to do some hitting station drills.

One of the inexperienced freshman players was pitching short toss batting practice behind an L- Screen when, as is typical for inexperienced players, he forgot to duck behind the screen after he threw a pitch. Murphy's Law took over, of course, and he was hit in the face with a line drive. The injuries cost the player the better part of the season.

Karma exacted its justice, however, when later in the day, the Head Coach was knocked down by a line drive that hit him in the forehead during batting practice on the full diamond when he was not paying attention.

Enough said.

Appropriate Emergency Assistance

The first piece of equipment you should unload from your car every day and the last one you should put in is the First Aid kit.

Check it frequently to be sure it is appropriately stocked for every and all contingencies. More importantly, know how to use everything in the kit. Constantly check for the freshness and usability of the items in the kit. Ice packs are notorious for becoming unusable after a period of time or if stored in too warm a temperature, for example.

A word of caution about the use of Advil or other types of Ibuprofen by high school athletes. They consume the pills like candy. Require that they get your permission before taking such medication….but monitor its usage very closely anyway. Over-consumption of Ibuprofen can cause health problems including stomach issues. You and your assistant coaches should update your CPR and first aid certifications every year regardless of the level or age you are coaching. (*See cprtoday.com*) Injuries can and will happen on all teams at any age. Assume you will have to give CPR to a player someday. It is likely to happen. Your player's life may depend on you being prepared for and competent to deal with this event.

Do not take any chances with any type of head injury. Any pain or dizziness as a result of contact with the head requires immediate physician evaluation and a written release by the physician for the player to return playing. No exceptions.

Pre-season screening and evaluation for susceptibility to such injuries for all players in a contact sport should be required by all Leagues at any level.

Of course, complete pre-season general physicals by competent physicians are, thankfully, standard everywhere.

Practice Day

If your message is being heard, you will inevitably have players arriving early for practice. Take advantage of this opportunity and use the time wisely. Teams of older players should first be sure their set up and field maintenance duties are done properly.

Even very young players should be trained to ask before every practice if there is something they can do to help and something should be found for them to do. If there is still time before practice, there are several things you can do to use the time wisely. Even during these pre-practice sessions multi-tasking is the key. During this time, the multi-tasking takes the form of mixing in conversation about how their day has gone up to that point and what is happening in their life. Do not accept "fine" for an answer. Ask specific questions about school, friends and family that cannot be answered with a "yes", a "no" or any one word answer. This is a critical rapport-building routine that falls into the category of *"They do not care how much you know until they know how much you care"*.

One of the first bad habits you will have to break baseball players of is picking up a baseball to begin playing catch before they have done their running form warm-up and stretching routines.

Baseball players warm up to throw. They do not throw to warm up.

Here are some of my favorite things to work on with baseball players when they arrive early (It is also a great "Rainy Day" practice list) :

Pitchers - grip drills, mental imagery drills, pitch sequence drills, pick moves with no throws and covering first base;

Catchers - framing, receiving, footwork for throws, pop ups, managing pitchers, game management, pitch sequence drills and umpire rapport;

Infielders - bag mechanics, ground balls with no throws, "wall ball" (fielding & reaction drills with the ball thrown by me coming off a wall) and pop-ups;

Outfielders - fly balls, triangle pop-up drills with infielders (an awesome drill, one variation of which is using a tennis racket and a tennis ball in windy conditions with the players having to catch the ball bare handed with only their glove hand.)

Footwork drills, reaction drills and "pass patterns" (catching fly balls bare-handed with only the glove hand thrown by a coach using a regulation size "softie" ball while the player is doing a long pass pattern.)

Hitters - bunting drills, "pepper", dry swing mechanics and "tic the tee" drills (swinging the bat at a tee with no baseball on it at different heights trying to barely "tic the tee" - a great swing plane control drill!)

Once in a while, just for fun, the players can simply play "flip". This a favorite game of baseball players where they stand in a circle, a player receives a "flip" of the ball from another player in the circle and then does a pre-determined number and kind of "flips" with the ball to himself without ever catching the ball before finally flipping the ball to another player.

The current players love it most because when they miss a "flip" they are required to turn their hat a quarter turn clockwise, so they get to violate the "no sideways hats" rule. Four turns of the hat and the player is eliminated from the competition. You can also do this game in teams with one team challenging another team to do a certain number and/or kind of flips in succession without a mistake.

Summary

Here are the elements to preparing for championship practices:

❖ In the off-season, get to know your assistant coaches, your players, and their families on a close, personal level. Get to know their social personality and their stress personality;

❖ Prepare your facilities and your equipment to be the best they can be.

❖ Have thorough and productive pre-season meetings with your players and their families.

❖ Begin your preparation for the current season the evening of the last game of the previous season by developing a "Need to Get Better" list. **That list needs to start with you.**

❖ Develop a plan and a vision for the current week's practices the Sunday prior to that week and work backward from the end of the week and from the end of each day.

❖ Divide each day's practices into timed segments which progressively build one upon the other culminating in a scrimmage or a game simulation competition.

❖ Have the players arrive at least fifteen minutes early for practice each day, have them run to the field, have them check the posted practice plan when they get there and ask what they can do to help set up or prepare for practice.

❖ Be a Christian role model for your players in every way - including the way you dress, the way you plan and organize for practice, your patience with teaching your players, the way you respond to adversity and your priority of serving others first.

❖ Do your homework in the off-season on the physical, mental and emotional needs of your players and how to improve their skills in a progressive, building-block manner.

❖ Be prepared to be flexible during practice due to changes in the weather and to player unavailability.

❖ Allow enough time for practice and always start on time so you can complete your teaching progression each day. Make wise use of the time prior to practice when players arrive early.

❖ Design your practices to have constant action by all players, have adequate repetitions of the fundamentals and numerous game speed, game-intensity competitions. The practices should have variety and flexibility, but should also have a familiar structure and feeling of predictability to the players.

❖ Multi-task during every part of practice to give them as much content and game relevance as possible;

❖ Be sure you have adequate help to set up and tear down stations before and after practice.

❖ Never compromise your standards when choosing assistant coaches.

❖ Choose the right coaching style to fit the particular players you are coaching that season. You adapt to their personalities and to their primary method of learning. They adapt to your standard of excellence.

❖ Teach your players how to teach and give all of them frequent opportunities to lead. Hold them accountable for doing so every day.

❖ Manage your risk very carefully when you design your practices and how you handle your relationships with your assistant coaches, players and their families. Always seek to educate the whole person, not just the athlete. Leave nothing to inference.

❖ Design specific life skill and personal integrity education into each practice.

When you do all of these things, you will be ready to execute championship practices.

Practices that will develop *Champions for Life*.

CHAPTER SEVEN

EXECUTING CHAMPIONSHIP PRACTICES

"But as for you, be strong and do not relax, for your work will be rewarded!"
2 Chronicles 15:7

Bill Self, the great basketball coach at the University of Kansas says that, *"Coaches should be judged primarily on two things: (1) How hard their team plays and (2) Whether the team thinks and plays unselfishly. You do not want to have to coach effort in a game, only execution".*

The pre-practice rules and requirements that I have outlined in the prior chapter set the tone for a coach to teach his or her team to do exactly those things.

Now that I have laid the foundation for a championship practice, I want to break down a sample baseball practice plan component-by-component to give you specific advice about how to put one together for the team you are coaching.

I will use and explain the principles that I have discussed in the prior chapter so it is clear how the principles apply to each part of the practice and to give you as many variations as I can without muddying the waters too much. *(Please refer to the Sample Practice Plan in Appendix L when reading this chapter.)*

As I have said from the beginning, I will not give much specific advice on how to throw, field or hit a baseball, but I will give you many tips on the keys to teaching those things.

I will also give you a few of my favorite drills for various parts of the practice. For many other drills and teaching techniques, please see the references in the Bibliography in the back of the book.

Always Start Practice on Time

This is so important I need to say it again. It is great to make full use of the time before practice to coach and to build rapport with players who arrive early, but watch the time carefully. It is imperative that you always start practice on time. You have broken down your practice plan into timed segments that build one upon the other in a progressive manner. The practice plan has been designed from the end of the practice game simulation competition or scrimmage backward. Therefore, staying on time and completing the practice is key to connecting the teaching points you are trying to accomplish.

Staying on time and on task every day is key to building trust with your players. Show them that you are true to your word and are reliable in your planning.

Quotes

Prior to, in between, and at the end of each of my practice plans are carefully selected quotes. Practice plans for younger teams may only have one or two quotes. The practice plans for my high school teams have several.

I have chosen these quotes because they illustrate the teaching points of the day's practice plan or "lesson".

Older players are required to read and memorize these quotes before practice starts. More importantly, they are required to internalize the relevance and meaning of the quotes. One of the competitions during the day involves players being called out to state the quote and to give an example of how the meaning behind the quote applies to the team or to the player's life.

The first quote sets the tone for the day and usually emphasizes the "get better every day" standard. The quotes prior to a section in the middle of the practice plan usually relate to work ethic and attitude.

They also frequently contain baseball concepts that we are trying to teach in the next part of practice.

The final quote of the day is generally something inspirational relating to how a person of high moral character acts in certain situations.

It sends a message to the players how to "go and serve the Lord" as they leave practice. *(See Appendix L.)*

Announcements/Illness & Injury Report/Prayer-Spiritual Testimony/Cheer

The field prep and station set up is done. The pre-practice drills and rapport-building are complete. It's time to start practice.

Announcements regarding upcoming events, reminders, general team or school issues and the like are made at the beginning and *again at the end* of practice. It is important to state them twice and to have them repeated by the players to assure they have any chance of being remembered.

If the information is vitally important, you need to send it in an email to their parents as well.

It is very important to ask your players, every day, who is sick or injured. They may not tell you, but it is very important from an "avoiding liability point of view" that you can truthfully testify later that you have a habit of asking them *every day*.

Do not rely on this inquiry as determinative of whether anyone is sick or injured. Be very vigilant during practice to watch for any signs of weakness or infirmity, physically or emotionally, among your players.

I cannot overstate the importance of prayer in my practices.

Without a spiritual connection, practices, like life, are meaningless. The players must be reminded that God is with them and cares about *why they are doing* what they are doing at all times.

Prayer time can take different formats at different times and with different teams. Sometimes, my assistant coaches and I will divide the team up and pray 1 v. 1 with 2 or 3 players each day. This way, by the end of the week, we will have prayed with all of the players on the team. It also allows us to get a closer look and understanding of what is going on in each player's heart and life.

If we do 1 v. 1 prayer, it is usually done before or after practice, otherwise it takes too much time away from the baseball part of practice. The prayer time with each player should last about five minutes. At other times or on other teams, we might pray all together every day, but a different player or coach will take a turn leading the prayer. The operative word here is "lead".

Everyone is encouraged to participate every day.

Once per week, I either separate the team into small groups for prayer, or an assistant coach and I will give personal witness and testimony about how our Faith has impacted our life in a way the youth can understand. These are short-- ten minutes or less--but can cover a wide range of possible subjects to illustrate how we are or have overcome challenges to do His work.

As I discussed in Chapter Four, whenever and however prayer is said, the same general format is used. First, always give thanks for blessings. No matter how tough life is and what crosses we are asked to carry, we always have many things to be thankful for. This is a key life lesson I teach to my players and the area in practice I "push the envelope" the most. Push them to enumerate the blessings in their life and the goodness in the world generally.

So many people only look at the negative in life.

We need to train our youth to always focus on the positive, the goodness (God-ness) in others, and in life.

Second, ask that they pray for the needs of others. On my high school teams, "others" to a freshman or a sophomore player, can be limited at first to his family, extended family and the people at school. But, "others" to a junior or senior player must be extended to the community, the State, country and the world.

Their sphere of awareness should be global by the time they graduate.

Finally, allow the players to pray for themselves. Youth team players, or freshman and sophomores on my high school teams, are allowed to pray for physical things like their health, their grades, good weather or whatever. Juniors and seniors can start with these things, of course, but are pushed to dig deeper to address overcoming fears in life, baseball, school or more personal challenges. They do not need to get too specific.

Respect their privacy, but push them to connect with the Lord to help them with challenges like relations with their parents, friends, teachers and teammates.

The next thing I do in this first part of practice is give the team a brief summary of why the practice has been designed the way it is, and what we hope to accomplish. I explain the progression of the practice and emphasize what we expect from them both generally ("get better every day through perfect practice") and specifically (how to do the next part of practice). Do not do too much talking here, however! Keep them doing, not listening too long.

Like most teams, we begin the activity part of practice by doing our team cheer. *Teams are families. Teammates must become brothers and sisters.*

Therefore, we do not cheer using the name of our team or our school mascot. At games and at practices, our cheer is "Brothers!"

One note that may be obvious, but cannot be overstated is that to maximize learning time and efficiency, the players *and coaches* must run from station-to-station for each part of the practice the *entire practice*.

From the moment everyone arrives at the field, the energy should always be high and hustle the norm. This habit will carry over to game day as well and will be a big intimidation factor working in favor of your team. Another key practical point is the players should carry their water bottles, gloves, bats and helmets with them to every part of practice. During a practice, a "water break" or a "go get a piece of equipment break" are unnecessary. This is the most common form of inefficiency in baseball practices. Everything a player needs to fully participate and keep safe should be with him at all times during practice.

Running Form Warm-Up

As I discussed in Chapter Three, some form of five-minute cardio or running form warm-up raising the core body temperature is essential before the body can be safely and effectively stretched. This warm-up can take many different forms for different teams and at different times of the season.

The basic warm-up routine for my younger baseball teams is set forth in Appendix D and is a series of footwork and running form patterns designed in a kinetically progressive way. This is our "default routine" for games and for the rare times at practice when the players have to start without a coach being present.

You will note that I said running "form" warm up. The running form warm up is another progression designed to work on the elements of good running form in a kinetically logical progression. The players are required to work on improving their running form every day. Warm-up does not mean just going through the motions!

However, once I have taught the basics of base running to my teams during the first few weeks of the season, I incorporate base running into the running form warm-up part of practice.

For example, for my older teams, their running form warm-up might start at home plate with me calling out the different base running routes from home plate to first base, i.e., ball-in-dirt on a third strike, ground ball to an infielder, ground ball that goes through the infield and a ball hit directly to the outfield.

For my younger teams, I incorporate many more reps of this routine so they have the nuances of base running perfected.

For their running form warm-up every day, I set discs or cones the same distance apart as the distance between bases in a game, say 70' for my youth players, and the players take a specific pre-determined lead before they do each run. (Multi-task at every phase of the practice!) I want to build "muscle memory" into my players about the distance of the base path so that it becomes second nature to them. This is a subtle advantage to particularly my younger players. Actually, even for my high school teams, our running form warm-up routine is usually done at 90' distances for the same reasons. The first run is started by a "designated lead" from first base. The next might be a steal lead. The next one a "one-way" lead and so on. The same would be true for second and third base. While doing the practice runs from third base, they do "safety" and "suicide" squeeze bunt leads and extensions and they do "tag ups" for fly balls.

Initially, because the players are young, leads are done without a coach as a pretend pitcher. Once they learn the basic leads, they will react to the movements of a coach pretending to be a right-handed or a left- handed pitcher. Then, I add "look ins" and reactions to first and third base coaches. When the players begin to get proficient at doing this routine, players are asked to volunteer and then be chosen to lead this routine by being at the front of the line and calling out the instructions to their teammates. *(Multi-task leadership skills!)*

The players do this routine in, at most, two lines. Therefore, six or seven players line up one behind the other in a vertical line and do the lead, extension and run at the same time. Otherwise, the routine takes too much time. Obviously, you need to allow more time for this at the beginning of the season when you are teaching it to the team. After a few weeks, they can just do leads from first base on one day, from second base the next, third base the next and a coach's choice from a variety of bases in random order the next.

Coaching Champions for Life

The fifth day your team practices base running can be Competition Day.

The basic format for my team's competitions

I divide my baseball teams into two teams for practice competitions - catchers and outfielders on one team and infielders and pitchers on the other. We do competitions at almost every part of practice on most days. Teams, as everyone knows, are only as strong as their weakest link.

So, we call our competitions "Weakest Link Competitions".

The first team calls out a player on the other team that they think is the weakest link for the drill for the other team. Then the other team does the same. The two players compete in whatever the drill is and the team who has the losing player on it suffers the consequence. The competition may have more than one round with the same two players competing or it may have several players from each team competing against one another in separate rounds.

Here's the catch, however.

A player who has been picked as the "weakest link" in one competition cannot be chosen again during that practice as a "weakest link" in another competition until all the other players on his team have been chosen. This prevents a team from picking the weakest player from the opposing team as the "weakest link" in every competition.

"Consequences" for losing competitions must be dreaded or the rewards for winning highly prized or there is no real pressure for losing. Competitions without pressure are useless.

Early in the practice, the consequences might be extra ab/core exercises or the assumption of clean-up duties during practice. Later in the practice, the winning team might get extra batting practice reps or some slight advantage in the "game simulation" competition.

At the end of practice, it might be extra running or the assumption of field "dress down" duties for the other team.

The possibilities are endless, but you get the idea.

The final "multi-task" I add to this part of practice, of course, is signs. Players take a particular lead not based on an oral command, but from a sign that we use for the lead in the game.

When it comes to base running and bunting, I sometimes reward players for challenging a teammate to a competition the day before a game. If he wins, he gets to substitute for the losing player during the game for one at bat or one base running opportunity of my choice.

This gives a "bench player" an opportunity to earn more playing time and does not disadvantage the team as long as the league allows "re-entry" of the substituted starting player.

It also assures that every player takes every part of their game seriously. No excuses for a "power hitter" being a poor bunter.

Stretching/Signs/Game Review/Daily Tutorial

Now that the players are adequately warmed up, the next progression in my practice is stretching. I discussed the importance and the specifics of stretching in Chapter Three.

It is always done before (and sometimes after) every practice and game and never lasts less than 15 minutes. Whether done "dynamically", i.e., in motion, or statically, i.e., while still, it is done with the same effort and concentration as every other part of practice and is done with the same "get better every day" attitude. It is also done symmetrically in a kinetically logical manner.

> *Even after the core body temperature is raised by the running form warm up, blood must be pumped into the specific muscle groups to be stretched prior to the stretching being done to avoid micro-tears from occurring.*

These things are true for all teams and all ages.

For my older teams, I use a warm-up routine that combines running form exercises, as well as, static and dynamic stretching exercises. A sample of this routine is set forth in Appendix E.

Make life skills education about topics like nutrition, positive thinking, spirituality and verbal and non-verbal communication a scheduled part of every practice.

Signs, game reviews and daily tutorials are three of the many things that can be done while the players are stretching to multi-task during this time. At the beginning of the season, teaching and reviewing signs are the obvious choice here.

The day after a game, I usually do my game review during this time.

Otherwise, most of the time, I do my daily tutorial here. I leave nothing to chance or inference in my programs. Therefore, *every* practice day I educate my players on specific pre-determined subjects that will help them be more well-balanced young people of high integrity.

Last season, this was our daily tutorial schedule:

Mondays - Nutrition, sleep, general health, physiology, sports training

Tuesdays - Positive thinking, mental conditioning (specific drills to condition the players to always see the "glass as half full", learning how to deal with fears, be more self-confident, have better mental discipline, etc.)

Wednesdays - Spirituality, Faith Sharing

Thursdays - Oral Communication - both in life and in baseball, including non-verbal cues for both

Fridays - Life Skills (how to give a proper handshake, how to carry on a conversation with someone you do not know well or have not seen in a long time, how to win or lose with class, how to get a job, etc.)

These "tutorials" are not just lectures, they are interactive. Subjects which require illustration on a white board are best suited for a classroom discussion at the end on an indoor practice rather than outdoors during stretching time.

Physical Conditioning - Part I

During this phase of practice, pitchers do a set routine to strengthen and protect their arms and shoulders.

I may vary the routine to do one set routine on Monday, Wednesday and Friday and another on Tuesday and Thursday, but the routines are set, are done with very strict form, and under close supervision.

The arm and shoulder conditioning routines involve the use of elastic bands, 2 or 3 lb. dumbbells, kettle bells and weighted balls. They do the same exercises for both shoulders regardless of whether they throw with their right or left hand.

Training is always done symmetrically. Great routines for this can be found in the references I have given you in the bibliography. Even my younger players do the basic four elastic band exercises every day.

> *It is never too soon to strengthen and protect a young pitcher's arm and shoulder.*

Our elastic band routine is done by our pitchers before they take the mound on game day as well. During the time the pitchers are doing their arm-care program, the rest of the team does their ab/core work. The pitchers do their ab/core work at the end of practice. Every day, exercises are done to cover the whole core area, i.e., upper and lower abs, obliques, lower back, core stabilization, etc.

I try to keep it fun and interesting by using a wide variety of exercises and training aids like weighted "medicine" balls.

Multi-tasking can be accomplished during this time by doing signs, pitch sequence drills, mental imagery work, other mental conditioning, visualization and game management drills during rest breaks.

Base Running

> *Big games, close games and championships are lost, not won.*

The team that makes the fewest mistakes usually wins. Most of the critical mistakes in these games are mental mistakes.

Frequently, in baseball, those mistakes occur during base running.

These may be subtle mistakes like taking a half-step too short a lead or getting a poor jump on a steal attempt. They may be very blatant mistakes like missing a sign, getting picked off a base, failing to "look in" for a coach's direction or running through a "stop sign". Subtle or blatant, base running mistakes are almost always a significant part of a loss in a close baseball game.

> *Base running must be worked on every day of practice and must be multi-tasked into as many drills as possible.*
>
> *Base running is not a lost art, it is a neglected one. Be sure your slower-running players do not believe that they cannot steal bases or that base running mechanics do not apply to them.*
>
> *If a player is going to run the bases and if you are going to win close games, everyone on the team must perfect their base running skills.*

You never know which run in the game will be the winning run.

Many players with much less than exceptional speed steal a lot of bases and score a lot of runs by studying the habits of pitchers and by perfecting their leads, reads and routes. Early in the season and until I am convinced the team can understand and execute the basic base running mechanics on command and by sign perfectly, I do base running as a separate part of practice and not just as a part of the running form warm-up.

Younger teams may do base running during both phases of practice. The pre-stretch base running will be done as a review of what we have covered so far that season and then we will cover new concepts in this part of practice. Base running fundamentals are taught like every other fundamental

,i.e., in a progressive building-block manner. The mental approach, footwork, posture and running form are taught first. Then, one base at a time beginning at home plate, what they do and *why they do it* are taught.

The mental routine a base runner must go through before every pitch is:

1. Find the ball and know where it is at all times. Never, ever take your eye off of it.

2. Flash the number of outs with both hands held high to the third base coach (this is done only when the runner initially reaches base safely or when another out is made while the runner is still on base.)

3. Know the score and the inning, i.e., the importance of your run.

4. Get your sign from the third base coach.

5. Check your defense for tips on what they will do and where you can get a jump or take an extra base if the ball is hit there; and

6. Take your lead when the pitcher steps on the rubber.

You must hammer this routine into the heads of your players in as many ways as you can think of every day to be sure every one of them do it on every pitch.

Championships cannot be won without this methodology!

At home plate, you must not only teach the basic routes from home plate to first base, but you must coach the subtle points as well:

- ❖ Where does the hitter stand and what does he do in the batter's box when a runner is stealing second or third base or home plate?

- ❖ What route does he take to first base on a ball in the dirt after a swing and miss with two strikes if the ball ends up on the first base side of home plate?

- ❖ What if the ball ends up on the third base side?

- ❖ What are the rules when a hitter swings and misses, but the pitch hits him or if the ball bounces first and then the hitter makes contact?

- ❖ What if the hitter makes contact, but one foot is out of the batter's box?

- ❖ What if the hitter makes contact with the ball twice and the second time he has one foot out of the batter's box?

- ❖ What if the ball makes contact with the hitter while he begins to run to first base?

- ❖ What if the hitter swings and steps out of the batter's box toward home plate to "protect" a runner attempting a steal of second base? Does it matter in that instance if he makes contact with the catcher?

- ❖ What does the on-deck batter do when a teammate is attempting to score a run?

- ❖ What does the "hole hitter" do when the on-deck batter approaches home plate to take his turn at bat?

- ❖ When does the hitter get his sign from the third base coach before the first pitch of his at-bat? *(Definitely not when he arrives at home plate when everyone is watching.)*

Multi-task base running into as many parts of your practices as possible. Knowledge of what to do by you and your players is not enough. To win championships, the habits must become instinctive.

These are just a few of the many, many things that frequently happen during baseball games that involve events occurring at or near home plate. You and your players need to know your rule book cover-to-cover.

> *More importantly, in all base running plays, everyone needs to be able to react instantly and instinctively to the event.*

Even the slightest hesitation can cost you the game.

When teaching the mechanics at each base, the building-block progression might look like this - mental approach, signs, non-verbal communication with coaches and teammates, posture, footwork, leads, reads of the pitcher, extensions, retreats, "look-ins", routes, multiple runners, run downs, tag ups, squeezes and sliding mechanics.

Yes, there are many, many details involved, but that is why base running must be worked on every day and must be multi-tasked into almost every part of practice.

Not multi-tasking base running into enough phases of practice is one of the most common mistakes I see in other coaches' practices. For example, my outfielders run from home plate to first base at the end of the session when my infielders take ground balls so the infielders have to perform at game speed and under the pressure of a runner running to first base.

Infielders run for my outfielders when we are working on relays or throwing to the correct base. Batting practice on the full diamond is almost always done with base runners and the base runners work on a pre-determined set of fundamentals at each base (*usually the fundamentals that were covered in the base running part of practice - progressions, progressions, progressions*).

Run downs or "hot boxes" are frequently mishandled or executed poorly by baseball teams. Usually, the runner either escapes safely to the base or if tagged out, is done so after too many throws are made so that other runners are allowed to advance to the next base.

I frequently work on run downs as a part of our throwing and receiving progression part of practice even if we are not doing base running as a separate part of practice. And, of course, run down mechanics are designed to be part of other parts of the practice like pitcher's picks to bases, 1st and 2nd bunt coverage, 1st & 3rd steal defense, "suicide squeeze" bunts, etc.

> *Multi-task base running into as many parts of your practice as possible and get better at it every day…or watch your championship dreams go up in smoke.*

Throwing and Receiving Progression

Next to stretching, the throwing and receiving progression part of practice is the one where I see the "perfect practice bar" lowered the most by inexperienced coaches.

They hurry through this part of practice and treat it merely as a warm-up. Then they wonder why their pitchers cannot throw strikes under pressure in games, for example.

> *Pitching is the art of refined throwing. Pitching does not begin on the mound; it begins every day during the flat ground throwing and receiving progression.*

Ditto for the mechanics of the infielders and outfielders.

Every part of this progression has a purpose or purposes and must be closely scrutinized every day. Throwing a baseball must be done perfectly every day.

As Coach Dedeaux said, "A throwing error is a *mental* mistake".

First, it bears repeating that *baseball players warm-up to throw, i.e., they run, they stretch and then they throw. They do not throw to warm-up.* Second, note how the title of this part of practice is "Throwing and *Receiving* Progression".

So many coaches focus so much on their players' throwing mechanics that they fail to remember that just as many runs are given up in games by poor receiving mechanics as by poor throwing mechanics.

> *A player should never throw a baseball in any part of practice unless he is throwing to a target and has a routine he is practicing for proper throwing mechanics.*

Receiving mechanics start, like everything else, with proper posture and footwork. The athlete must start with the proper "athletic stance", weight on the balls of the feet, a slight bend in the knees and at the waist, arms extended but slightly flexed out front and the hands spread shoulder width apart.

If the person throwing the ball does not see his partner in this position, he should not throw him the ball. This is a critical point of accountability by teammates.

The person receiving the throw must be watching the throwing mechanics of the thrower and the person throwing the ball must watch the receiving mechanics of the receiver - every throw of every day. I like to pair players who have similar bad habits so it is easy for them to spot what their partner needs to improve upon and also remind them of what they need to work on.

The target of the throw is the receiving player's chest, not his glove. We talk about "soft focus" and "hard focus" (some coaches call them "broad focus" and "narrow or fine focus") as keys in visualization techniques. Different players and different coaches have slightly different cues for "soft" and "hard" focus points, but all good players and coaches use them.

When I refer to "soft" and "hard" focus below, I am referring to the ones that I teach my players to use at first, but they are free to change them to something that works better for them.

A player starts the process by being aware of the "soft focus" and at a certain point switches to the "hard focus".

The "soft focus" in general, flat-ground throwing is the receiving player and the other players around him.

The "hard focus," i.e., the specific point of focus or target, is a button or letter on the receiving player's shirt. The "hard focus" is picked up when the thrower reaches his "balance point" (i.e., standing on his back leg) in his throwing motion.

The concepts of "soft" and "hard" focus are very important parts of a baseball player's mental training. In hitting, I teach that the "soft focus" is the pitcher and the hitting background in center field. The "hard focus" is the letter or letters on the pitcher's hat. The hitter picks up the "hard focus" when the pitcher starts his motion and then transfers his focus to the release point when the pitcher is about to release the ball.

Some pick up the "hard focus" when the pitcher breaks his hands. It is very important not to begin the "hard focus" too early, however, because a person cannot maintain his "hard focus" with complete concentration for more than 2 or 3 seconds.

In pitching, the "soft focus" I teach is the catcher and the "hard focus" is the catcher's glove or a quarter-size orange dot in the middle of the glove. Like other defensive players, the pitcher picks up the "hard focus" point when he reaches the "balance point" of his delivery, i.e., when he is balancing on his back leg or "posting foot".

Good receiving mechanics dictate that the player receiving the ball has a slight swaying movement to his body while waiting for the throw so he can have an explosive first step in moving to the ball. He should always expect a bad throw, not a good throw. It is easy to receive a good throw, but the receiver does not want to be surprised by a bad throw.

The receiver must move to catch the ball chest high in the trunk of his body, never "outside the box". He must receive the ball with both hands together with the bare hand going underneath (*throws above the waist*) or over the palm of the glove hand (*throws below the waist*), not around the glove, to take the ball out.

The glove is held with the fingers pointing up for balls received above the waist and fingers pointing down for throws received below the waist. The ball must be taken out, i.e., transferred, as quickly as possible on *every* reception.

Finally, the player's weight must be on his back, throwing side foot as he receives the ball so he can immediately push off on his "power leg" to make the return throw.

However, until the players are doing the "rapid fire" portion of the progression, the player should not return the throw immediately. Rather, they should just make a quick transfer of the ball from the glove to throwing hand, break their hands as if to throw and check to see if their weight has been properly transferred to their back leg. Then they should stop to allow their partner to get into the proper receiving position and to allow them to think about their proper throwing mechanics.

> Quality before quantity, always.

I will state the order of our throwing progression, the purpose(s) of each throw in the progression and the keys to teaching it, but I will not detail the mechanics of each and every throw.

That is the subject of another book .

I took the time to specify the details of receiving mechanics because they are rarely discussed in the "how to" books and are frequently ignored by inexperienced coaches.

Dart Throws

The first thing I work on in our throwing progression is "dart throws", i.e., the throws used in executing "run downs" and short overhand throws. The throws themselves are also taught in a progressive manner. Early in the year, pairs of players do them from a stationary position about fifteen feet apart.

Then they progress to starting at the distance of the base path in a game and the person with the ball runs at his partner *at game speed*. When the receiving player catches the ball, he tags his partner as he runs by him. In other words, the thrower becomes a runner after he makes the throw so the receiver can practice his tags. Many balls are dropped by the player making a tag in a game so it is imperative that tags are worked on in practice.

Once the basics are mastered, I have outfielders become runners so that the progression is completed by a game simulation drill.

Of course, to be efficient, we have three or four "run downs" being done simultaneously by different groups of players.

Finally, pitchers start the run downs by running at the runner and dart throwing the ball to the "hot box" player who is standing near the base once the runner has committed to going toward a particular base and is within the last third of the base path.

It is critical that the pitcher not run at the runner and try to make the tag (unless, of course, the runner freezes and gives up without trying to run to a base) because this frequently leads to pitchers or players making the throw from outside the "hot box" throwing the ball too late to the "hot box" player.

This will "handcuff" the receiving player causing him to drop or miss the ball.

Square Offs

Second in our throwing progression are "square offs".

Two players face each other about fifteen feet apart and throw a "two color" ball to each other. A "two color" ball is one that has simply been colored black on one of half the ball. (*I just use a "sharpie" pen to do this. A black piece of tape or thick stripe down the middle of the ball will also work.*)

This ball is used so the throwing player can check that he is using the proper grip before he throws and has the proper pronation of his hand when he executes the throw.

In other words, he stops to look behind him to look at his throwing hand before he throws to check his grip and arm position. Then he watches to see when the ball is travelling to his partner if there is a sharp black line down the middle of the ball indicating he threw the ball correctly, i.e., pronated his hand upon release of the ball.

> **TIP** - Players use the two-color balls for the entire throwing progression every practice until I am sure that the player's grip and release mechanics are sound.
>
> The receiving player must again use all of the proper receiving mechanics before and after the ball is thrown. He must also catch the first five of these throws with the back of his glove so that he learns to use his glove as a pad and not as a trap.
>
> This is how hand transfer mechanics are multi-tasked into the throwing mechanics.

The goal is also to be able to have all players own or have actual "hand-pads" to use in place of their gloves for the first few phases of the throwing progression. "Hand pads" are mini- gloves or pads that do not bend so that the player must use both hands to receive the ball.

He must also learn to receive the ball with "soft hands" within the trunk of his body or he will drop the ball. At a minimum, all catchers must start the season using "hand pads" for the first few phases of the throwing progression so they begin immediately working on improving their ball transfer skills.

By the way, catchers suit up in their catcher's gear prior to the beginning of the throwing and receiving progression and they wear their gear for most of the remainder of the practice when the team is doing defensive drills.

A catcher must adapt to wearing his gear at all times while doing defensive drills so that the gear becomes just another part of his body.

Catchers hate this, but the same is true for the running and SAQ drills. They do them all with their gear on!

Stride Outs

"Stride outs" are begun with the player facing sideways to his partner and his feet about double shoulder width apart.

The back foot is perpendicular to his partner and his front foot is at a slight angle just short of straight on toward his partner.

The toe of the front foot is 1-2" open, i.e., to the glove side, of a straight line between the toe of the back foot and the target.

The arms start together in front of the chest and the player sways his body in a back, front, back and then throw manner.

The player "breaks" his hands and arms open in an "equal and opposite" position during the last phase of when the player rocks his body back, front and back.

When the player throws the ball, he does not move except for rolling over on to the toe of the back foot. The coach watches to be sure the player is initiating the throw with his hips, is keeping his shoulders and eyes level, his head steady and pointed straight toward his target and not leaning to the side, and that he keeps his glove over his front knee at least waist high at release point.

Once the player has mastered the basic motion and throw, he then adds an explosion forward toward his target after releasing the ball by pushing off of his front stride foot and kicking the heel of his back foot high into the air. In this variation, the player's heart will travel toward the glove during the explosive finish. The coach needs to be sure that the player's glove does not trail to the side or behind the player. Advanced players should also add a variation where they start at release point and work on the wrist snap and leg kick portions of the drill. These throws are done over a very short distance, however.

> **TIP** - To help the players master these mechanics, I have them do this drill, without the explosion and wrist snap variations, while standing on 2x4 pieces of wood. The pieces of wood are about as long as the players are tall.
>
> The pieces of wood I use on hard surfaces or indoors have a "T" piece at the back end of it to help stabilize it. The length of the "T" is about 1/3 as long as the main piece of wood.
>
> The ones I use outdoors on grass do not have a "T", but have three holes in them spaced equally apart through which I drive 10" nails into the ground for stabilization. (Be careful of those irrigation lines!)
>
> The player must obviously do this 2x4 drill indoors or outdoors while wearing tennis shoes and not his baseball cleats.

Step Behinds

The next throw in the progression is a "step behind".

This is executed by the player starting again sideways to his target with his hands together in front of his chest and his feet shoulder width apart. His weight and all movements are on the balls of his feet with a good athletic posture. First, he takes his back, throwing side foot and "steps behind" his front, glove side foot. Simultaneously to the footwork, he crosses the hand with the ball in it underneath the glove hand. The motion is smooth and rhythmical, but with a momentum-building energy to it.

The player then takes another rhythmical step uncrossing his feet and arms and now is in the "stride out" position he just did in the "stride out" throw of the progression and then he makes his throw. These throws start at about half the distance of the base path in a game and progress to greater distances every two or three throws until the players reach the distance of the full length of the base path. I add two variations of this throw to the progression once the player reaches the distance of the full length of the base path.

The first one is the "power leg" throw. This is done by the player hopping three times on his back leg before he throws the ball. The coach must carefully watch to be sure the player maintains a good athletic posture during the hopping and does not lean back when executing the throw. The player must stay in a good vertical alignment above his power leg and must learn to push off with that leg when initiating the throw.

Arm strength, power and distance when throwing a baseball starts with this power leg push off, are then facilitated by the torso and core rotation of the body and are completed by arm speed and wrist snap. The player will do 3-5 throws of this type of throw.

The second variation is called "front leg" balances.

After the player throws the baseball 3-5 times doing the prior variation, he will balance on his power leg again after he completes his throw. He must hold his balance on one leg for a count of three before he is allowed to use his other leg for balance. The player will only be able to hold his balance on one leg consistently if he does the following mechanics correctly: starting his motion in a balanced, athletic and vertically aligned position; he has stepped in a straight line to his target; has not leaned left or right during his throw; has kept his head and shoulders square to his target; his eyes level; and has kept his glove over his front knee at release point and in front of his heart after releasing the ball.

"Crow Hop" or "Bicycle Step" Throws

Once the player has completed his "power leg" and "balance leg" throws, he then starts a series of throws where he will start facing his target and take 3 or 4 steps to get momentum into his throw.

The player will get explosiveness into the throw by doing either a "crow hop" (turning sideways to the target upon receiving the ball and doing a hop on his back "power leg" to propel his throw) or a "bicycle step" (jumping off of his glove-side foot upon receiving the ball and doing a bicycle motion with his feet in the air giving him maximum momentum to make his throw) just prior to the throw.

The distance for these throws starts out at the full base path distance. The player then takes two or three steps back with every throw until he reaches a point where he can no longer throw the ball with good form and not too much arc. As such, the maximum distance for these throws will vary with each pair. A coach must carefully monitor this because the competitive nature of the players will cause them to want to throw the same distance as their teammates.

> *A player should not throw a ball a distance that causes him to "lean and launch," for example, or he risks developing bad habits and an injury.*

The throwing motion and mechanics for the "long toss" throws must be identical to those of the shorter throws and the arc of the ball should not exceed about two (most of the throws) or three times (only the last few throws) the height of the player.

The only differences in the long toss throws as compared to "step behind" throws is the amount of momentum, i.e., number of steps, prior to the throw and "long toss" throws are begun facing directly toward your partner.

The emphasis on these throws should be on "stretching out the arm" by keeping the motion fluid and comfortable. Velocity is not a concern with these throws.

TIP - One point frequently overlooked by young coaches in these throws is the footwork after the follow through.

Once the player lands on his power leg after releasing the ball, the player should continue his momentum by hopping forward two or three times on his power leg. If the player's throwing mechanics are solid, the hops will be in a straight line toward his target.

If they are not, the player will fall off to the side (usually his glove side) or he will usually not be able to hop on one foot at all.

Relay Mechanics/Long Hop Throws

Once the players have completed the "long toss" part of their throwing progression, the infielders go back to the distance of the base paths and work on relay mechanics.

The outfielders, on the other hand, increase their throwing distance to about 10 - 15 feet beyond the distance they can throw with the ball not exceeding twice their height and work on "long hop" throws.

Relays

"Relay mechanics" are the same as receiving mechanics, except when the player moves himself into position to receive the throw chest high, he turns his body to receive the throw on his glove side. He needs to be sure he is receiving the ball with the weight on his "power (throwing side) leg" so he can be ready to immediately push off to make the relay throw.

The first part of this drill is, again, done in pairs with the player with the ball having his back to his partner. His partner calls out instructions to move him to the right or left (e.g., "left two!" or "right three!") the player with the ball follows the instructions, pretends to receive the ball with good receiving mechanics and throws the ball in his glove to his partner.

The person receiving the ball does so with proper receiving mechanics and pretends to throw it to another player as he would in a game. Then he will become the initial receiving player and the process will start over again for the next throw.

These are not rapid fire throw sequences. They are done very deliberately and are closely scrutinized by both the coaches and the player-partners.

If time allows, this drill can be turned into a team competition by putting three or four infielders in the middle of a line of players spaced out at a normal game relay throw distance with a catcher and an outfielder at the end of each line.

The teams will throw the ball to each player in their line, using all of the proper physical and verbal mechanics, up and back two or three times to complete the competition. The team that does so first wins. After a best 2 out of 3, or 3 out of 5 series, the team that loses suffers the "dreaded consequence".

If the ball is not caught by the next player in line, the ball must be returned to that player before the sequence may continue.

Each player in the line must receive the ball each time through the line for the series to count. Coaches can "raise the bar" as the season goes along by disqualifying or not counting series where the mechanics were not done correctly even if the ball was caught sequentially by each player in the line.

> *Progressions, raise the bar, hold them accountable - this is the coaching process.*

"Long Hop" Throws

Infielders receiving the ball from a long throw at a bag or a catcher receiving a long throw at home plate where the ball bounces, want the bounce or "hop" to be a long, high one so they have an easier time seeing and handling it.

"Short hops" will usually "handcuff" the receiving player and he will have a much greater chance of not catching the throw and making a smooth tag.

Umpires, by the way, are "rhythm performers".

If the throw, relay, reception and tag are done smoothly and keep the umpire in his rhythm to make the call, you have a much higher chance of getting an "out" call on a close play. Any awkwardness by a defensive player will usually result in a "safe" call by the umpire because "it just didn't look and feel right".

The outfielders will initially do "long hop" throws in pairs working on all of their throwing, grip and footwork mechanics.

I highly recommend that they use two-color balls for this drill so that they can be sure they are getting a 12-6 rotation on the ball.

A 12-6 rotation (i.e., long seams of the ball rotating perfectly parallel to one another from top to bottom) will cause the ball to give an easy-to-receive high hop to the receiving player.

If the ball is thrown correctly, but the player's fingers are across the *narrow* seams, the ball will skid when it hits the ground and will hop up at the last second, again "handcuffing" the receiver.

(The momentum of the ball hitting the seam is what causes it to hop.)

The "long hop" throw drill can be multi-tasked with infielders receiving the throws at their bags working on "tag mechanics" and by catchers receiving throws at home plate. Finally, runners can be added to the drill to make the tags more "game-like" and so the runners can work on their different types of slides and base coaches can work on their sliding signals.

Rapid Fire/ "Do or Die" Mechanics

Next, infielders position themselves about half the distance of a base path apart in a staggered stance with their glove side foot forward and "rapid fire" the ball back and forth a pre-determined number of times. They use hand pads and regulation size "softie" balls at first until they are proficient at the drill. Then they can use their normal gloves and regular baseballs. The key coaching points here are be sure (a) the player's hands are close together (I say that their wrists are in handcuffs) as they are receiving the ball; (b) their bare hand goes over or under the palm of the glove hand and not around the glove, (c) the glove is used as a pad, (d) the "exchange" occurs out front and not behind the head and (e) the throw is received with the player's weight on his back "power" leg.

Pairs of players compete at the same time to complete a certain number of throws first, e.g., 15-25, without dropping or missing the ball. A drop or a miss requires the team to start their count over. One player is required to call out the team's "count" on each throw. A competition is usually a best 2 out of 3 or 3 out of 5 series. Be sure to mix up the pairings each day so that all players get accustomed to each other's rhythms.

Getting accustomed to a teammate's throwing and receiving rhythm is a key to middle infielders working well together on double play throws, for example.

Again, the best players must be frequently paired with the weakest players. This is how the best players learn to teach and how to handle defeat with grace. This is how weaker players learn that they can succeed and improve when they are pushed out of their comfort zone.

Another variation of this drill is to put four players on a team in a square with the throws being done the first time around in a clockwise (HP to 3B to 2B to 1B to HP) manner and then when the ball reaches the catcher or the first player to throw again, the ball is thrown in a counter-clockwise direction with reverse pivot footwork being used.

The same teaching keys are important, particularly receiving the ball with the player's weight on his throwing side foot.

This variation can be expanded to the full-size diamond at the end of the throwing progression in a drill called "four corners".

At first, the drill is done with only throws, and then tags are added on the next round. At this time, we also work on the throwing routines we use in games after a strike out or after a ground out with no runners on base and less than two outs.

TIP - After doing the four corners drill, we usually work on catchers' footwork and throws to bases with the infielders working on tags. One coaching tip here is to be sure that your infielders are not standing at the bag while the catchers are making their throws. This is also true for your pre-game infield routine.

In a game, the catcher will rarely make a throw to a base with the infielder already at the bag *during the time the catcher is making the throw*. The infielder may be stationary at the bag when *receiving* the throw, but he is almost always moving toward the bag when the catcher is in *the process of throwing*.

Therefore, the same should be true of all practice routines, i.e., the catchers need to get accustomed to throwing to an "open bag" trusting that the infielder will get there when the throw is received. This is one of the two most common reasons why catcher's throws in games are not as accurate as they are in practices.

The other reason, of course, is that they do not make enough throws in practices at game speed and under game-like conditions.

While infielders are working on "rapid fire" throws, outfielders are working on "do or die" mechanics and throws. These are throws which are used by an outfielder when they need to charge a ground ball or fly ball aggressively so they can field it quickly, but efficiently and throw a runner out at home plate usually with no relay.

The same basic mechanics are used here as in "long hop" throws, except in this next step in the progression, the footwork and fielding mechanics are added.

The teaching progression for "do or die" mechanics are: (a) as usual, footwork, with no baseball; (b) "ball in hand" drills where the players do the proper footwork and ball transfer skills with the ball starting in their glove; (c) throwing short ground balls and fly balls, again only working on receiving and transfer skills and no throws; (d) game-like ground balls and fly balls; and (e) add throws to the progression after everything else has been perfected.

Base runners are multi-tasked into "do or die" drills.

When they run from second base, they are working on leads and extensions from second base, routes to home plate, reading signals from the third base coach and sliding mechanics at home plate. For safety reasons, my catchers and runners do not make contact on these plays. I lay down a second home plate for the runners to slide into and the catcher practices his tag at the original home plate.

> *Remember to teach your base runners that you slide aggressively into home plate because unlike slides into second or third base, a base runner does not have to worry about sliding past home plate, only touching it.*

Catchers practice tags on runners at other times during another part of practice when runners are not running full speed. Runners from third base work on leads, extensions, tag ups and slides.

Appendix N is one of my favorite games to play after the throwing and receiving progression. This is called, "continuous 1st and 3rds".

This game basically works on first and third team defense, but instead of just one player stealing from first base and third base, runners continue stealing until certain things occur or three outs are made. The game requires multi-tasking on throwing and receiving skills, pitcher pick skills, runner's leads, reads and sliding skills and defense run down and tag mechanic skills.

Most importantly, the drill is done at game speed. The only concession, again for safety reasons, is the runners slide into a separate home plate since they are running at full speed.

Short Hops/ Blocking Drills

The last series of throws in the progression are short hops done by the infielders, digs by the first baseman and blocking drills done by the catchers. The outfielders assist the infielders and the catchers with these drills.

There are two basic types of short hop drills that we do with the infielders. The first is done with pairs of players facing each other about ten feet apart and the players remain down in their ready-to-field position at all times. They throw short hops to different locations, both forehand and backhand, to each other.

Coaches should be sure that the players are challenging each other with the pace of the ball being thrown, varying the location of the short hop and the severity of the short hop.

Also, I require that each of my players in the pairing keep an extra ball within arm's reach so that if a ball is missed, the players are not allowed to rise up from their fielding position until they have successfully completed a high number, e.g., 20 or more, of throws without missing a reception.

A missed reception means the count starts over.

While the second baseman, shortstops and third baseman are doing the first short hop drill, three or four of the outfielders are helping the first baseman with "digs", i.e., short hops at first base. Three outfielders are alternating throwing short hops from varying distances and from the three angles the first baseman is receiving the throws from infielders during a game.

To save time and maximize efficiency, each outfielder starts with five baseballs so that after the first baseman makes the "dig" he does not need to return the throw, but simply tosses the ball behind him to one or two other outfielders who are backing up the throws.

While the infielders are working on short hops and digs, three or four other outfielders are helping catchers with various blocking drills.

The system they use is the same as for the infielders, i.e., the outfielders are throwing the balls to the catchers while other outfielders are backing up the throws to be sure as many quality reps are being done as possible in a short period of time.

I want to emphasize again that the outfielders are not just helping with the drill; they know the correct mechanics to be done, and are *coaching* their partners to be sure that they are getting better every day.

The next short hop drill is done with one outfielder paired with one infielder. The infielders are at their positions and the outfielders are standing on the infield grass 20' back of the infield dirt and are alternating throwing high arcing tosses that the infielders charge, field on the short hop and make a throw to first base.

Outfielders are actually doing three things during this drill -- throwing the high arcing short hops, backing up the throws to first base and running from home plate to first base to ensure the drill is being done at game speed and with game-like pressure.

You can see that the throwing and receiving progression part of practice is much more than a "warm-up". An incredible amount of teaching, learning and development needs to occur during this time. If it does not, the remainder of practice is largely a waste of time. *(Appendix O is a summary of my throwing and receiving progression.)*

Position Fundamentals

The next two parts of practice deal with position fundamentals and team defense. These parts can vary day-to-day depending on what your goal is for the game simulation competition at the end of practice and on how many coaches and players are on the team.

If players are playing several positions during the season, or if it is a young or inexperienced team, I almost always have a separate part of practice for the whole team for pitchers' and catchers' fundamentals. Otherwise, pitchers and catchers simply do their individual skill work during this part of practice.

> **TIP:** The better and more developed your pitchers and catchers are, the more games you will win. You need to spend time every practice being sure their individual skills are improving.

Furthermore, having everyone participate in some way in these drills, whether or not they are a pitcher or a catcher, will make them better players and better able to help their teammates during practice.

You will recall, for example, in the throwing and receiving progression part of practice how I said that outfielders help catchers in their blocking drills and that they do much more than just throw the ball; they also coached the catchers on their mechanics. Well, this is where young players learn those mechanics.

I usually pair up infielders with pitchers because they are natural partners for drills involving things like picks to bases. Outfielders help the catchers.

Pitchers - We stress seven different general concepts to our pitchers:

(1) Throw strikes, especially first pitch strikes. We want a 2:1 strike-to-ball ratio in general and I want them to throw first pitch strikes at least 70% of the time. I want the batter on or out in 3 pitches 50% of the time.

   With your talented, power pitchers, it will be a tough sell convincing them not to try to strike everyone out.

   Actually, the best pitch in baseball is not just a first pitch strike, it is a first pitch pop-up to the infield - minimum wear and tear on the arm, no throw required for the out and a runner cannot safely advance.

Pitchers become most effective when they not only throw a high percentage of strikes, particularly first-pitch strikes, but also when they stop trying to strike every batter out and make them hit the pitch they want them to hit.

Sandy Koufax said that he became a great pitcher when, "I stopped trying to strike everyone out and I started making them hit the pitch I wanted them to hit". Today, we call these pitchers "contact pitchers" or pitchers who are not afraid to pitch to contact.

(2) Work quickly, but in a rhythm that has been successful for you in the past. This will keep your defense alert and will give the hitter the minimum amount of time to adjust to the pitch sequence.

(3) Changes speeds - have at least two different speeds for your fastball and your curveball or breaking pitches. One key to h*itting is timing and one key to pitching is upsetting that timing.*

(4) Change location - never throw the same pitch at the same speed in the same location during the same at-bat to a good hitter, unless he has looked overmatched on a particular pitch and location.

Work on developing your pitchers' mechanics every day, the mental as well as the physical. Developing their character and integrity off the field will lead to great things on the mound.

(5) Command the mound with a confident presence at all times. This can only be done if the player has been taught to be a "glass half-full", always positive type of person in all areas of his life.

You cannot become on the mound what you are not in life.

(6) Maintain your composure at all times - think "this pitch, this moment". The past is over and done. The future, the umpire's zone, the weather, my teammate's actions, the crowd noise, etc. is out of your control, but you can always have a positive mental approach. Visualize and think success with this one pitch.

No matter what has happened in the past, the future can be perfect, but it must be achieved one pitch at a time.

(7) Field your position - know where you are going to throw a ball hit back to you or what base you are covering or backing up if it is not hit back to you before you step on the rubber.

At least one of these seven concepts is discussed by me *every day* before I begin drills with our pitchers.

Here is the order of training I do with our pitchers and a few of the drills we work on with them:

(1) **"Dry mechanics"** - I break down the pitching delivery into phases, including the pre-pitch routine before he steps on the rubber, and we work with him on each phase with no baseball or throwing involved.

(2) **Mechanics drills** - "towel drills," throwing off of 2x4's, various flat ground drills to engrain proper throwing mechanics;

(3) **Flat ground throwing** - throwing fast balls, first 4-seam, then 2-seam, from a short distance to learn command of the inner and outer third of the plate. I start at a distance of about 2/3 of the game distance and work our way back 5' every week or so until the game distance is reached and the pitcher can command his fastballs. Only after he has command of his fastballs do I start over at the 2/3 distance with change ups.

Finally, I do the same routine with curveballs. I want our pitchers to have two different curveballs, one a "get me over curveball" that has about 90% of the velocity of his best curveball that he can throw for a strike at any time, and his "strike out" curveball which is thrown at 100%, but is designed to land, most of the time, on the ground just behind the back corner of home plate.

For both the change up and the curveball, we experiment with several different grips because different players have different size hands and the same grip does not feel comfortable for every pitcher.

At the high school level and above, if the pitcher throws mostly four-seam fastballs, the first grip he should consider for his change-up should also be with his fingers across the long seams so the spin of the ball as he delivers the pitch looks the same for both pitches. Likewise, if the pitcher throws mostly two-seam fastballs, he should consider griping his change-up along the long seams like he does his fastball for the same reason.

For the change up, I start with being sure that the speed differential (85 - 90% of his fastball) is perfect on every pitch.

Ideally, of course, you want the pitcher's arm speed to be exactly the same for all his pitches so he does not "tip" what pitch is coming. However, I have learned that in youth baseball, including most leagues at the high school level, a change up with perfect speed differential, movement and location, in the proper pitch sequence will get the batter out even if a pitcher's arm speed is *a little* slower.

Work on the grip, throwing mechanics, location and pitch sequence first and focus last on perfecting the arm speed factor once the pitcher's confidence is high regarding the other things. Also, work on the speed differential first, i.e., being comfortable with the grip and releasing the ball palm before fingers with the ball coming primarily off of the ring finger, then work on the movement, i.e., hand pronation at release point and then the location.

All of the factors are important and need to be mastered, but perfect speed differential and the proper pitch sequence are the most important factors to begin with.

For the curveball, I start with visualization drills telling my pitchers to visualize the arc of their own curveball in a ball, ball, ball super slow-mo video replay that they see on TV when watching college or professional games. Then we work with different grips working on getting a tight spin on the ball with 12- 6 rotation (generally, it's not actually 12-6) always landing the ball in the catcher's glove which is on the ground behind the back tip of home plate.

To perfect the spin on the curveball, we start by throwing it with only the middle finger on a long seam and the thumb directly beneath the ball on another seam.

Develop the change-up before the curveball and when delivering it, be sure the ball comes off of the ring finger.

The index finger does not touch the ball. One-finger curveballs are thrown from distances shorter than regulation game distance. Two-finger curveballs are thrown from game distance after one finger curveballs are perfected. Once the best grip and tight spin are accomplished, I work on throwing curveballs with two different speeds starting again from a short distance and working our way back gradually to game distance.

Command the fastballs first, then the change up and then the curveballs.

Pitchers 12 years old and younger should work exclusively on commanding the fastball and change-up pitches.

If the strength training and stretching routines prior to and during the season are sound, the nutrition and sleep habits are proper and the grip and throwing mechanics are sound, no pitcher older than age 12 should hurt his arm throwing a curveball as long as it is not thrown more than 10-15% of the time.

If any of these factors are not sound and proper, a pitcher can hurt his arm or shoulder throwing any pitch, even if he throws exclusively fastballs.

Ideally, all of the work in sections (1), (2) & (3) are to be completed prior to the start of regular season practices!

(4) General Pitching Strategy and Pitch Sequence Rules *(See Appendices P & Q)* - I spend a lot of time on these areas and I multi-task them into as many parts of practice as possible.

My pitchers and catchers call their own game. I do not call pitches for two reasons. First, winning is not as important as the self-esteem of my players and winning is only worthwhile if it is accomplished as much as possible by the players themselves. Second, *the best pitch at any given time is the one the pitcher believes in his heart is the one he can throw to look like a strike in the proper location.* What I think, or what "the book" says is the right pitch at that time, is irrelevant.

Teach them what to do, trust them to execute it and be prepared to accept the outcome with dignity and class.

Three of my favorite drills in this area are the "countdown" drill, the "set sequence" drill, and the "glove only" drill.

In the **"countdown" drill**, the pitcher throws the first pitch of a pre-determined sequence of pitches. If the pitcher throws the pitch in the designated spot, he scores a "1". If not, he throws the pitch again and again, up to four times, until he hits the spot.

The pitcher's score for that round is the number of pitches it took him to hit the spot. The pitcher with the lowest total number of pitches at the end of the sequence of pitches wins the competition. The number of pitches per round and the total number of pitches in the sequence depends on the age of the pitcher and the time during the season the drill is done.

The **"set sequence" drill** is just that, i.e., a pre-determined number and sequence of pitches that a pitcher must throw.

You can start out by just having the pitcher throw the pitches for a strike and then later in the season require that he throw them in certain locations. The final and best variation of this drill is to give the pitcher a hypothetical batter and situation and let him call his own sequence of pitches depending on whether he throws a strike or a ball pitch-to-pitch. After he throws the third strike, you stop the drill momentarily to evaluate his sequence selection before you give him a new hypothetical situation. You can increase the challenge of the drill by adding changes to the situation in the middle of the sequence, e.g., the hitter and runner show bunt and run after the first pitch or the runner at first steals second base on the first pitch, etc.

This will help you evaluate how well your pitchers and catchers "think on their feet" and adapt to changes in the flow of the game. For both the "countdown" and "set sequence" drills, hitters can stand in or near the batter's box and work on "soft focus", "hard focus" and tracking skills. This one of the most overlooked components of training hitters. They do not see enough "live pitches" other than fastballs during batting practice.

Seeing and tracking the ball is a huge key in hitting.

Practicing tracking all types of pitches from release point to the catcher's glove is a critically overlooked part of hitting. It needs to be multi-tasked into as many parts of practice as possible. The **"glove only" drill** is where a pitcher throws a bullpen session to a catcher with no home plate involved. Pitchers need to learn that the target is the catcher's glove (or rather the quarter-size orange dot in the middle of the glove) and not the plate. This is a great drill to reinforce that concept.

Being able to track the ball clearly from release point to point of contact is one of the most important skills in hitting. Have your players track pitches during a pitcher's bullpen work often.

Coaching Champions for Life

Bullpen sessions are practice sessions for both the pitchers and the catchers. I am amazed at how many coaches waste valuable practice time by focusing only on the pitcher during a bullpen session. Catchers pretend on every pitch or every other pitch, when the pitcher is pitching from the stretch, that a runner is stealing a particular base so you are also multi-tasking them working on footwork, receiving and transfer skills.

Catchers work on their "splitting" the plate mechanics on every pitch and on their blocking skills on every pitch in the dirt. Most importantly, catchers work on giving positive verbal feedback to the pitcher. They need to be sure that his confident mound presence and his composure remain intact at all times.

After a bullpen session is complete, the pitcher and catcher always shake hands and congratulate each other for a job well done.

Let me say a few words here about pitch counts. I am definitely in favor of them for all pitchers. The 12 x 5 > 60 x 1 rule applies here as well. When learning to pitch and for the health of a pitcher's arm, pitching fewer pitches more frequently is better than pitching a lot of pitches in one game...and not all pitch counts are the same. In other words, 75 pitches thrown in five innings in a 15-15-15-15-15 sequence is much easier on the arm than a 20-10-20-10-15 sequence.

Think of it in strength training terms:

If you curled a 40lb barbell for five sets, after which sequence above would you be more tired, the sequence with the same reps in each set or the one with the varied sequence?

Pitch counts are determined by the age of the pitcher, his physical condition and maturity, the time of the season, the weather and maybe, most importantly, by how sound the pitcher's mechanics are. Remember, the pitches in the bullpen prior to coming into the game and the pitches between innings need to be monitored closely too. The weather may dictate more or less pitches in these situations. The arm knows only the total number of pitches, not when they were thrown.

TIP - If a pitcher is taken out of a game before he reaches his pitch count, have him continue throwing in the bullpen with the pitching coach until he reaches the count and/or to work out any mechanical issues to get his confidence back. Have your pitchers end the day on a positive note feeling good about themselves!

(5) Holding runners on and picks to bases - Again, the sequence of teaching here is footwork first, once the footwork is mastered, then work on footwork with short throws, then full distance throws and finally full distance throws with base runners.

The pitchers work on varying the type of pick, number of picks and duration of time in the set position prior to the pick so they will be unpredictable to the base runners. The runners work on leads and reads of the pitcher's moves. The pitchers also work on minimizing the time it takes from first movement of their delivery to the time the catcher receives the ball (this should be <1.3 seconds for high school pitchers).

"3-in-1 Drill - Picks"

My favorite drill here is one of many "3- in- 1" drills, i.e., three things being done simultaneously. (Please see Appendix R) I use three pitching rubbers spaced out on *flat ground* with enough room between them for three pitchers to work comfortably at the same time.

The pitcher on the right side rubber is working on picks to first base. The pitcher on the middle rubber is working on picks to second base and on minimizing his delivery time to home plate (Actually, all three pitchers can work on this if you have three catchers). The pitcher using the left side pitching rubber works on picks to third base. Bases and a home plate are used and are at game distance from the pitching rubbers.

I multi-task using base runners working on leads, reads and retreats, but to avoid injury they do not dive back to the base that the pitcher is throwing to. At first base, I use several "throw down" bases lined up behind the first base the pitcher is throwing to so several runners can work at the same time. If control is not an issue with the pitcher, you can also have a hitter stand in at home plate. He will, of course, not swing at any pitch, but he can fake bunt to try to break the concentration of the pitcher and the catcher or he can just work again on his "soft focus", "fine focus" and tracking skills.

After a pre-determined number of pitches in this 3-in-1 drill, the pitchers rotate to a different pitching rubber so they get practice working to each base. No one stands around watching. The other pitchers, for example, while listening to the coach's instructions to the pitchers doing the drill, are practicing their footwork for each pick move or a "slide step" to home plate.

Coaching Champions for Life

(6) Defense - Specifically, I work on fielding bunts, covering first base on balls hit to the right side of the infield, covering home plate after a passed ball or a wild pitch with a runner attempting to score from third base, backing up third base or home plate on relay throws and executing run downs after successful pick offs or pitch outs on "suicide squeeze" plays.

"3-in-1 Drill - Bunts"

Here are some of my favorite drills for working on these things.

For fielding bunts, one of my favorite drills is another 3-in-1 drill. Again, three pitching rubbers are spaced out on the ground with enough space for three pitchers to work comfortably at the same time.

In this drill, you must also have enough room for one catcher to work with each pitcher.

The pitcher and catcher using the right side rubber are working on communication and fielding bunts for the plays at first base. The pitcher is also working on covering first base for balls hit to the right side. The middle pitcher and catcher are working on communication and fielding bunts and "comebackers" for plays with the second baseman and shortstop at second base.

The left side pitcher and catcher are working on communication and fielding bunts for plays with the third baseman at third base.

Outfielders stand in foul territory outside the base lines and receive throws from the infielders after they receive the throws from the pitcher or catcher. The outfielder standing in foul territory then throws the ball to another outfielder who is standing behind one of the catchers and is in charge of throwing the bunts or "comebackers" or of hitting the balls to the right side of the infield to start the drill.

Extra outfielders and infielders are involved in the drill as base runners working on base running mechanics and sliding techniques. The runners also give the drill the necessary "game speed" component.

The "communication" part of the drill starts before the ball is hit or thrown, just like in a game, with non-verbal communication between the pitcher and infielders regarding where the ball will be thrown, to whom and any "exchanges" that might be necessary.

An "exchange" is where one player covers the base for another player because that player has had to vacate his base to field the ball. For example, catchers "exchange" with third baseman with a runner stealing from first base when the third baseman has had to charge hard toward home plate to field a bunt so that the runner does not continue to third base with no one covering the base. In this instance, the pitcher covers home plate while the catcher "exchanges" and covers third base while the third baseman is fielding the ball and throwing it to first base.

On short ground balls between third base and the mound where the third baseman fields the ball, the pitcher "exchanges" with the third baseman and covers third base. On balls hit between third base and shortstop which are fielded by the third baseman going hard to his left, have the shortstop "exchange" with him and cover third base. Finally, the same is true for pitchers and first baseman on short ground balls hit between the mound and first base. A pitcher never chases a ball hit beyond his reach there. He always continues straight forward to cover first base and lets the first or second baseman field the ball.

In this 3-in-1 drill, as in the previous one, pitchers rotate after a pre-determined number of pitches to the next pitching rubber so they get practice working on each type of situation.

For working on **pitchers covering home plate** after a passed ball or wild pitch with a runner attempting to score from third base, I like to use a **drill** that has pitchers lined up in a line behind the pitching rubber and four balls pre-placed on the ground in foul territory behind or to the side of the catcher. One of the balls is on the third base side, one is directly behind the catcher by about two feet, one is behind the catcher by 15' and one is on the first base side.

The drill begins with the catcher in his normal crouch behind home plate and the pitcher pretending to throw a pitch to him. As the pitcher finishes the delivery of his "pretend pitch", he charges home plate while shouting instructions to the catcher to tell him where the ball is located. The pitcher can choose any ball for the catcher to pursue, but once he begins to yell the instruction and point in the direction of the ball, all the other pitchers and players yell the same instruction. It will take more than one player during a game to overcome the noise from the crowd.

My teams use only one word "verbals" to communicate in baseball. More than one word is unnecessary, takes too much precious time and can be confusing. For this drill, I use "1!" to tell the catcher that the ball is on the first base side, "2!" for a ball behind him a good distance, "3!" for a ball on the third base side and "feet!" or "plate!" for a ball behind or under him but near his feet or near home plate.

An advanced version of this drill can be done using a pitching machine that throws curveballs. Set the machine so that it throws sharp-breaking curveballs in the dirt in front of the catcher. Now the catcher must work on his blocking skills to start the drill. Of course, to maximize your multi-tasking, you will have a hitter at home plate and runners at second and third base.

The situation is two strikes on the hitter and less than two outs in the inning. Therefore, when the hitter swings and intentionally misses the ball, the catcher has to make a choice. If he successfully blocks the pitch from getting by him, he will have to hold, i.e., "look back" the runner at third base before he throws the ball to first base to get the hitter out. If the ball gets by him, the pitcher and infielders will have to tell him where it is and he will need to field and throw the ball to the pitcher covering home plate. The runners must read the situation and either advance to the next base or hold at their current base.

Catchers - The complexity of learning the pitchers' and catchers' positions are about the same, but there are usually many more camps and personal trainers for pitchers than there are for catchers. Therefore, it has been my experience that catchers are a little more behind in their skill development than are pitchers. If this is the case for the catchers when they arrive on my team, I schedule individual skill fundamental training as a part of every practice and I multi-task them into as many parts of practice as possible.

Last season, this was our weekly schedule for training catchers during this part of practice:

Mondays - Sign calling and receiving mechanics.

Tuesdays - Footwork for throws, throws to bases, pop-ups.

Wednesdays - Blocking

Thursdays - Relay mechanics, receiving long hop throws, tag mechanics.

Fridays - Managing pitchers, game management/non-verbal and verbal communication, leadership, umpire rapport and pitch sequences.

Here are three keys to the catching position that many coaches overlook and that will help your pitchers get more called strikes:

(1) Be sure your catchers do not set up too far behind home plate. This will make it more difficult for the umpire to see and judge the outside corner pitch. It will also cause the catcher to give up more passed balls on pitches landing just behind the back tip of home plate that should be blocked.

If your catcher is giving up passed balls on pitches landing in the dirt in front of him, he is probably set up too far behind home plate. He should not be more than one arm's length behind the back elbow of the hitter. I am amazed at how many catchers set up in the exact same spot for every hitter when not all hitters stand in the exact same place in the batter's box. Catchers need to adjust the location of their set up position for every hitter.

(2) Be sure the head of your catcher or the glove of your catcher do not rise to catch the pitch. The raising of the catcher's head will again cause the umpire to have a difficult time seeing the pitch on the outside corner. The rising of the catcher's glove to catch a curveball, for example, may take a pitch that would otherwise land in the strike zone out of it. When receiving the pitch, be sure the catcher moves only his arm and glove, not his whole body. The catcher should receive the ball with a flexed arm in front of his body just beyond the bend in his knee, but he should not lunge his whole body forward to receive it.

He should let the ball come to him and not be too anxious to reach out to get it.

(3) One of the most overlooked skills of a catcher is rapport-building with the umpire. This relationship, like all others, must be built on trust. Therefore, a catcher should not frame pitches by attempting to drag pitches into the strike zone in an attempt to fool the umpire.

This will only cause the umpire to feel like he is trying to be "showed up" and will cause him to lose trust in the catcher. This will cause his strike zone to narrow for that pitcher particularly on close pitches in key situations. Catchers should split the plate at first movement of his pitcher, should catch the ball in front of, but within the distance of his knees (this is where umpires are taught a strike lands) and should be sure that their glove remains solid when the pitch hits it and does not trail off.

When your catcher's receiving mechanics are rock steady, the umpire will have the best view of the plate and the strike zone will expand. Work on improving your catchers' fundamentals every day.

__Infielders__ - Hall of Fame manager, Leo Durocher was fond of saying, "There are no bad hops. It was the way the infielder played or misplayed the ball".

Well, as hard as balls are hit off of bats by exceptionally skilled players, that may be a harsh assessment at times, but the fact remains, all of the players known to be one of the best defensively in his league have at least one thing in common; they fielded thousands and thousands of ground balls in practice, and, when everyone else was done, they fielded a thousand more.

All of the basics of fielding ground balls: bending your knees while on the balls of your feet so that your thighs are parallel to the ground; fielding the ball out front and getting your nose over the baseball ("smelling dirt"); using "soft hands" with the glove acting only as a pad; transferring the ball from the glove directly to your throwing side ear without funneling it into your stomach; starting and staying low to the ground while getting to the throwing side of the ball; using quick feet, smooth strides and efficient "to and through" footwork (right, left pick up, right, left throw), etc. cannot be learned except by fielding thousands and thousands of baseballs. Before practice, after practice, during this part of practice, during batting practice, whenever a spare moment exists, practice.

Here are some of the things I think are keys to developing good infielders. First, as always, is the mental side of the game. Good infielders (like all players) want the ball hit to them, expect that the ball will be hit to them on every pitch and are confident that they will make the play, particularly in the pressure moments because they have done their homework and have taken those thousands of ground balls to get ready for the moment. They have studied the scouting charts to know the tendencies of the hitters and know how their pitchers are going to pitch the hitters. They know what pitch is coming and have shifted their mind and body accordingly.

> *Tall infielders like Cal Ripken, Jr., who for their size had surprisingly great range, know that "great instincts and anticipation are no accident".*

The basics to the mental part of defense, for all defensive players, is as follows:

(1) What do I do if the ball is hit to me, either directly or to my left or right?

(2) What do I do if the ball does not come to me, i.e., where I am backing up?

(3) Communicate with the other defensive players verbally and/or non-verbally.

   I work on verbal and non-verbal communication skills as a designed part of practice at least once per week. Catchers must learn to communicate with the pitcher and all infielders. They must also see that the outfielders are communicating with one another. Catchers should never take their crouch or give a pitch sign until they see that all necessary communication has been done by all defensive players. Infielders must communicate with the players next to them, to the pitcher, to the catcher and to the outfielders behind them.

   The outfielders must communicate with outfielder(s) next to them and to the infielders in front of them;

(4) Get in your set position and be ready to execute your "set, ready, creep step" routine. This routine is hands on your knees when the pitcher is on the rubber getting his sign (i.e., "set"). Be in an athletic position on the balls of your feet with your hands out front when he begins his wind up ("ready"), take a few shuffle steps forward as he releases the ball and stutter step when the ball reaches the strike zone ("creep"). *Every* player,

other than the pitcher and catcher of course, must be trained to do this on *every* pitch for the entire game.

A static defense is a worthless defense.

Second, the other work that needs to be done before the infielder ever gets to the field is the physical conditioning work.

Jump rope routines with various footwork patterns are fantastic conditioning and development tools for ball players.

The same is true for **agility ladders**. I do agility ladder work as a part of almost every practice for all of my teams regardless of age. The mistake a lot of coaches make with agility ladders, however, is not insisting that their players use the same posture while doing the agility ladder routine as they expect them to use when fielding a ground ball. This is true for all SAQ work.

Take a long rope and have two players hold it on either end at the height you expect the player to maintain when moving to a ground ball and make him do his SAQ work at the same height. Also, multi-task by incorporating a baseball toss into the drills. For example, when the player exits the agility ladder, have a teammate on one knee about fifteen feet beyond the end of the ladder toss a baseball to one side or the other that the player exiting the ladder will have to react to and catch. Ground balls can also be tossed by a teammate as the player exits the ladder moving laterally. Early in the training on the ladder and when no baseballs are being used, be sure the player exits the ladder with an *explosive* series of steps and not decelerating steps.

Explosive steps are condition precedents to great plays.

The third tool that should be used to train infielders (actually all baseball players) before they take ground balls on the field is "wall ball". Concrete walls are great training aids that coaches can use for hundreds of drills. However, while "wall ball" can be great for obtaining thousands of reps in a much shorter period of time than hitting baseballs on a field, it can also mislead a player into believing that quantity equals quality. Most players rapid-fire reps off of the wall without using proper form to field the ball or without any real purpose for the toss.

They are just wearing out their arm and the ball with no improvement to their skills. Worse yet, they are usually just reinforcing old bad habits! Monitor these drills carefully. Slow it down at first. Perfect practice, perfect practice, perfect practice. *(Appendix S is my wall ball routine for infielders from last season.)* I have already discussed the skills and mechanics we work on at the field, but prior to taking ground balls on the normal infield, i.e., the throwing and receiving progression and drills like short hops, digs, relays and four corners.

Once at the normal infield, one great drill you can do is what I call the **"mirror" drill.** This is done by having all of your infielders line up in 3 or 4 lines triple-spaced apart on the dirt area of the third base side facing the coach who is located on the infield grass. The coach calls out and does all of the footwork patterns for fielding ground balls and making the various plays that infielders have to make while the players do them simultaneously mirroring the coach's moves. The coach and players repeat the footwork patterns over and over again moving around the infield from left to right until they end up on the first base side. "Mirror" techniques have been used in coaching in many sports for many years. I remember taking my first downhill skiing lessons as a young man and my instructor lining us up to ski behind him to simply "do as I do".

Of course, the first couple of skiers located immediately behind the instructor were doing much better than those at the end of the line who were simply copying the mistakes of the students in front of them. But it still was a very effective technique as long as the students rotated their order in the line frequently.

TIP - Here is a tip that I wish I knew from the time I first started coaching baseball many years ago - The wear and tear on your body every time you bend over is cumulative and takes a toll even when you are too young to feel it.

Therefore, no matter your age and no matter if you are hitting fly balls or ground balls, if you are retrieving the balls from the bucket yourself, stack the ball bucket on top of another bucket so you do not have to bend over every time you get a ball.

This one tip will add another ten years to your coaching life!

You are finally ready to hit some ground balls. If possible, have two coaches, or a coach and a player, or two players hit the ground balls at the same time so that many more reps can be done in a short period of time.

The ball buckets are stacked on home plate.

The person hitting the balls from outside the left hand batters' box hits ground balls to the third baseman and the second baseman. The person hitting the balls from outside the right hand batters' box hits the balls to the shortstop and the first baseman. The players receive the balls in the first round or two wearing hand pads and not their gloves and do not make throws.

They simply field the ball and get into the proper fielding and throwing positions, check themselves and then simply toss the ball into a pile in foul territory or in the outfield grass behind second base. I divide the hand pad phase early in the season or with young players into two phases.

During the first round of balls, the players have to stop completely after the ball hits their hand pad and they cannot move until a coach or a teammate has checked their mechanics and has approved or corrected what the receiving player has done.

During the next round the players can add the throwing mechanics to the drill. For young players, actual throws are not added to the drill until the players field the balls with their gloves. During the first round of throws, all throws go to first base with the players or coaches synchronizing the hitting of the balls so that the next coach hits a ball after the player who has just received the prior ball has released his throw.

The next round is usually a **2-in-1 round** i.e., two things happening at once just like the 3-in-1 drills described previously.

Your imagination will be able to come up with many possibilities for these drills. For example, while the third basemen are fielding bunts and slow rollers and making throws to a first baseman at the bag, the shortstops and second baseman can be turning double plays and throwing to another first baseman who is located in front of a 7x7 screen. The 7x7 screen is set up 20' short of first base so it is out of the way of the other first baseman working with the third baseman.

Pitchers can also alternate and work with third basemen on covering bunts or covering first base on balls hit to the first baseman.

Of course, the three most important things to do when working with infielders, like everything else, are to keep it fun, constantly have the players compete with one another and require the players perform at game speed.

Great Play Friday

At the pre-high school youth level, my teams traditionally have "*Great Play Friday*".

This is a fun game looked forward to all week by the players, but one which gets them thinking "outside the box" and to taking chances that they normally would not take (within reason for safety purposes, of course). Sometimes the competition is done individually and sometimes in pairs or in teams. The prize for the winners is usually something special like gift certificates to a yogurt shop, but it does not have to involve something that costs money.

Here is an example of a "Great Play Friday" game and how it peaked the imagination of my players. I hit slow rollers to my team of 11-12 year-olds who were divided into teams of two, third baseman and first baseman.

The winning team on this particular day had its third baseman charge and field the ball (requested by the player to be "medium bounces" like in kick ball) by bouncing the ball off of his t-shirt, which he had pulled tight like a trampoline, into his bare hand which he then threw off-balance off of his right foot to the first baseman who caught it in the stretch position in his hat!

Not bad thinking for 11-12 year-olds!

Position players compete against each other for the most or most consecutive receptions in a round. Right side infielders compete against the left side infielders, etc., etc.,. And, of course, our outfielders and catchers compete in **"weakest link" games** against the pitchers and infielders.

One such game might be where an outfielder hits a ball off a tee to a "weakest link" infielder with the outfielder running to first base to try to beat the throw. Every outfielder and pitcher hits a ground ball one at a time to the same infielder and keeps track of how many times the infielder makes the catch and throw to first base without an error, e.g., 8 out of 10 or whatever. Then the infielders and pitchers pick a "weakest link" outfielder.

The outfielder must catch a routine length fly ball and hit a relay man, i.e., an outfielder partner, who must make an accurate throw to the catcher before the infielder/pitcher runner has tagged up and scored from third base. The team with the most number of successful plays out of ten, or whatever, wins.

Spring Training with Alex Rodriguez

The key to incorporating pressure and game-speed into the drills is having base runners involved. I remember going to Spring Training to watch Alex Rodriguez take ground balls with his teammates when he was with the Texas Rangers.

What impressed me most was not the number of ground balls they took, 100-150 each, but that Alex made a game of the drills by pretending on *every throw* that Ichiro was running. If one of his teammates would double tap his glove after fielding the ball or take an extra shuffle step before throwing it, Alex would exclaim, "Eee's safe maaan. Ichiro's runnin'. You no haf time for tat maan!"

And the Rangers were not even playing Ichiro and the Mariners that day! Alex was going to set the bar as high as possible every day for his teammates and was going to hold them accountable to it on *every* ball hit. Say what you want about Alex, but it is no accident that he is a superstar athlete.

The other drill I like my infielders and outfielders to do, as I mentioned before, are **pop-up drills**. First, I love them to have to catch tennis balls hit high in the air with their bare glove hand (or with two hands for younger players) in really windy conditions. If it is windy, my players know that I am getting out the tennis racket and we're catching pop-ups!

On non-windy days, I feed balls into the machine so that I can have them field many, many balls hit at maximum height.

On rainy days, I use machines for pop-ups to infielders, outfielders and catchers when doing ground ball work is not practical.

When fielding pop-ups, I have my players in triangles or squares. One square or triangle is on the right side of the infield and outfield and one is on the left. The infielders are, of course, at the front of the triangle or square running backward and the outfielders are at the back running forward just like they would be in a game. I do not wait until the ball is caught by the team on one side before I feed another ball into the machine for the other team. I have two balls going at once so they get to field as many balls as possible in a short time. When I hit pop-ups to catchers, I am sure to multi-task by doing it at home plate with pitchers, first basemen and third basemen at their positions doing the drill as well.

Obviously, communication is a huge part of baseball and of these drills so you want to make the drills as game-like as possible. I also multi-task by having the remainder of the team involved in the drill by requiring them to yell out the location of the ball on each one put into the air.

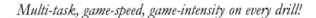
Multi-task, game-speed, game-intensity on every drill!

Multi-tasking is one of the most important keys to running an effective and efficient practice. Bunting, blocking, base running, communication and bunt defense, for example. And in every bunting drill, bunt only strikes.

Outfielders - The teaching here again starts with footwork early in the season and, for younger teams, at the beginning of this part of practice every practice. I line up my outfielders in one or two lines triple spaced apart facing me. I have them do their set, ready, creep pre-pitch routine and then I point straight right, straight left, over their right shoulder or over their left shoulder.

Depending on how I point, the players are required to properly execute cross-over steps or drop back steps. I start with them having to do one

Coaching Champions for Life

quick reaction step and then we add multiple steps when the reaction steps and pivots are perfect.

Once they master the basic steps, I will ask them to go back doing a drop back series of steps and then come forward as if they are catching a fly ball and having to make a throw to a base.

In addition, I will have them move laterally in a proper arc to field a fly ball or a ground ball so they are pointed straight toward the base when they field the ball. Then we will add "do or die" mechanics to the drill. Still no ball involved in the drill at this point, just footwork.

Next, I add a drill called **"reaction tosses"**. I kneel down in front of two players standing together facing me.

The person receiving the ball toss is standing 25' or so behind the two players in front of me, but he cannot see me. He does his set, ready, creep routine and then I toss a ball from behind the 2-player screen that he must react to quickly using the proper footwork that we just worked on.

Another favorite drill at this point is the **pass pattern drill** I described generally in the previous chapter. Here are the basics and some variations of that drill. The drill can be done with one line of players or two. The players start 20' or so out in front facing you.

If there are two lines, one player starts to the right of you and the other to the left.

Again, to ingrain good habits into them for games, they always start with their set, ready, creep routine.

Then I point the direction I want them to run and they must do so using the proper drop step or cross-over step we worked on in the footwork session. This is a conditioning drill too so I make them run 75'-125' to catch the ball.

We use regulation size "softie" balls for this drill so they must catch the ball with their *bare glove hand* only. In a "combo run", they have to run hard for the first ball going out or laterally, catch the ball in their bare glove hand, transfer the ball to their throwing hand while they run back toward me as fast as they can to receive a second toss that they receive preferably below waist high.

These are called "out and backs". The "out" part of this drill can be done vertically or laterally. If it is done vertically, it can be done with a normal drop back step and run, or the end of the run can have a "wrong way turn"; i.e., a snap of the head to change directions as I throw the ball over the opposite shoulder from the direction the player is running.

Regardless of what type of pattern they are running, to emphasize the conditioning part of the drill, the player must run the ball all the way back to me and place it in my hand behind my back. They are not allowed to toss it to me.

I do not wait for them to get to me to toss another ball.

Even if one player at a time is doing the drill, as soon as the first player catches the ball and while he is running it back to me, I send the next player on his pass pattern. Two players can also do the drill at the same time receiving separate balls from me or they can work on communication by calling for a single ball thrown by me between them.

Again, this can be done in two parallel vertical lines or it can be done with two lines facing each other 200' apart starting out 120' or so in front of me. The first players in each line in this variation of the drill run toward each other as fast as they can, I throw the ball in the middle of the distance between them and they must communicate so one of them can catch the ball before the two players collide into one another.

The easy variation of this drill is that they can carry the ball back to the end of the line with them (the line opposite to where they began so they get work running both directions) and put it in a pile there for gathering at the end of the drill.

The tough variation is that both players have to run the ball back to me and then run back to the end of their lines for another turn.

If the lines are stationed 125-150' out from the coach tossing the ball and the players are required to run the ball back to him each time, this can mean that the players are continuously running a large triangle for the duration of the drill if the coach starts the next two players running as soon as the ball is caught by one of the two previous players and he does not wait for the ball to be returned to him.

Some of the areas young or inexperienced coaches neglect is how to play balls in the sun and how to handle fly balls and ground balls hit to the wall. These can be worked on indoors and outdoors. Use the big indoor lights to act as the sun for "sun mechanics" and the concrete walls for playing balls at or off the wall.

Also, multi-task oral communication drills for your outfielders as often as you can throughout practice.

Outfielders fail to communicate more often than any other players on the field and therefore make the most mistakes in throwing to the wrong base or failing to back up a base.

> *When outfielders do communicate, they tend to think only of "what do I do if the ball is hit directly to me?" They fail to think of what to do if the ball is hit between him and the outfielder next to him. A ball hit in the gap may require that the outfielder throw to a different base or relay man.*
>
> *Catching a fly ball is pure joy. Knowing what to do with it after you catch it is a business.*

Designing A Drill

I want to be sure that you are clear about how to design specific drills for your practice using the principles I have been discussing. Let me give you an example of the difference between the way I see almost all youth team coaches run a drill and the way I recommend running a drill incorporating these principles.

The other day I watched a youth coach hit ground balls to six of his players at shortstop so they could work on fielding mechanics. The way he ran the drill is the way I see most young youth coaches run the drill. His assistant coach handed him balls out of a bucket and he hit balls to the players one at a time while the remaining players waited in line for their turn.

The player fielding the ball would simply throw it back to the assistant coach. When the players made a mistake, either in fielding form or in throwing the ball, the coach, his assistant coach or both yelled out to the player who made the mistake what the player did wrong. The remaining players probably did not hear what was said because since they were not involved in the drill, they were talking to each other and not paying attention. More importantly, the player who made the mistake felt embarrassed and deflated. The other players, assuming they were paying attention, were dreading their turn.

The first mistake made by this coach is he set his players up for failure because he failed to teach his players in a progressive manner. As you know, my coaching technique is one of crawl before you walk, walk before you jog, jog before you run, etc.

As it relates to fielding ground balls, hitting the players ground balls is one of the last steps in the progression even for experienced players.

I watched practice from the beginning and this coach had no separate part of practice for throwing and receiving mechanics.

The players simply threw a ball back and forth for a few minutes "to warm up". There was also no separate position fundamentals part of practice where the players were taught how to properly field a ground ball focusing step-by-step on footwork, glove mechanics, transfer mechanics, throwing mechanics, etc.

As you now know, the proper progression is dry mechanics (*i.e., no ball involved at all*), ball-in-hand drills, ball rolled to the player from a short distance by a partner or by the player to himself off of a wall and then, as a last step, balls hit to a player with a bat.

The players must attain a certain level of proficiency at each step of the progression before they are allowed to move on to the next step. The players who attain the requisite level of proficiency move on to the next step. The ones who do not, stay at the prior step until they achieve the requisite level of proficiency by doing more work in practice or more on their own time outside of practice.

Doing practice in this progressive style is important for several reasons. First, you set the players up for success not failure because they are succeeding at every phase of the process.

This will increase their desire to learn more and to work harder because they are experiencing success more often. Second, they learn easier and more quickly having the process broken down into manageable steps. Third, the players have more fun because the initial steps in the process, while done individually, are done all at the same time so everyone is actively involved.

> *"Tell me and I forget. Teach me and I remember. Involve me and I learn". - Benjamin Franklin*

Finally, as each player has more fun and learns more, they will want to teach their teammates more so everyone can have fun together.

When you finally progress to the point of the process where the players are ready to be hit ground balls, keeping everyone constantly involved and multi-tasking as many skills mentally and physically into the drill as possible are the keys.

Here is how I would have run the drill even though the coach was working with 11-12 year olds in an early season practice.

First, two buckets are stacked one on top of the other so one coach can easily retrieve balls from the top bucket freeing up the other coach to be next to the players fielding the ground balls.

This will allow the coach next to the players to do a better, more direct job of coaching them. Second, the players will work in groups of three. Three players fielding ground balls and three players receiving throws, one receiving throws at first base, one receiving throws at second base and one putting the balls in a bucket behind second base.

Here is how the drill works. Before the coach tosses the ball into the air to hit it, *all five* players not receiving the ball tell the player who will receive the ball "you can do this, you will make this play". Even the coach standing next to him will say something like, "Want the ball. It is the bottom of the last inning and you want the ball hit to you. You will make this play".

This builds team chemistry and a positive feeling in the player about ready to make the play and in the team supporting him.

Also prior to the coach tossing the ball into the air, *all six* players must get into their ready-to-field position. The coach holds the ball until all six players are ready.

It's a team game and the players must learn that we all must focus at the same time all the time. As Benjamin Franklin told his "teammates" at the time of the drafting of the Declaration of Independence, *"We must, indeed, all hang together or, most assuredly, we shall all hang separately"*. Once the ball is tossed into the air, all six players take their creep step forward as if they will receive the ball just like in a game. Once the ball is hit to the player in the front of the line at shortstop, the next player in line is his back up and the third player in line is that player's back up in short left field. This accomplishes sending the message that in a game everyone is doing something not just watching the player field the ball.

If the player fielding the ball does not field it cleanly, he must tell the coach why he made the mistake. Notice - he tells the coach, the coach does not tell him. This is how you teach players to think and this is how they learn to teach.

Then, the player takes a deep breath, turns to the outfield, wipes his foot across the ground wiping away the memory of the error and then turns to the second baseman to say, "We are going to turn a double play with this next ground ball". All of his teammates then say to him, "No worries. You will make the play on the next one. This play, this moment". This dialogue proactively practices how *the team* will handle adversity in a game and it builds team chemistry by requiring that they support one another every play of every day.

If the player fields the ground ball cleanly, he throws the ball to the first baseman. The first baseman catches the ball and then throws it to the second baseman who makes a tag on a pretend runner at second base. The third player in that group is backing up the throw to the second baseman.

Once the second baseman makes the tag, he throws the ball to his back-up player who puts the ball into the bucket.

Then the process starts over again.

If the throw to the first baseman is not accurate, the first baseman must do everything in his power to stop or block the ball if at all possible. Just like in all receiving mechanics drills, he must not stretch for the ball until he is sure the throw is accurate. His heels must remain against the base and he must remain in an athletic receiving position until the throw is released. If the throw is not accurate, he must stop the ball so that the runner will remain at first base and not advance to second base.

Teams must learn how to perform under pressure, so here are the consequences of the possible physical or mental errors in this drill. Failing to field the ground ball cleanly, an inaccurate throw to first or second base or a dropped throw for *this age group* are physical errors and result in three push-ups for the *entire team*.

> *Baseball players must learn to like getting dirty so the push-ups are done in the dirt, not the grass.*

Failing to back up the missed ground ball or the throw to second base or failing to attempt to stop a bad throw to first or second base are mental errors and result in the team doing five push-ups. Multiple errors on one play may result in more push-ups than the young players can do, so you may substitute sit-ups (done again in the dirt) for the push-ups or a combination of both. For older, more experienced players, like Coach Dedeaux said, throwing errors are mental errors and result in greater negative consequences.

As a last step to the drill, I would have only one shortstop and one first baseman in the field. Everyone else would run one at a time to put pressure on the fielder to have to make the play with a runner running to add game-like conditions. The fielder would stay at his position until all four runners have run. The fielder who made the most errors would lose the game and suffer a consequence. First baseman who failed to attempt to block a ball and players who did not say something positive to the fielder before and after the play would have an error added to their total. You need to build team chemistry and to multi-task at all times!

I think it is obvious how many more things are accomplished by running the drill the way I have described it. First, everyone is involved at all times. By the time the drill is complete, in one fifteen or twenty minute segment, fielding mechanics, throwing mechanics, tag mechanics, bag mechanics, back-up duties, base running, team chemistry, handling adversity, mental focus, work ethic and performing under pressure are all practiced at the same time!

Now if you design your practices to have every segment of every practice of every day to be that effective you will build a championship team composed of *Champions for Life*.

Hitting Fundamentals

As you know, there are plenty of resources discussing the fundamentals of hitting and giving you drills to teach them. I have listed of few of them in the Bibliography. In this section, I want to give you my keys to teaching hitting fundamentals and how to integrate them into an effective and efficient practice.

In my opinion, here are the four most important keys to being a good hitter:

(1) The hitter must believe that no matter who is pitching and no matter the situation, he will hit the ball hard somewhere.

There is an old saying that the most difficult thing to do in sports is to hit a baseball. Good hitters do not believe this.

They believe they will hit the ball hard every time up.

(2) Get a good pitch to hit. *Hitting is timing and pitching is upsetting that timing.* Good hitters hit the pitch that is in their "zone".

They are patient to hit the pitcher's mistake. They do not swing at pitches in the pitcher's zones until they have two strikes.

A word of caution here. Pitchers are taught to *"get ahead and stay ahead"* in the count. They are taught how important first pitch strikes are. Therefore, in my opinion, it is a bad habit for a hitter to always take, i.e., not swing at, the first pitch in the name of "patience" or "to see what stuff the pitcher has".

The first pitch may be a fastball thigh-high right down the middle - it may be, and frequently is, the best pitch the hitter will see the entire at bat. If the first pitch is "fat", the hitter should not waste the opportunity and he should hit the ball hard somewhere. That is why and two different curveballs or breaking balls that he can throw for strikes at any time.

A pitcher does not always want to "get ahead" in the count with a first pitch four-seam fastball.

(3) The hitter must know his job before he steps up to bat and must adjust to a potentially new job as the at-bat progresses.

Most of the time, coaches think a hitter has done a great job if he has found a way to advance runners (e.g., bunting, hitting behind a stealing runner, hitting a sac fly to score a runner, etc.) or simply finding a way to get on base while not causing any other outs. One of the most common mistakes of average hitters is over-swinging to get an extra base hit when a simple ground ball to the right side of the infield or a single to right field to advance a runner into scoring position or to third base will suffice. *Good hitters know their job and execute it.*

(4) Tracking the ball well for as long as possible after release point. The most common thing you will hear a "hot hitter" say when he is hitting well is "I'm just *seeing* the ball so well right now. The ball looks like a beach ball when it is travelling toward me". I am a big believer that having hitters stand in the batter's box during a pitcher's bullpen session (or behind a screen in the batter's box if control is an issue) is a huge key to developing good hitters. When tracking the ball, the hitter should call out whether the pitch is a strike and its location before the ball hits the catcher's glove. This will help the hitter recognize when to hit that "outer half" pitch to the opposite field, for example! Hitters need to track balls off of live pitching from release point to the catcher's glove as often as possible-- thousands and thousands of balls. Hitters do not practice tracking enough non-fastballs. They see fastballs during batting practice, but rarely do they see a lot of change ups and the variety of breaking balls that they will see in games.

Not having hitters stand in to simply track balls during pitcher's bullpens is the single biggest mistake made by coaches in teaching hitting!

Great hitters believe that they will hit the ball hard every time up. This confidence has been built through years of perfect practice using a building block methodology.

When my hitters go into a "slump", here is my "slump buster" routine (my apologies to the movie "Bull Durham" and other such traditions in baseball, of course) to get them back to hitting well. The primary emphasis of this routine is to get the hitter to see the ball well again. Of course, the first step to change is always changing your thinking from negative to positive. When asked if his hitting woes of late meant that he was in a "slump", Yogi Berra said, "Slump? I ain't in no slump! I'm just not hitting".

My **"slump buster" routine**, in addition to believing that good things will happen today, is every day for five consecutive days:

(1) Track 25 fastballs;

(2) Track 25 curveballs;

(3) Successfully bunt 25 fastballs down each line;

(4) Successfully bunt 25 curveballs down each line;

(5) Do 10 "tic the tees" at three different levels, 30 swings total;

(6) Hit 20 half-swing line drives - letting the ball "get deep" in the zone, i.e., seeing the ball a little longer, is a key to good hitting. Taking full force (do not ease up on the swing; take a normal swing from starting point to contact), controlled half-swings is one of the best tools to let balls "get deep" and one of the best hitting drills I know;

(7) Hit 10 full-swing line drives up the middle off of fastballs; and

(8) Hit 10 full-swing line drives up the middle off of curveballs.

Do this routine for five consecutive days *in addition to* the other keys to hitting that I mentioned above and the hitter's slump will be over. I promise.

My players must master the fundamentals of bunting before they are allowed to hit. They must successfully execute their bunts in batting practice before they are allowed to swing away. They are allowed a certain number of total swings in batting practice beginning with different types of bunts in different locations. They must successfully execute all of their bunts before they are allowed to take full swings. Every extra attempt it takes to successfully execute a bunt, they lose a full swing from their round. Some days, a hitter may not bunt well and will not be allowed to take any full swings. This will certainly motivate him to spend a lot of extra time on his bunting! The beginning part of the progression is not done just at the beginning of the year.

This reminds me of a coaching tip regarding teaching bunting. One aspect of setting the "perfect practice" bar for bunting is requiring that the hitter only bunt strikes, always, no matter the drill. Yes, on "suicide squeeze' plays, the hitter is required to bunt any pitch, but this is a much easier adjustment during a game than laying off a letter high fastball when the hitter attempts to bunt that type of pitch all the time in practice. Watch this very carefully especially when players are working in pairs or small groups. Make the consequences severe for poor bunt discipline!

We do dry mechanics and tee drills every day we do hitting. Great hitters like Tony Gwynn and Don Mattingly did the same thing. They spent time in front of a mirror or reviewing video tape looking at their mechanics every day. They hit hundreds of balls off of a tee every day *and then they started batting practice.*

Tom House, the noted professional and college pitching coach, has done extensive research on the biomechanics of baseball players. He has discovered in his research that the human eye can only see about 32 frames per second, while most of the critical movements in pitching take place at 250 to 750 frames per second.

Master the fundamentals. Crawl before you walk, walk before you jog, jog before you sprint. Championship teams are built this way.

Therefore, you need to own video equipment and know how to use it proficiently.   Use it and review the CD's frequently.

I review tape on each of my hitters and each of my pitchers at least once per week regardless of the level I am coaching at. Having the ability to "break down" the throwing and swing mechanics of my players frame-by-frame is a huge key to improving my players' skills.

However, do not show the tape to the players, especially young players, too often.

Visuals can be very helpful for older players, but even they can get *paralysis by analysis*, or simply bored, with watching tape too often. At every level, you need to find the balance between being technical and being "hands off" and between being verbal and being physical.

Please review my comments on the different learning styles that I discussed in the last chapter as well. For example, instead of telling a pitcher to get his release point out front or not to land on the heel of his stride foot, tell him simply to "land softly" on his stride foot. By trying to "land softly", he will naturally not land as severely on his heel (in my opinion, it is preferable for most pitchers to land initially on the inside ball of their foot) and his arm will travel forward more, prior to releasing the ball.

As I mentioned before, instead of getting too technical with my pitchers regarding throwing curveballs, we simply visualize and practice throwing them to land just beyond the back corner of home plate.

You will be amazed at how many technical things a player will do naturally by practicing good visual cues.

Here are some keys to teaching each phase of the hitting progression.

The "load, stride, back knee trigger, i.e., begin to rotate the back heel" routine or whatever you teach, must be done *at each station every day* so that it is a permanent habit in games. A player cannot casually swing at balls in batting practice drills and be expected to have a sound pre-pitch methodology in games. One way, the right way, all of the time.

TIP - One of the biggest keys that inexperienced coaches overlook is not insisting that the hitting routine be done for every phase of the progression. No exceptions, ever!

This is a big problem even for professional hitters.

Watch closely pre-game batting practice at a professional game some time. You will see that most of the pitches thrown to the hitters are waist high and the hitters take their swings with a different, less athletic posture than they do in a game. Is it any wonder why they struggle in a game when they have to swing at pitches at or near their knees?

Secondly, hitting is usually one of the player's favorite parts of the practice day. Therefore, this is another area where the "quantity over quality" problem rears its ugly head.

Be very careful to monitor this problem. One thing I do is to prohibit the hitter's partner from tossing or throwing him the ball unless he does every part of his pre-swing routine correctly. If the hitter does not, his partner stops, no pitch is made and the routine starts over.

Another technique I use to ensure quality is to reward execution.

Hitting line drives or hitting to the opposite field, in general, or for older players, a certain number of times, is rewarded with extra swings in the round.

Wood bats have a smaller "sweet spot" than non-wood bats. Therefore, if players learn to hit the ball on the sweet spot of a wood bat, they will get maximum results when they use a non-wood bat. However, they should also use their game bat at least part of the time during the last hitting practice before a game because their game bat and their batting practice bat may have a different feel. Both bats should be the same length and weight.

When using an aluminum bat, be sure a player rotates it slightly after every swing so the seal of the bat will last longer and the warranty will be honored by the manufacturer if the seal breaks prior to the expiration of the warranty period. In other words, unlike a wood bat, an aluminum bat should not be hit by the ball on the same spot over and over again. The downside, of course, to wood bats is they break easier than aluminum ones.

When choosing a wood bat, be sure it has a very large, tight grain pattern on each side of the bat. The more area of the bat that has a tight grain pattern the more difficult it will be to break, if it is held correctly. To properly hold a wood bat, the label of the bat should face upward when the bat is held at the contact point of the ball over the plate so the ball will be hit on the side of the bat with the tight grain pattern.

Dry Swing Mechanics - With regard to dry mechanics, have the players do them in front of a mirror as often as possible.

Set the tone early in your relationship with your players. Partners and teams who do not take this "coaching each other" responsibility seriously should face serious consequences.   Teach them how to teach and hold them accountable for it!

Hitting Tee - Teaching the tee should always start with **"tic-the-tee" drills.**   Learning how to *barely* tic-the-tee with no ball on it at different heights, beginning always with the load, stride, back knee trigger routine, is one of the best swing flaw detectors there is. A player's goal should be 9 out of 10 perfect tic-the-tees at three different heights (thigh high, belt high and barely above belly button high - remember we are training to hit pitcher's mistakes in the strike zone).

Pair your players together who have similar mechanics to improve and hold them accountable for getting better every day.

Tee drills should always involve multiple tee heights and should always require that the player hit to all fields not just straight away. There are times when hitting into a net is sufficient, but also frequently give the player the chance to hit balls off of the tee into an open field so he can watch the spin on and flight of the ball. This was one of Cal Ripken Jr.'s favorite drills.

These things will give him important feedback on swing flaws.

One of the most common mistakes I see when working with the tee is the player simply looks at the ball on the tee the whole time. The player should do his pre-pitch routine while looking straight ahead, *not at the tee*.

> **TIP** - The player should pretend to track the ball from an imaginary pitcher's release point to the tee before every swing.

Soft Toss – Slow your soft toss drills down! Have your players take fewer swings and take more quality swings. Again, hit to all fields and toss the balls at different heights. Have a purpose for every toss. Don't forget to mix in **"loft tosses"** (tosses above the player's head that the player must keep his weight back and wait for the toss to enter the strike zone) to simulate change- of-speed pitches.

Holding two balls of different colors in one hand one on top of the other and throwing them simultaneously with an instruction by the pitcher just prior to tossing the ball to hit only the ball of a certain color, or to hit the top or bottom ball if their colors are the same, are favorite soft-toss drills of all my teams.

These drills are done with the pitcher very close to home plate so that the balls are tossed straight up vertically and therefore, should only be done by older, very experienced players.

Short Tosses - One key to doing short tosses starts from the very first time a young boy swings a bat.

Probably the worst habit a young hitter learns when an adult is throwing a ball to him underhand is leaning backward.

When an adult tosses a ball underhand to a child, the child is tracking the ball in a low-to-high arc. Therefore, the child's natural tendency is to lean back to hit the seemingly rising ball.

Bingo. Such is where the bad habit of loss of "dynamic balance" is born.

> **TIP** - Almost all parents who play baseball with their children toss the ball underhand to them to hit the ball. This is a bad idea unless the player will be a softball player. Use an overhand dart throw to baseball players!

Tossing the ball underhand to an older player is not a problem as a station drill. Just like tee drills, however, be sure to toss the ball from all three angles, not just straight ahead. When tossing the ball from behind a screen on the first base side, toss it to the outside corner of the plate and have a right hand hitter hit the ball to the opposite field. Obviously, left hand hitters pull the ball in this situation. Conversely, when you are tossing the ball from the third base side, toss it to the inside part of the plate.

Right hand hitters work on pulling the ball and left hand hitters work on hitting to the opposite field.

And I cannot say it enough. Don't just toss the ball. Be sure you have a routine that allows the hitter to do his load, stride, and back knee trigger pre-pitch routine!

Here is one of my favorite drills for working on change of speeds in a short toss drill. Hold a regulation size Wiffle baseball and a badminton birdie in each hand , but hidden by a slight turn of your chest as you do your wind up so the player does not know which one you will toss. The Wiffle ball acts like a fastball and the badminton birdie acts like a change up or an "off-speed" pitch. It will take some practice by everyone to throw both the Wiffle ball and the badminton birdie at the proper speed to be strikes and hittable, but it's a fantastic drill that the player's love in teaching them how to maintain balance while tracking the pitch.

The only negative to the drill is that the power generated by an older player swinging an aluminum bat tears up a lot of birdies and Wiffle balls.

Use the drill once every two weeks or so for older players.

A great drill to improve focus and concentration is to hold three Wiffle balls at the same time, two green ones and one white one. Again, the short toss pitcher should turn his body to hide which ball he will throw.

Hitters are instructed to hit the green balls, but to take the white one. Instead of hiding the ball being thrown behind a turned body, the hitter can keep his eyes closed on a command of "relax" by the pitcher and open them on the command of "ready" when the pitcher's toss is at the release point.

> *"When my swing is mechanically sound, my front leg is stiff and solid, and I'm deriving my power from the drive of my back leg". - Hall of Fame player, Tony Gwynn*

If you study the swings of all the great power hitters frame-by-frame, you will see that they all rotate their back hip while the front leg is stiffening and straightening and then the back leg drives forward to add more power. Mantle and Mays had huge "backside drives". Aaron, Ruth and Ken Griffey Jr. had medium ones. Ted Williams and Joe DiMaggio had smaller ones…but *all of them* did not rely exclusively on backside rotation. All of them come out of the back foot hole and derive additional power from driving their back leg forward after their hip is fully rotated so that the laces of the back foot shoe are facing toward the pitcher.

Be careful when teaching backside drive, however. Players using non-wood bats do not really need it. Only when you swing a wood bat do you see how essential backside drive is for power.

Ever watch players who grew up swinging aluminum bats try to hit for power using wood bats? Ever wonder why they are as strong as or stronger than we were at the same age, but hit with so much less power with a wooden bat?

The answer…no backside drive!

But like I said, be careful that your players do not get so obsessed with learning backside drive that they get their swing sequence out of order.

The sequence after the stride is made should be: (1) back heel rotation begins, (2) then back hip rotation begins and front leg stiffens, (3) the swing is started, (4) back hip continues to rotate so that the laces of the back shoe face the pitcher, and (5) the knee of the back leg drives toward the front leg.

In fact, as I said before, the back leg drive does not begin until the back hip is fully rotated with the laces of the shoe on the back foot facing the pitcher. The time between each step is a fraction of a second and may seem simultaneous to the hitter, but most inexperienced hitters start their hands too soon causing their back shoulder to dip, their swing plane to be improper and their chances of solid contact and their power are decreased.

Study the swings of any great power hitter frame-by-frame and you will see what I mean about proper swing sequence and backside drive for power.

When you're sure a hitter has his swing sequence perfected and you want him to learn backside drive, a great drill for this is **self-toss.** Albert Pujols loves this **drill**. Every player of my generation grew up hitting thousands of balls tossed to himself or tossing up rocks to be hit by a broom stick.

We learned that to self-toss and hit for power, you needed to get a couple of rhythm steps for momentum into the swing before you hit the ball. When done correctly, the last thing that happens is the back leg driving into a stiff front side and leg, i.e., "backside drive".

Start out by having the players do self-toss and hitting line drives straight ahead. Like the other drills, eventually have them learn how to do it hitting to all fields. They will naturally learn very important adjustments with their body in relationship to the ball when they hit to all fields doing self-toss.

Similarly, a hitter can learn backside drive by walking up to a ball on a tee or balls thrown to him by short toss, by a machine or by a live batting practice pitcher. One of two footwork patterns can be used to do these drills. The hitter can simply take a short jab step forward with his back foot, then stride into his normal stride out stance with his front foot and then drive his back leg into a stiff front side at and after contact. Or, he can again take a short jab step with his back foot and then do a step behind with his back leg behind his front leg before he strides into his normal batting stance and hitting sequence.

He will again finish by driving his back leg into a stiff front side, *after hip rotation occurs*, at and after contact. Players today call this last footwork pattern and drill "Happy Gilmores" after Adam Sandler's golf ball driving technique in the movie with the same name.

Hitting Machines and Batting Practice Pitchers

Many coaches believe that taking batting practice off of machines is bad for hitters because they get no timing off of a pitcher's delivery and they do not get to track the ball from different release points. All very true. There is no substitute for batting practice off of live pitching. When done correctly, it is the best form of batting practice, but it's not essential every time you do batting practice either.

Sometimes it is not even possible because there are not players or coaches available who can throw strikes consistently for the whole team to take batting practice.

In all my years of coaching, our lowest *team batting average* was .323. It is usually around .370. We hit off of live pitching less than 20% of the time. The advantages to hitting off of machines is they consistently throw more strikes *lower in the zone*, they can be set to throw in a single zone, pitch after pitch, so that a certain type of hitting, e.g., hitting to the opposite field, can be worked on and they can throw an unlimited number of curveballs or off-speed pitches. Batting practice pitchers throw way too many very high pitches, some strikes and some not, but the players swing at them anyway. Hence, really bad pitch discipline can be developed.

As I said before, most batting practice pitchers for youth teams cannot vary speeds and simply cannot throw consistently with enough velocity to mirror game conditions. They certainly cannot throw enough curveballs for strikes to the entire team day after day.

> **TIP** - The single biggest key is to set the machine so the ball comes out of it at exactly the same distance a pitcher would release the ball in the game - not the pitching rubber distance, the release point distance! This will ensure that the hitter's timing in batting practice is the same as the game.

This is another problem with live batting practice. I do not know many batting practice pitchers for youth teams who can consistently throw from a distance and at a speed to adequately simulate game-speed pitching. We use our JUGS radar gun to measure the speed of the pitches, both fastball and curveball, to make sure that the machine is throwing the same speed as we expect to see in our next game.

Second, do not just show the ball to the hitter above the machine and put it into the machine prior to the hitter's swing.

You must have a pre-pitch routine that allows the hitter to do his "load, stride, back knee trigger" routine on every pitch.

This is almost never done by other teams I watch taking batting practice off of machines. The hitters just swing away without any pre-pitch routine at all. Actually, as I said before, this mistake is made by many teams for almost all of the hitting stations.

Since this is usually one of the parts of practice that you allocate the most time, you will want to multi-task during it as much as possible. The possibilities are endless, but here are a few tips and variations that I use. First, carefully design and monitor your hitting sessions so that safety is the priority.

Be sure all players are protected with screens or by other players in front of them wearing their gloves.

> **TIP** - Again, all players carry all of their gear (hat, bat, batting helmet, glove, batting gloves and water bottle) with them at all times. So much valuable time can be wasted by players running back and forth getting their equipment from the dugout or wherever.

Never, ever run a batting practice where everyone other than the hitter is shagging balls and every ball is being shagged. At most, have 2 or 3 players in the outfield shagging balls or have everyone shag balls after the round is over. Make it a competition to do so. The pair or team that gathers up the most baseballs after a round is the next team to hit.

The only ball that needs to be shagged after it is hit during a round is one that could get lost or would be a danger if it is not shagged right away.

On the other hand, when outfielders are shagging in the outfield, a "no ball touches the ground" rule is a good habit to get into for them.

> *There is no better practice for an outfielder than fielding live fly balls off of a hitter's bat.*

Next, batting practice on the baseball diamond is always done with base runners. They work on a pre-determined series of leads, extensions, reads and routes from each base.

This includes picking up signs, look-in signals and tag up directions from a third base coach.

> **TIP** - In practice, use your players as base coaches. It will shorten their learning curve significantly!

Base running has to be more than pro-active; it must be instinctive. For it to become instinctive, it must be practiced at game speed every day. Base running during batting practice is a great way to achieve this.

One of my favorite batting practices is a combo batting practice and scrimmage. Base runners start at bases for pre-determined purposes. All nine defensive players are in their positions, communicating, fielding balls and backing up bases under game conditions. The first round, for example, a runner may start at first base and the hitter lays down a sacrifice bunt toward the first baseman to advance the runner to second base.

When the runner is at second base, the hitter bunts toward the third baseman to advance the runner to third base. When the runner is at third base, the hitter and runner execute "squeeze play" mechanics.

In the second round, when the runner is at first base, the hitter tries to hit a ground ball behind the runner on a hit and run play. Regardless of the outcome, the runner runs next from second base and the hitter again tries to hit behind him to advance him to third base.

The runner works on executing the "ground ball rule", i.e., any ground ball hit at the runner or to the runner's left after he takes his extension, he advances to third base; any ball hit to his right, he retreats to a point where he cannot be thrown out by the defensive player fielding the ball and he extends again or attempts to advance to third base after the defensive player releases the ball to first base. When the runner reaches third base in round two, he executes the "contact rule" on ground balls, i.e., advance immediately to home plate on seeing the down angle of the ball off of the hitter's bat and executes "tag up" rules on fly balls.

During the third round, the hitter is free to swing away and the runner reacts to and runs on *every other hit* so the round keeps moving along. In this round, during the at bat when the runner is not running, the defense works on non-verbal communication with each other. Then the ball is "live" and game conditions exist when the runner is running. Of course, during all rounds, multiple runners can be used and many different situations can be predetermined to be worked on by the offense and defense. As I said before, no balls are shagged until the end of a player's turn at bat except if they are hit at a defensive player or ones that would be lost or pose a safety hazard if they were not shagged.

Appendix T is a sample batting practice designed to combine hitting, base running, fielding and game simulation at the same time. In the 4th rotation, only every other or every third ball is played "live" to keep the round moving along. This batting practice is great for mid-to-late season or any time for older, experienced players. The batting practice in Appendix L is used early in the season or for younger, inexperienced players. It's also good for "getting back to basics" for older players. Keep the rounds short, however, to maximize concentration, minimize fatigue, and simulate game conditions.

Quite frankly, even if you follow every bit of advice that I have given you in this section, hitting quality pitching is not easy. To develop good hitters, you will need to spend hundreds of weekend and after-practice hours, both in-season and in the off-season, working with your players.

Team Defense and Offense

This part of the practice is, of course, where you work on things like your bunt defenses and offenses, your double steals and defenses of them when runners are at 1st & 3rd , relays, etc. - all the special situations that require tactical plays, offensively and defensively, during games.

> *Executing tactical plays win close games. Failing to execute these plays loses championships.*

Work on them every day, their execution needs to be instinctive and perfect.

Here are some of the mistakes inexperienced coaches make in this part of practice. First, they are not proactive. They wait until their team loses a key game to work on these plays to perfect them.

Second, they do not lead up to them in a progressive, building-block manner during practice. If your team defense drill in practice that day is going to be bunt defenses, everything leading up to the drill must involve the components of the drill. *(Please refer again to Appendix L.)*

Third, many coaches fail to start with perfecting the verbal and non-verbal communication part of the drill. Also, few coaches, when it comes to bunt defenses, coach their pitchers on the pitch sequence for such situations.

We don't want to make it easy for the bunter by giving him a thigh-high down the middle fastball to bunt. If you don't want to risk a passed ball or a wild pitch by throwing the hitter a curveball, throw him a letter high fastball.

You will be surprised how many young players do not have the discipline to let it go by and will bunt a letter high fastball for a pop up leading many times to a double play.

Finally, even in this part of practice where you are breaking down the play component-by-component, end the session with game-speed base running to test the defense. Build the confidence of your defense by starting with your slower runners, but be sure to end the drill with your fastest runners.

You are preparing to play your toughest competition every day regardless of when you play them next.

Game Simulation

Everything you have done in practice has been building toward this part of practice. Everything has been a logical progression toward this point. All of the fundamentals and mechanics in all of the other parts of practice are in preparation for this part of practice. This is where the team hopefully puts it all together.

This is where you learn if they can execute and apply what you have tried to teach them. What is the difference between the "Team Defense" part of practice and this section? In this section, after explaining to the team what you are working on and the specifics of how it will work, *you stand aside and be quiet.* Let the team show you what they know and what they have or have not learned.

Coaches talk too much during the scrimmage or game simulation competition part of practice.

This is the biggest reason why coaches are surprised by how their team plays as compared to how their team practices. Talk at the beginning and at the end of this part of practice. Otherwise, stand aside, be quiet and watch carefully, no matter what happens. Let the players take charge and coach themselves.

Every practice should conclude with a team scrimmage or game simulation where you do nothing more than stand back and observe what your players have learned.

Tear Down Stations, Dress Down Field, Pitchers Ab/Core, Bag up Equipment

The components of this part of practice are not done randomly. There is as much planning and training in this part of practice as there is in any other part of practice. All of the players have pre-assigned daily duties and they are trained how to do them *perfectly*. They also know that if a teammate is absent, the absent player's duties are done by the rest of the team, perfectly.

Therefore, just like in a game (and in life) there is no excuse for not being prepared to assume additional and different roles.

If field equipment is limited, pitchers do their duties first so they can get to their ab/core work asap.

Physical Conditioning - Part II - Long Run, SAQ, Sprints

No substitute exists for running. However, for baseball players, that running needs to take many different forms for both training reasons (athletes need both aerobic and anaerobic training) and just to keep it fun. More often than not, one of the conditioning sessions during my practice involves a SAQ drill and one involves an endurance drill.

The SAQ drill, as often as possible, involves the handling of a baseball to make the drill as relevant as possible. Here's a coaching tip that will definitely set your players apart from those on other teams. I don't know why, but baseball players stop using their arms to help them run when they run with their glove on. Using your arms in an aggressive and efficient manner is an essential part of maximizing your speed.

> **TIP** - When you have your players run their sprints, have them wear their gloves so they get accustomed to using their arms when they run with their glove on.

The endurance training is not just long runs, but involves a change of speeds, e.g., Fartlek Runs and Native American Runs. Appendix U is a list and a description of a few of my favorite conditioning drills. As always, this part of practice, like all of the others, almost always involves competitions of some kind, pairs, teams or "weakest link". The team must be required to perform under pressure at all times.

Review, Announcements, Homework, Heart-felt Handshake

At the beginning of practice, tell your players what you are going to teach them. During practice, teach it to them. At the end of each practice, take a minute or two to tell them what you think they should have learned and what they need to work on during their own time.

Remember, if you expect them to remember an important announcement, you better tell it to them both at the beginning and at the end of practice. Particularly important information needs to be emailed to their parents in addition to telling it to the players.

Give your players homework. Require that they invest some of their "free time" into learning more about their sport and the concepts you are trying to teach them. Make them understand that your program is a classroom, the school of baseball and of life.

The possibilities here are endless. For young players, I frequently ask them to research the meaning of key concepts like "tenacity", "synergy" or any of the words on the list in Appendix A and think of an example of how that concept applies to our team. I love to give homework to all of my players that requires them to research the history of baseball, its players, managers, owners, development of the fundamentals of the game and how the development of baseball paralleled the development of our country. Increase their "Baseball IQ" and make them "students of the game".

Finally, as I discussed in Chapter Five, this is where we pair up and give each other a "heart-felt handshake". The possibilities for what someone could say to his partner include not only what that person did that day that his partner is proud of him for, but could also include things that the person speaking wants help to improve, physically, emotionally or whatever.

The partner's response could be one of advice or simply a promise to support him in the quest. The themes could be individual ones, team ones, school ones or whatever. You can set the themes or your players can suggest them. Use your imagination. Better yet, listen carefully during prayer time and the Lord will guide you to what your heart-felt handshake theme-for-the-day should be.

Summary - A Championship Practice

So, you've spent an enormous amount of time preparing for it, but how do you know if it was a *championship* practice? Every day ask yourself these things:

❖ Did you see your players and assistant coaches smile and laugh? Did they see you do the same?

❖ Were your players and coaches comfortable enough to share something from their heart during prayer time?

❖ Did someone new step up to demonstrate leadership skills?

❖ Was everyone committed to and held accountable for the TEAM getting better today?

❖ Did everyone attempt to "practice perfectly" at every phase of the practice?

❖ In what ways did you and your coaching staff push your players out of their comfort zone to be mentally and physically tougher?

❖ Was there a consistent high energy from beginning to end?

❖ Did the execution of the practice plan in its flow and progression match its design?

❖ Could you have defeated your toughest competition today?

❖ Were YOU better today than yesterday?

❖ Did everyone act excited to come back tomorrow?

If you can answer yes to each of these questions every day, you are executing championship practices. More importantly, you are training *Champions for Life*.

CHAPTER EIGHT

DEVELOPING COLLEGE-BOUND CHAMPIONS

"Get all of the advice and instruction that you can and be wise the rest of your life. You can make many plans, but the Lord's purpose will prevail." Proverbs 19:20-21

In my opinion, *at least* sixty percent of high school Varsity athletes have the physical potential to play a college sport.

While most of those athletes would love to play a sport in college, less than five percent of those athletes will do so. This is true despite the fact that receiving a college athletic scholarship is a goal for the athletes and their families from the moment the athlete steps on campus as a high school freshman.

Here's how to help more of your athletes achieve their goal of playing a sport in college.

Preparatory Meeting

First, you need to have a meeting with your freshman athletes and their families as early in their first year as possible.

The most common mistake made by coaches and athletes is they start the athlete's preparation for playing college sports much too late in the athlete's high school career. The majority of coaches either never have a meeting with their athletes and the athletes' families specifically discussing how to prepare for obtaining a college scholarship or, if they do, it doesn't occur until the athlete's junior or senior year. By then, it is usually too late. The athlete and his/her family just has too much ground to make up. I'm not saying the athlete can't still pursue it, but a whole lot of valuable time has been lost.

If the athlete has exceptional and elite natural skills, sufficient time might still exist, but for the overwhelming majority of athletes, this will not be the case.

Get them started as early as possible!

Four-Year Process

In your introductory meeting, emphasize first to your athletes and their families that the pursuit of a college scholarship is a *four-year* process. *Every day* during that process is important.

There can be no wasted, unplanned days. I'm not saying that every day is a training day. That would be counter-productive and very detrimental to the athlete's health. Rest and stress-free time just to be a kid are essential, but even those things need to be part of the annual plan.

It's okay to start preparing for college entrance exams in the athlete's sophomore or junior years, but not for obtaining an athletic scholarship.

Information v. Knowledge

The next thing for them to be told is that 80% of what they will hear from other sources about what it takes to get an athletic scholarship is wrong-- completely false.

> *The high school experience, both for youth and adults alike, is full of people with tons and tons of information and very, very little knowledge.*

You'll hear everybody talking about athletic scholarships and they'll all have a story about someone they allegedly knew very well who obtained one. However, the generalizations they make from their "information" are not applicable to most people.

Furthermore, most of their "information" is full of lies, "half-truths" and just plain bad information. I'm sorry, but it's just of fact of the "information age" we live in - there's a whole lot of self-proclaimed "experts" on almost every subject, but in fact, they really don't know much at all. Unfortunately, too often this applies to "academic advisors" at high schools as well. Although they are very well-meaning people, they provide families with a lot of misinformation about college entrance and scholarship requirements. Verify and triple check everything you are told by anyone. An erroneous reliance on one piece of information can lead to irrevocable hardships.

In short, everyone is looking for quick and easy answers to everything. Well, obtaining an athletic scholarship is neither quick nor easy for most athletes. This process takes a whole lot of hard work over a long period of time. It can be done, but persistence and commitment are the keys to success.

The Physical-Ability Component

Let's be clear about the physical-ability component. You do not need exceptional and extraordinary ability to play college sports.

Above-average ability to start with will do. And, if the Lord has put the love of the sport and the passion to pursue it in the athlete's heart, hard work, desire and commitment may overcome a lack of initial ability.

Give every athlete the chance and the benefit of the doubt and put the rest in the Lord's hands.

On the other hand, however, it's important to address up front the common misconception that you are not playing an athlete because he is short or undersize or the like. Parents of these athletes love to use this reasoning to try to "guilt you" into giving their son or daughter more playing time.

Set out clearly at the beginning of the season what an athlete needs to do to succeed and keep a record of the athlete's work and progress with those expectations.

You can then overcome these shallow objections with objective facts.

Student-Athletes

Athletes are student-athletes…and the student comes first.

Many athletes fail to play sports in college or fail to play at a level commensurate with their athletic ability because of poor grades and/or poor entrance exam scores. I remember vividly standing in the living room of a close friend in high school during our senior year and having an assistant coach from UCLA tell my friend that they could not offer him a football scholarship because his grades were not high enough.

He had seen my friend play the night before and was very impressed, but after a visit to the high school's administration office to verify grades and class pre-requisites, my friend's academic performance did not meet UCLA's minimum standards for admission. And despite what you might hear to the contrary, exceptions are not made for athletes.

You either have the grades, the class requirements and the entrance exam scores or you don't. If you don't, no admission, period, end of story.

I remember sitting in the stands last summer watching a game at a high school baseball "showcase". I was sitting next to ten to fifteen college scouts when one local high school coach whispered to a scout, "Wow, Rob, that kid has looked good the entire day. He's going to make some college coach really happy". Rob replied, "Maybe so, but sadly it will not be me".

The coach look puzzled and said, "Why? He obviously has a good glove, exceptional speed and can hit for power".

Rob pointed to the player's line on the background info sheet given to all of the scouts and said, "Yeah, he has all of the tools except the one most often absent". Rob was pointing to the athlete's 2.9 grade point average.

"I need at least a 3.2," Rob sighed sadly.

The high school coach just shook his head in disappointment.

> *The key point that athletes need to understand is they cannot afford to get off to a slow start with their grades in high school.*

The athlete's *cumulative* high school GPA after their junior year will be the primary influence on whether they meet the minimum requirements for college admission. If after their junior year, their GPA is too low, they will not be able to take enough classes in the first half of their senior year to bring it up significantly.

In addition to college acceptance, an athlete's GPA and entrance exam scores can also significantly impact the amount of "tuition assistance" that some schools can give. Most people know that college tuition is not affordable for most families.

What most people do not know is that the amount of "tuition assistance" that some schools can give is directly related to the athlete's high school GPA and entrance exam scores.

For example, at the Division III level, college coaches cannot give *athletic* scholarships. However, many of them can give *"academic tuition assistance"* to their athletes based on an "academic grant". That grant could be pre-existing or it could be created just for that athlete. In any event, the amount of that grant could be $5,000 per year for an athlete with a GPA of 3.2, but jump to $10,000 for a GPA of 3.4 or 3.5. For a GPA of 3.8 or higher it can jump to as much as $15,000 or more!

Furthermore, some colleges offer academic scholarships of $10,000 or more for students who place in the top 3 in single "core studies" (math, history, English composition, etc.) exams held prior to the student starting school at the college. Most students don't take advantage of these opportunities or don't even know about them.

The main message to the athletes when it comes to academics is to take it very seriously right from the beginning. In the "student-athlete" discussion, two other components are also very important. First, athletes should not assume that every year the difficulty or ease of their classes will be the same. Class difficulty can change every year, for *each athlete,* for a variety of reasons. One student's "easy" year could be the most difficult for another student. To be safe, an athlete should always assume that next year will be more difficult and the athlete should do everything he can to get the best grades possible every year.

Secondly, an athlete needs to continue working on improving and ingraining strong study habits. This is even more important than the grades ultimately achieved. Grades are only one teacher's assessment of a student's performance at one given point in time. They can be very subjective and dependent on the level of competition in that one class.

Good study habits are timeless and are universally beneficial in school and in the work place after graduation.

> *Good study habits and a passion for reading are the keys to academic success.*

Choosing a College

Another common mistake made by the athletes and their families is getting caught up in what the college will provide athletically and not giving equal or

deration to what the college will provide socially and
An athletic career can be over in a second for a variety of

should always ask himself, "If my playing days were over, would
this ⌣   ;e be the best fit for me given my other career goals?"

> *An athlete needs to choose a college first as if he or she were not an athlete.*

Here are some of the questions the athlete needs to consider:

1. Are the location, community and student body environment ones that I am comfortable with?

2. Do I like the weather (year around, not just the day they visit), the living accommodations, the extracurricular activity opportunities and the campus setting?

3. Is the surrounding community and its business and social environment stimulating to me?

4. Am I comfortable and compatible with the school's mission statement, rules, policies and philosophies?

5.   Are there career majors and departments at the school that interest me and that are *nationally* recognized for their excellence?

6.   Am I comfortable with the racial and social diversity or lack thereof of the student body?

    ...and, here's a huge one that almost everyone overlooks...

7. How successful is the placement department at the school in placing students in internships while they are in school and in placing students in fulfilling jobs after graduation? A great education is an important first step, but it's not usually very satisfying without good job opportunities after graduation.

The Athletic Fit

It is important at this point that we review again what an athlete must do to develop physically to his or her optimum level.

An athlete must choose the sport he wants to play in college as early in his high school career as possible. It takes years of planning and training, not months, to achieve this goal. And while playing multiple sports can be beneficial, year-around training in the sport of choice is essential. This

Coaching Champions for Life

juggling act will take careful and extensive planning and support by the athlete, his parents and his coaches. The off-season training must include four-to-six months of getting bigger, stronger and faster, as well as, hundreds of hours mastering the fundamentals of the sport. In addition, one month of complete "down time" away from all training (but not away from proper nutrition and sleep) is also critical.

The athlete must have complete compliance and commitment to the principles outlined in Chapter Three regarding stretching, strength training, nutrition, supplementation and sleep. Choosing appropriate friends and role models during this time is critical to an athlete's ability to stay "on task".

> *The athlete should remember that most of his friends and peers will not do at all, or will not be committed long-term to do what they need to do to successfully obtain an athletic scholarship.*

I discussed earlier some of the questions to consider when choosing a college. Once you are sure that a college is a great fit for your athlete in every other way, here are the questions to consider from an athletic perspective (every athlete should have a copy of the booklet from the NCAA entitled, "Guide for the College-Bound Student-Athlete"):

1. What positions will I play on your team? This is not always obvious. Most coaches want to be flexible, so the athlete might not receive a definite answer. The athlete should also be flexible and have an open mind to playing a position different from the one he played in high school, but the answer is good to know up front.

2. What other players may be competing at the same position? The response could give the athlete an idea of when he can expect to be a starter.

3. Will I be "redshirted" (i.e., asked to practice with the team, but not allowed to play in games with no loss of eligibility) my first year? The school's policy on redshirting may impact the athlete both athletically and academically.

4. What expectations do you have for training and conditioning? This will reveal the institution's commitment to a training and conditioning program.

5. How would you best describe your coaching style? Every coach has a particular style that involves different motivational techniques and discipline.

The athlete needs to know if a coach's teaching style matches his learning style.

6. When does the head coach's contract end? How long does the coach intend to stay? Do not make an assumption about how long a coach will be at a school. If the coach leaves, does this change the athlete's mind about the school/program? The same questions should be asked about the athlete's position coach. The ability of the athlete to get along with his position coach may be even more important than liking the head coach. Be careful of the situation in which the head coach is also an athlete's position coach. Many times the position coach needs to be a "big brother" mentor and personality-buffer between the athlete and the "tough love" tactics of the head coach.

7. Are preferred, invited and uninvited walk-on situations allowed? How many do you expect to compete? How many earn a scholarship? Situations vary from school to school.

8. Whom else are you recruiting for my position? What other athletes, both at my position and in general, have committed to your school for the upcoming season and what current athletes plan to transfer to another school and why?

   Coaches may consider other student-athletes for every position. The athlete needs to get an idea early on about his competition and the strength of the college's recruiting class overall. Playing time is great, but the potential of winning some championships is also important.

9. Is medical insurance required for my participation? Is it provided by the college? The athlete may be required to provide proof of insurance.

10. What happens if I want to transfer to another school?

    An athlete may not be able to transfer without the permission of his current school's athletic administration. Ask how often coaches grant this privilege and ask for examples of situations in which permission was not granted.

11. What other factors should I consider when choosing a college? Be realistic about the athlete's athletic ability and the type of athletic experience he would enjoy.

    Some student-athletes want to be part of a particular athletics program, even if it means little or no playing time. Of course, the ideal is to choose a college or university that will provide the athlete with both the educational and athletic opportunities he wants.

12. Is the department in my major nationally recognized for its excellence? How many students are in the department? What is the average class size? Are classes taught by the professors themselves or by teaching assistants?

How available are the professors for consultations outside of class?

13. How available are working internships during the time I attend the school? How many graduates are successfully placed with the help of the school in well-paying jobs after graduation?

14. What percentage of players on scholarship graduate? This response will suggest the school's commitment to academics.

15. What percentage of incoming students eventually graduate?

16. What is the current team's grade-point average?

17. What academic support programs are available to student-athletes? Look for a college that will help the athlete become a better student.

18. If I have a diagnosed and documented learning disability, what kind of academic services are available? Special academic services may help the athlete achieve his academic goals.

19. How many credit hours should I take in season and out of season? It is important to determine how many credit hours are required for the athlete's degree and what pace he will need to follow to obtain that degree.

20. Are there restrictions in scheduling academic classes around practice? NCAA rules prohibit an athlete from missing class for practice.

21. Is summer school available? If I need to take summer school, will it be paid for by the college? The athlete may need to take summer school to meet academic and/or graduation requirements.

22. What is a typical day of a student-athlete? The answer will give him a good idea of how much time is spent in class, practice, study and travel. It also will give him a good indication of what coaches expect.

23. What are the residence halls like? The response should give him a hint of how comfortable he would be in his room, in study areas, in community bathrooms and at the laundry facilities. Also, ask about the number of students in a room, co-ed dorms, the availability of "Christian" dorms and the rules governing life in the residence halls, and most importantly, the type and amount of supervision in them.

A quiet, comfortable study environment will be crucial to an athlete's academic success and to him maintaining his athletic eligibility.

24. Must student-athletes live on campus? If "yes" ask about exceptions, e.g., only after freshman year?, sophomore, never?

25. How much financial aid is available for both the academic year and summer school? What does a scholarship cover?

26. Under what circumstances would my scholarship be reduced or canceled? Coaches should be able to give an athlete some idea of how players are evaluated from year-to-year and how these decisions are made. The institution may have a policy governing renewal of scholarships. Ask if such a policy exists and read it.

The "Full Ride" Scholarship

Most people think a "full ride" is good for four years, but most athletic financial aid scholarships, i.e., those governed by the NCAA, are given only on a one academic-year renewable basis! The four-year scholarship is optional at the discretion of the school.

Unless a player has been specifically granted a four-year scholarship in writing, the school can refuse to renew a player's scholarship after one year for any reason even if the player has fulfilled all of his obligations academically and has played well athletically.

If the coach has recruited players whom the coach thinks will help the team win more games, for example, he may refuse to renew the scholarship of a "lesser talented" returning player. This is a key point to remember.

Sports at the DI level, at least in the major sports, is many times viewed as a business; and that business is winning, not academics. In these cases, DI athletes are not recruited as student-athletes, only athletes. If the athlete also happens to graduate and gets a good education too, it's merely icing on the cake in the view of the athletic department of these schools.

The moment an athlete stops being the best viable option to help the team win…he becomes expendable.

---

27. Are there academic criteria tied to maintaining the scholarship? Some institutions add academic requirements to scholarships (e .g. a minimum grade-point average).

28. What are my opportunities for employment while I am a student? Find out if an athlete can be employed in season and out of season or during vacation periods.

29. Exactly how much will the athletic scholarship be? What will and will not be covered? It is important to understand what college expenses a family will be responsible for so a payment plan can be arranged.

   Educational expenses can be paid with student loans and government grants, but it takes time to apply for them.

   Find out early so something can be lined up.

30. Am I eligible for additional financial aid? Are there any restrictions? Sometimes a student-athlete cannot accept a certain type of scholarship because of NCAA limitations.

   If an athlete has been awarded other scholarships or grants, let the coaches and the financial aid officer know so they can determine if additional dollars can be accepted.

31. Who is financially responsible for medical bills and expenses if I am injured while competing? The athlete needs to understand his financial obligations if he suffers an injury while participating in athletics.

32. What scholarship money is available after my eligibility is exhausted to help me complete my degree? It may take longer than four years to complete a college degree program. Some colleges assist student-athletes financially as they complete their degrees. Ask how such aid is awarded.

   The athlete may be required to work with the team or in the athletics department to qualify for this aid.

33. What scholarship money is available if I suffer an injury ending my athletic career? Not every institution continues to provide an athletic scholarship to a student-athlete who can no longer compete because of a career-ending injury.

34. Will my scholarship be maintained if there is a change in coaches? A coach may not be able to answer this, but the Athletic Director should be able to do so.

The Recruiting Process

Serious Recruiting Interest

One of the most common questions I receive from parents and athletes is, "When do you know a college is seriously interested and not just 'stringing me along' prior to making me an offer?"

This is a great question because good athletes will receive a lot of general interest letters and forms which have been personalized to make it seem like the college is very interested in the athlete. These are not indicators of serious interest regardless of how personalized they are!

They are nearly always a mass-marketing scheme to get the athlete to attend one of their "camps" which are mostly held as fundraisers for the program.

The college may also make telephone calls to current and former coaches and to scouts seeking information about the athlete's ability, work ethic, coachability, etc. These are indicators of "medium interest" by the college.

Of course, you know that a college is getting pretty serious when the head coach and/or an assistant coach comes to one of the athlete's games to specifically watch him or her play.

However, in this day and age, probably the best indicator of when a college is very serious about recruiting an athlete is when a coach from the college asks to exchange cell phone numbers with the athlete. If this doesn't happen, the athlete is probably not very high on their list.

> *Once an athlete starts talking on a regular basis with the coaches on his cell phone, he knows he is receiving serious consideration by the college to play for them.*

Ownership of the Process By the Athlete

But, let's not get ahead of ourselves here. What does an athlete need to do to get recruited once they have fully complied with and been committed to the program outlined in Chapter Three?

First, while obtaining information and help from multiple sources is important, the athlete needs to take the primary responsibility for obtaining the scholarship.

Being very proactive and double-checking all information throughout the process is critical. Colleges want to hear primarily from the athlete, not the athlete's parents or coaches. Colleges want athletes who are mature and grounded enough to stand on their own. After all, the scholarship will be given to the athlete alone and to no one else.

Governing Body Websites

The websites:

www.ncaa.org, www.naia.cstv.com, and www.collegeboard.com are very valuable resources during the recruiting process and should be referred to often.

Among other things, these websites provide athletes and their families with rules regarding when and how college coaches are allowed to contact recruits (usually they are not allowed to do so before July 1st of the athlete's junior year), protecting an athlete's amateur status and the acceptance of gifts. Does the NCAA prohibit me from accepting t-shirts or tennis shoes or the like when I attend college camps and "showcases"?

Make a List of Potential Colleges

The next step the athlete should take is to develop a list of potential colleges he may want to attend. Have the athlete develop this list using the criteria I set forth above regarding the important things to consider if you were *not* an athlete.

Try not to be influenced by what he has seen during a sporting event telecast. Obviously, what a college is really like may be nothing like what is portrayed on TV. A football game between two long-time rivals may be very exciting to watch on TV, but the fact that the weather was 90 degrees with 95% humidity may not be disclosed. An athlete may not want to live in an environment with a harsh climate for four or more years of his life. The athlete should, however, keep a broad perspective geographically when composing his list of potential colleges.

> *Be sure to ask if equal opportunities are given to "out-of-state" athletes as compared to "in-state" athletes.*

Looking at the current and former rosters of the team and where their players are from will give an athlete a good idea how open that team is to players from other states. If the athlete feels strongly that the college is a perfect fit for him, but there are no players from his state or area on the team, he should contact the recruiting coordinator and ask why not.

The prospective recruit should also talk to current and former players about this issue. The current coaches will almost always say they are willing to give a fair shot to anybody and that it is merely budget considerations that keep them from casting a wider recruiting net, but in reality, the reasons may be very different.

"Camps" and "Showcases"

Here are some crucial things everyone needs to know about "camps" and "showcases". First, they are most often held by colleges primarily for *fundraising* purposes and not for recruiting prospective players. Camps or showcases that are open to anyone for a fee are merely fundraisers, despite their fancy names or promotions. I would encourage an athlete to attend one of these during an athlete's sophomore year to get a feel for what goes on. But the athlete should not count on being recruited as a result of his attendance.

> *Don't be surprised if the head coach gives the welcoming address to the athletes at the beginning of the camp and is never seen again.*

In fact, for an athlete's first camp, I recommend attending one the athlete is reasonably sure will not be attended by coaches on the athlete's list of potential colleges. I am not saying that the athlete should not take the camp seriously or prepare for it properly. On the contrary, you never know what the future holds. The athlete should take it very seriously so he can be sure to receive the best preparation possible for the next camp or showcase where the right scouts will be in attendance.

(Appendix V has the list of things I tell all of my athletes to do so they can be successful at camps.)

Here is how to select a camp or a showcase to attend that the athlete wants to be sure will be worth his or her time after the initial "introductory" one they attended just to get experience.

First, do not be a camp "junkie". More is not better. Be very selective. Some of these camps will have scouts from the same colleges. It is very important that a scout sees significant improvement in the athlete every time he sees him. Old news is not good news when it comes to recruiting athletes.

Next, in their sophomore year or in the summer between their sophomore and junior years, the athlete should choose a camp where the emphasis is on instruction and is not just a talent "showcase".

Second, if possible, when choosing a camp that is not a teaching camp but is primarily a talent "showcase", choose camps that are very selective about whom they allow to attend.

> *If the selection criteria includes grades, even better.*

Coaches from the premier college programs are more likely to spend their valuable time attending a camp they know will only have the "cream of the top" talent showcased versus an "all-comers" fundraiser. Be sure to check with current and former elite athletes and coaches about which camps they know to be the best. Most importantly, the athlete should contact the recruiting coordinator coach at the colleges the athlete may want to attend to find out which camps they will send a coach to scout.

If the athlete wants to attend a good camp, but has not received confirmation from his preferred colleges whether they will send a scout or has not yet developed a list of potential colleges, he should ask the camp director what college coaches and scouts have *committed to attending the camp that year.*

Do not be fooled by statements by the director that certain college coaches and scouts will probably attend because they have done so in the past. The past is the past. The athlete wants to be sure that he knows who has committed to attend the camp he will attend. The camp director needs to supply the athlete with the list of coaches and scouts who have committed to attend that year *prior to* the athlete paying for the camp.

If you are not sure what colleges you want to attend, but you want to attend some camps anyway, select camps that will have coaches from a variety of colleges and colleges at all different levels, not just DI colleges. If you are not sure about the level of your talent, ask your coach and the top coaches at other programs that have seen you play more than once at what level they think you are most likely to play at in college.

An athlete should not be in a hurry after his first "introductory" camp to attend other camps.

"You only have one chance to make a good first impression" is a very important axiom in this arena too.

Be sure the athlete has developed his talent to as close to elite levels as possible. For example, in baseball, some of the things college scouts look for generally are athletes who can run a 60-yard dash in less than 7.0 seconds, left-handed pitchers who can throw > 82 mph, right-handed pitchers who have a working velocity of > 85mph, catchers whose "pop times" for their throws from home plate to second base are less than 2.0 seconds, third basemen who can throw from the outfield grass behind third base to first base on a line without taking any steps and outfielders who can throw 220+ feet on a line to home plate.

It needs to be emphasized, however, that guidelines are very general and are not applicable to all situations. A sub-seven 60-yard dash time is not very important for a catcher, for example. It is much more impressive for a catcher to have a sub 4.30 SPARQ shuttle time.

Also, everyone knows it is the entire package that is important. And the difference makers are as often intangibles like hustle, confidence, composure and leadership as they are physical qualities. But to be sure, the athlete must stand out as being exceptional from his peers in the fundamental skills of his sport. If the athlete, for whatever reason, is not likely to do so, he should stay home and work on his skills or should, at a minimum, choose another camp with scouts from lower level colleges.

Do not, however, be told by anyone that it matters at what level in high school the athlete plays.

Elite talent is elite talent. Scouts today will find it and will recognize it when they see it. You do not have to play at a large school or at a premier program to be recruited by a top college program.

Yes, of course, a recommendation from an elite coach at a premier high school program will mean more to a scout than one from unknown sources. Extraordinary stats from small schools at lower level leagues will generally be discounted or disregarded. But scouts know talent when they see it.

If you are a high character person with exceptional skills they will find a place for you in their program. Just ask Boston Red Sox star Jacoby Ellsbury who is from the small town of Madras, Oregon.

It goes without saying that you should attend a camp or showcase to display your skills, not abuse your body. I have heard of occasional stories where the athletes at a camp were asked to do an unhealthy number of reps when performing drills and were injured while doing so.

It is obviously better to listen to your common sense by stopping the drill and walking away from the camp where you are being asked to do an excessive number of reps or to perform in dangerous conditions (field, weather, etc.) than it is to ruin a career by sustaining an injury.

Register With the NCAA

At the beginning of the athlete's junior year, he/she should register their information with the NCAA "clearing house" (see www.ncaaclearing house.net) so that college coaches and scouts can easily obtain all of the necessary background information on the athlete and the athlete will not have to redo the information for every school.

In fact, the NCAA requires this registration for all athletes who desire to play college sports at the DI or DII level. (It is not required for other levels of college sports, but each institution may have its own requirements.)

The athlete can merely refer college coaches and scouts to his NCAA Eligibility Center ID number and they can get most of the basic information they want.

Again, refer to the www.ncaa.org website for details. Click on "Academics & Athletes", then click on "Guide for the College-Bound Student Athlete".

The Letter Writing Campaign

Here is the letter writing campaign that an athlete should do to get recruited by the college of his/her choice. At an "off time" of year for the college coach (e.g., late October or early November for college baseball coaches), the athlete should write a short letter of introduction to the coach who is in charge of recruiting at the college with copies of the letter to the Head Coach and the position coach, if applicable.

The letter should state why the athlete is interested in being a part of their program and why the athlete is a good fit for them. The letter should include cumulative GPA numbers, advanced placement classes taken, SAT/ACT scores (if taken), extra-curricular student activities and church, civic and charitable activities.

TIP – In other words, when writing a letter to a college coach, the whole person, not just the athlete should be promoted.

This is another reason why it is so important that you should meet with the prospective college athlete in his/her freshman year. The athlete needs to know what will be expected of them in all phases of their life so they can get involved early!

This first letter should not include any stats or accomplishments relating to the player's sport. It should simply be a promotion of the character and integrity of the player and why they are a good fit for the program and school.

The athlete's coach should help the athlete write this letter and the coach should write a letter of recommendation for the athlete as well to be sent about a week after the athlete sends his letter. (Appendix W is a sample recommendation letter that I wrote on behalf of one of my pitchers in his sophomore year.)

Again, the coach's letter should be sent to the college coach in charge of recruiting with copies to the Head Coach and the position coach. The coach's letter should not only evaluate the player as an athlete, but should promote the whole person.

It should also include a copy of the athlete's high school career stats, significant accomplishments and awards and the upcoming season game schedule. As you can see from my sample letter, the stats should be carefully broken down into meaningful categories.

For a baseball pitcher, for example, the % of first pitch strikes, strike-to-ball ratio and the strikeout-to-walk ratio are very important stats to a scout. The game schedule should be sent to the coaches every few weeks of the season and an email sent every time a change to the schedule occurs or when a pitcher recruit is scheduled to pitch.

Keep in mind that college coaches are very busy and their time is very limited. If you can recommend that the coaches attend a game with more than one college prospect playing in it, your chances of them attending the game will increase dramatically. (The scouts call this "block booking".)

By the way, this is a great teaching point to the other athletes on your team. Many college recruits are discovered while the scout is attending a game initially to watch other players!

A Scout's Eyes

A scout's eyes are not selective by name, only by ability and by character. Furthermore, many times a scout will only stay for part of the game for the initial viewing. As I said before, a scout's time is very limited and valuable.

> *Whatever skills the athlete has, they had better be displayed in warm-ups and by the third inning of the game. After that, the scout may leave to catch the end of another game.*

What the players do between innings is equally important to what occurs during the game. Catchers' "pop times" will be recorded on their throws to second base between innings just like they will be during the game. In fact, if no runner attempts a stolen base during the time the scout is at the game, the "pop times" recorded between innings may be the only ones recorded period!

Ditto for the double play turns of the infielders.

Most importantly, know that the scout's eyes do not miss anything and are *always* on the recruit, particularly before the game starts and while the athlete

Coaching Champions for Life

is in the dugout or on the bench when the athlete may let his guard down and show a different character. Leadership, composure, hustle and being a tenacious competitor until the very end of the game no matter the score are the key intangibles the scout is looking for.

Remember to remind your athletes that being the best player on the field that day is not good enough. The athlete must be one of the 4 or 5 best players the scout has seen or will see *anywhere* that entire recruiting season!

Prepare a Skills Tape

Now that the athlete has developed his skills to the best they can be (hopefully to an elite level) he should prepare a tape of his skills to send to the college coaches along with one of the follow-up letters.

The tape should be short with a clear index of what is on the tape and how the coach can quickly access the different skills if he is only interested in some of them. College coaches receive tons of these tapes and they do not have time to view all of them or any that are more than a few minutes in length.

The tape should be *unedited* and clearly marked as such. Do not send game "highlight" tapes. A scout or a coach need to analyze a myriad of details that can only be discerned from viewing the tape of a player for an entire game. Better to send a short skills tape made in a non-game setting and let the scout come to watch an entire game. Finally, the tape should be sent to the recruiting coordinator coach and the position coach, not the Head Coach. The Head Coach is almost always too busy to view such tapes.

The tape should be previewed by the player's high school coach or other knowledgeable coach prior to it being sent to the college. After the coach reviews the tape, it should not be edited, but it may need to be redone completely. That would be unfortunate and inconvenient, but well worth it considering the scholarship dollars at issue.

Pre-Camp/Showcase Letter

Once the athlete knows what camps or showcases the college coach will attend, he should send the coach a short email or letter notifying him that the athlete also plans to attend and he looks forward to meeting him at the camp. (Know your NCAA contact rules, however! The coach may not be able to initiate the contact or feel comfortable talking directly to the athlete if the camp is during an NCAA contact "dead period".)

A reminder email or note should be sent to the coach by the athlete the week of the camp stating that the athlete is looking forward to seeing the coach at the camp.

Talking to College Coaches or Scouts

In addition to strict adherence to the guidelines set forth in Appendix V, when an athlete talks to a college coach or scout, he should just focus on being himself and not worry about saying all the right things. A good firm handshake, good upright, confident posture, maintaining eye contact throughout the conversation, good listening skills, smiling and "yes sir, no sir, thank you sir" will mean a whole lot more than anything in particular the athlete says.

In addition to those things, the athlete should have an air of energy about him and should be excited and positive about everything--the weather, the opportunity to participate in the camp, the opportunity to learn something new and to meet new people and coaches.

Nothing even close to a negative word or comment should leave the athlete's mouth. If the conversation occurs after the workout and the workout did not go as well as the athlete hoped, the athlete should still be upbeat and confident in his ability knowing he will do better next time. He should definitely show his coachability by asking the coach what he thinks the athlete needs to work on so he can improve.

Whatever the coach says, the athlete's response is always "Yes, sir" and never in effect, "My coach wants me to do it differently".

"If he asks you to jump, you say how high on the way up" is the old saying that applies.

The answer to the question of whether the athlete is open to playing other positions is always, "Yes sir, whatever I can do to help the team".

Many athletes play different positions in college than they played in high school for a variety of reasons, the principal one being the needs of the team.

Finally, hustle is important here too. The athlete should run to greet the coaches and he should run to return to wherever he is going next.

Hustle, hustle, hustle, energy, energy, energy - the college coaches love this!

(Appendix X is a list of questions you can expect college coaches to ask you when recruiting your athletes.)

Coaching Champions for Life

Post Camp/Showcase Letter

Following the camp, the athlete should send a letter to the scout and to the coaches who conducted the camp. This letter should include how much the athlete enjoyed the camp, how much he learned, how he will recommend it to other athletes, how much he enjoyed meeting them and how he looks forward to staying in touch.

Negotiating Your Scholarship

If an athlete has fully complied and been committed to the principles in Chapter Three and has carefully followed the recommendations in this chapter, there is a very high probability that he will be offered an athletic scholarship or tuition assistance to play his chosen sport in college. How does he go about negotiating the best deal?

Negotiations Are a Process

First, realize that the recruitment and scholarship process is a *negotiation* and the college's first offer or second offer may not be their best offer even when they say it is "their best and final offer".

They may not be able to offer you any more tuition assistance, but they may be able to offer you money for books and housing.

Also, their *athletic* resources may be tapped, but there may be other academic grants or assistance available through the college or independent sources.

Research your Financial Aid Options

Athletes need to spend a substantial amount of time researching financial aid options on-line, through the college itself, through their high school advisers, coaches, and athletic director.

Of course, the athlete should also talk to as many of their peers and their peers' families as possible about how they financed their college expenses and how they negotiated their athletic scholarship. The athlete should not just talk to other athletes - he should talk to as many people that either attend college or will attend college in the next year or so.

Just forewarn the athletes again that they should not rely solely on the information from any one source. Everything should be checked and double-checked. And they should not be surprised or dissuaded about how many people have such little knowledge about the whole process.

Quantity Limitations

Next, the athlete must understand that athletic scholarships are limited not only in amount, but in number as well. In baseball, for example, DI colleges can only give out 11.7 scholarships per year for 27 players on the team with 8 more players being on the roster, but non-scholarship.

That's right, 11. 7 scholarships total per year. Thus, scholarships are, most of the time, not full scholarships. They might be 1/3, 1/2, 2/3 scholarships or whatever. *(They are required to be at least 1/4)* Yes, different schools have different philosophies. I traveled out of state to a DI college last year with one of my pitchers and when we asked the pitching coach about what their recruiting philosophy was he said, "when it comes to financial aid, we offer big money, for big talent".

However, generally, the college coaches need to offer financial aid to as many athletes as possible.

Very few families can afford the cost of college.

Be Realistic About the Athlete's Talent

It is critical that the athlete is realistic about his talent and his relative value. No athlete is irreplaceable. Very, very few of them command a "must have ticket". One reason for this, of course, is that the talent level is getting better every year.

Second, recruiting methods and information are improving every year. Another reason, however, is that in the major sports, if the athlete is truly elite, he will not be around for four years in college. He will be drafted into professional ball long before he graduates. Colleges today are realizing more and more that they would rather have two really good athletes at 1/2 scholarship each who will stay for three or four years, rather than one elite athlete on a full scholarship who may only stay for one.

The bottom line, as usual, is the athlete should not get greedy.

He probably should not take the college's first offer and should "play one offer against another", but once he has been offered enough for his family to afford the college experience, he should not hold out for more.

If he does, the school may just move on to one of their other options. Trust me, they almost always have other good options. An athlete should be very aware that there is definitely only a window of opportunity to take advantage of an offer.

Once scholarship money has been committed by a college to athletes, all other athletes are "left out in the cold". Early signing may be necessary for all but the most elite athletes. But, after accepting an offer, an athlete should continue to investigate all other financial aid options outside of the athletic department!

"Letters of Intent"

Once the athlete signs a "letter of intent" to play for a particular college, all other colleges *within that division* are required to stop recruiting the athlete.

For example, if the athlete signs a letter of intent to play at a DIII college, no other DIII college can recruit him after that point, but DI, DII, NAIA and community colleges can still do so. Of course, no one should be authorized, formally or informally, to speak on behalf of the athlete except the athlete or his/her parents. The athlete should never sign anything without it being carefully reviewed by the athlete's parents or guardians, the athlete's coach and Athletic Director.

Warning: Never rely on an oral commitment from a college. A commitment is not a binding commitment unless it is in writing! Many athletes get burned by relying on an oral commitment early in their Senior year, for example, only to be told at the end of the year that the college has given the scholarship to another athlete.

Community Colleges

If the passion to play the sport in college is deep in the athlete's heart and the athlete is not offered enough assistance to make attending the college of his choice feasible, the athlete should strongly consider attending a community college (called "JUCO's", i.e., Junior Colleges) for a year or two.

Some of the best DI college and professional players, like Evan Longoria, got their start at a community college. Players get to grow and develop to their full potential while they are there. Physically, athletically and emotionally there is a HUGE difference between an 18-year old and a 20-year old. These two years can make a big difference in the opportunities and performance of the player later at the DI or DII level.

Furthermore, the athlete may need more time to improve his study and academic skills. A talented athlete does not do a college any good if he cannot stay academically eligible. More importantly, the athlete's job opportunities may be better if he graduates from a better college after first improving his academic abilities at a community college.

Parents who are worried about a community college not being academically challenging enough for their student-athlete should consider this - it is also possible for an athlete to attend a four year college, take a class or two at the local community college and play baseball for a year or two at the community college to improve his skills enough to hopefully play baseball one day at the four year college!

The "DI Mentality"

It is also crucial that the athlete understand how coaches at many elite DI colleges think. Winning the conference championship is a good year, but the only truly acceptable year is winning a National Championship. It is very much a business-like "what have you done for me lately" philosophy.

One or two bad outings as pitcher, for example, and the player may find himself on the bench or relegated to pitching only during "mop up time" in a hurry. The player may be happier at a lower level college with a good reputation for teaching and development.

A patient, two-to-four year approach to developing the player by the lower level college may also improve his draft prospects as well! The athlete should talk to as many current and former players who played for the current coaches as possible.

It may be more enlightening to talk to the "bench players" rather than the starters to see how fairly they think they were or are being treated.

Summary

Many more athletes have the ability to earn an athletic scholarship than currently do. The athlete does not need extraordinary physical or athletic ability to accomplish the goal. The keys are an early commitment to the principles outlined in Chapter Three, to good study habits and grades and to extracurricular student and civic activities.

The athlete, and not his parents or coach, should take the primary responsibility for the research and college contacts although he will need much help and support from both of them.

Careful planning and research from as many sources as possible will be required, but great care should be taken to double check and verify all information before relying upon it. The athlete should carefully protect his amateur status and know the contact and "gift" rules thoroughly by becoming very familiar with www.ncaa.org.

Financial aid for college can come from many sources other than an athletic scholarship and can be assisted by good grades and entrance exam scores. A college should be chosen first based on academic and community fit and only secondarily based on the athletic program. A wide geographic search should be done and colleges at all levels, including community colleges, should be considered, but it should be clear from the college coaches that athletes from all areas will be given a fair opportunity to succeed.

Camps should be attended only when the athlete's skills are at or are approaching exceptional levels. Instructional camps should be attended first and "showcases" should only be attended when the athlete is sure that admission to them is highly selective or will definitely be attended by scouts from his chosen colleges.

A systematic and thorough promotional campaign and contact follow-up program is essential. When the athlete starts exchanging cell phone calls with the coaches at his colleges of choice, he will know that he is close to the goal. When he receives his offer, he should know what he is worth and what the college can do for him.

He has worked hard and he deserves the best, but he should not be greedy. He wants a college that cares about patiently developing the whole person and not just an athlete.

After all, they are getting a *Champion for Life*.

Coaching Champions for Life

CHAPTER NINE

LET CHAMPIONS PLAY

"Shepherd God's flock among you, not overseeing out of compulsion but freely, according to God's will; not for money but eagerly; not lording it over those entrusted to you, but being examples to the flock. And when the chief Shepherd appears, you will receive the unfading crown of glory." 1 Peter 5:2-4

Good coaches are good teachers. They teach the fundamentals of their sport through progressive building-block methodology.

And they teach by modeling appropriate behavior and habits for life skills in general. Some coaches put so much emphasis on the former that they forget that the latter is much more important. For example, a coach whose coaching methodology is to yell and yell louder in attempting to get his players to master the fundamentals of playing the sport is doing a very poor job of modeling how to appropriately handle adversity.

"They may forget what you said. They may forget what you did. But they will never forget how you made them feel."

Very few athletes will have the opportunity to be a professional in their sport. The most important thing they will derive from good coaching along the way is high self-esteem by accomplishing things individually and/or as a team they may have initially thought were not possible. However, building an athlete's self-esteem is very difficult if the coach is micro-managing every step and thought of the athlete every minute of the game.

> *Let the athletes play. Practices are for the coaches to teach. Games are for players to demonstrate what they have learned.*

If a coach is calling out instructions to the players every minute of the game, the coach is doing several negative things.

First, he is sending a message to the players that he has not taught them well enough for them to do it on their own when it counts. The message is, "Don't trust my coaching". Second, he is sending a message that he does not trust his players to think and act on their own, i.e., "You're not good enough". Third, he is implying that his own self-esteem is not strong enough to handle losing. He is sending his team the message that the outcome of the game is more important than the self-esteem of the players in the game. The coach is implying that his needs are more important than the needs of his players. Fourth, coaches are always telling their players to "flush it" and remain in the moment after a mistake has been made.

However, if a coach yells out to his team or to a player after every mistake is made, it will be very difficult, if not impossible, for the team to remain in the moment. Many times, I think coaches yell out to their players during a game in hopes that they will impress the audience with their knowledge of the sport.

In fact, the only thing the coach is really doing is poorly modeling composure and embarrassing the player, the team and the player's parents.

Finally, if a coach is also constantly yelling out encouragement to the players to the point where the players themselves are relatively quiet, he is emotionally rescuing them from their own feelings. Learning to self-soothe and to deal appropriately with one's own emotions are some of the most important life skills than can be learned from sports.

The same can be said for a player helping other players with different personalities and maturity levels than his deal with their emotions.

Positive reinforcement and encouragement are always appropriate. However, the older the player, the less a coach should yell out encouragement in a game. Let the players take the primary accountability for supporting one another.

Coaching Champions for Life

This pitcher, in his Junior year, pitched 32 innings and had a 0.00 ERA. He alone decided what pitch to throw on every pitch. Teach them well, but let your players play.

In baseball, I recommend that during the defensive half of an inning, the players stand at the front of the dugout and the coach stands *behind the players* so the players are in charge of the emotion and communication with the team during the inning. If you can do this, you know you have reached the pinnacle of the cooperative style of coaching and you are truly elite among your peers. One of my cardinal rules of coaching is *a coach must be brave enough to let your players play and to accept the outcome.*

As a baseball coach, I would rather lose a championship game by letting my pitchers and catchers call the pitches in the game than to win the game with me calling all of the pitches. The game, even a championship game, is just not that important. Winning is not anywhere near as important as the message to my players of my trust and faith in them. If a team loses a championship game, a wonderful opportunity is presented to the coach. He can teach his players about seeing "the glass half-full" by pointing out all of the positives they did in the game. He can model being gracious and classy in defeat. He can teach how one game does not define a season or an entire career. *And finally, he can teach that the outcome of a game, win or lose, does not define a person. It is how they react to winning or losing that defines a person and a team.* Obviously, winning is much more fun and a great goal. But learning to deal with defeat may be a much more valuable lesson in the long run. If I am unhappy with the pitch sequences of my pitcher during a game, I can call time out to have a mound conference with him, I can talk to him between innings or I can do a better job of teaching him during practice.

Other than those things, the most important thing I can do during the game is to stay positive and set a good example by focusing on all of the things he is doing right.

By the way, this will also have the added benefit of making you feel better as a coach. When the pitcher pitches a no-hitter or a perfect game or our team wins a championship, the self-esteem of the players has been built as much as possible because they know they accomplished it largely on their own. Striving for external rewards and being "successful" in life tempts many people to focus on "me," "our side," material things and just plain being selfish. This, in turn, causes those people to blame others, to focus on the "glass half empty" and to be negative in general.

We will be much happier and more successful in life if we learn to focus instead on having a charitable heart, on what is right with others and with the world. We need to send athletes out into the world with the self-confidence that they can perform well under pressure against great odds on their own and that they can help others do the same.

To do these things, we need to keep quiet more often during games and *let champions play.*

CHAPTER TEN

COACHING CHAMPIONSHIP GAMES

"I don't say this out of need, for I have learned to be content in whatever circumstances I am. I know both how to have a little, and I know how to have a lot. In any and all circumstances I have learned how to be content - whether well fed or hungry, whether in abundance or in need. I am able to do all things through Him who strengthens me." Philippians 4:11-13

"This is the day the Lord has made; let us rejoice in it and be glad." Psalm 118:24

My teams have finished first or second in League play 13 out of the last 15 years. In the interest of full disclosure, however, I will admit that I have lost as many championship games as I have won. My friends support me by saying that I have to be doing a lot of things right if my teams are consistently in the championship hunt. My detractors point out that I have lost the last two State Championship games in a row.

They also point out that we had not lost to the last team that beat us in the State Championship game in almost three years.

We had beaten them seven consecutive times, three times in the past season, twice during League play and again in the League Championship game. The combined score in our favor of the three games against them in the last season was 38-6.

Yet, in the State Championship game they beat us 14-9 in *eleven innings..* We played a good game, but they played a great game.

They outplayed us in every phase of the game and deserved to win. As all good coaches tell their players, *"You don't have to be the best team in the State to win a State Championship. You just have to be the best team on the field that day"*.

On that day, they were the best team.

No excuses. (Of course, it helps to remember we were one of the two best teams in the State for two consecutive years!)

We lost and, as I said in Chapter 1, when we lose, particularly in a close, extra-inning game, I tell myself there were things I could have done in training my players and in game management that could have made a winning difference.

And as I said in the Preface, the information I have given in this book comes from the times I have done things right and from the times when I learned what I should have done.

So, here is what I have learned coaches need to do to have their team play their best in Championship games.

1. Practice and execute fundamentals before flash.

Remember what got you there. Do not implement any last minute "gimmick plays" at the expense of perfecting the fundamentals. The first thing you do when you practice trick plays is send your team a message that they are not currently good enough to win the championship game by doing what they have been doing that got them there in the first place. I cannot think of a worse message to send to your team.

They have worked so long and so hard and yet they still aren't good enough in their coach's mind to win the big game. Huge mistake.

However, be careful in pre-championship practices that you don't practice fundamentals so much that you leave your team too exhausted to play their best in the game.

Too many reps may also send your team the same self-defeating message (i.e., that you do not think they are good enough to win) that practicing trick plays would send them.

You will have to make a key judgment call on how much and how long to practice leading up to the championship game based on the players' age, their maturity, their commitment to proper nutrition and sleep, etc. so they are at their physical and mental peak to play their best.

Secondly, trick plays are rarely, if ever, the difference maker in championship games. Trick plays are called and will sometimes work, but the team that does a better job of executing the fundamentals will win the game – blocking and tackling in football, pitching and defense in baseball, etc.

You will notice, however, that I implied not to implement any *new* gimmick plays. If you have unique plays or defenses that have worked for your team in certain situations in the past and you have practiced them to perfection, by all means, use them if the situation calls for it in the championship game. That is part of "what got you there".

In short, "do what you do," do it better than you have ever done it before and you will have the best chance to win.

2. **Most championship games are lost, not won.**

Many more physical and mental errors are difference-makers in big games than are home runs hit off of great pitches, for example. And of the two, mental errors are the bigger culprit because mental factors like inexperience with dealing with pressure and adversity, self-doubt, insufficient practice time at game speed and game intensity all lead to the physical errors that lose championships.

Furthermore, spend the majority of your time perfecting your defense. In most sports, great defense wins championships. Offense, scoring lots of points, runs or whatever, is exciting, but good defenses (I'm including pitching when I say good defense in baseball of course) shut down good offenses. The reason is not just physical, but mental too.

Ask yourself this, what fires up your team more in football and takes the heart out of the other team more, a long touchdown pass by your offense or a goal line stand by your defense? In soccer, a "header" off of a corner kick for a goal by your offense or a penalty kick save by your goalkeeper?

A grand slam home run in baseball or a double play with bases loaded to end the inning turned by the defense?

Make mental preparation, competitions with real pressure and perfecting your defense the emphasis of your practice time and you will win championships.

3. **Know your team's strengths and play to them.**

John Wooden said, *"Never let what you cannot do interfere with what you can do"*. In football, you may wish that your quarterback had a stronger arm to allow your offense to "stretch the defense" more often, but that is not essential.

Vary the looks of your run options and mix in short and medium range passes to different targets and you will succeed.

In soccer, you may wish you had exceptional team speed and could attack more vertically and directly, but again this may not be what got you to where you are.

If not, then patience, good defense and counter-attacking are the keys to your victory.

In baseball, I wished some of my teams had more power to score runs in bunches with the long ball. But we succeeded with playing a less-exciting brand of "small ball" where we scored runs by putting pressure on our opponent's defense and forced them into making mistakes.

In fact, this is another key to winning big games. Use your offense to force the defense to make plays.

Versatility never hurts, however. Sometimes other factors may force you to occasionally modify what you do.

In the last two State Final games, my teams hit 12 balls that would have been home runs in almost any other ballpark with a fence that we played in all year. But because the State Final games are played in a professional ballpark with major league distance fences, the 370-380' "bombs" my players hit were merely extra-base hits, or worse, long outs in the State Final games.

We did not hit a single home run in those games and if we had played them at any of our usual opponents' ballparks, we would have hit 12 of them and would have won both games easily. A "squeeze bunt" or a hit and run play in one instance or two in those games may have yielded much better results.

We were "rope-a-doped" by the large ballpark and my poor game management.

I'm not saying you should go away from your usual routine, but coaches need to remember all factors, including field conditions and dimensions, when formulating their game plans.

Equally as important is to know and attack your opponent's weaknesses. You must also prepare to defend your own team's weaknesses. Good scouting of your opponent by yourself, your assistant coaches and by qualified volunteers may provide your team with valuable information with how to attack your opponent's weaknesses and what they are likely to do to attack yours.

Information about a team's and a player's "tendencies" in certain situations or just vulnerabilities in general can definitely be a difference-maker in a championship game.

4. Perfect Your "Special Teams" Play.

Every sport's games have key moments that require special teams, special personnel, special offenses and special defenses. Prepare your team to execute them perfectly.

I am amazed at how many times I hear sports commentators and "experts" analyze an upcoming Super Bowl matchup or NCAA National Title game and they spend almost all of their time analyzing the "skill position" players. Then, inevitably, you watch the game and the key plays are caused by mental mistakes, e.g., penalties and turnovers, and by great plays or poor play by the "special" (punting and kicking) teams. The same is true for "set pieces" (e.g., free kicks and corner kicks) in soccer and for base running, bunt defense and 1st and 3rd defense in baseball.

Championship teams make very few, if any, mistakes in these "special" situations and they know how to get the most out of their personnel to help them succeed in these areas. In baseball, for example, one of your starters may not be your best bunter or best base runner and may need to be substituted for in special situations to let a bench player come in to do a key job to help the team.

In most sports, the starting player is allowed to re-enter the game after the bench player has done his job. Special teams and special situations are special for a reason.

They win championships.

5. **Expect the unexpected in everything and be prepared to deal with it – the weather, injuries to key players on your team, the level of the other team's play, bad calls by the officials, etc.**

The biggest mistake I think that is made by most coaches in preparing for championship games is the assumption that they and their teams have seen it all and have experienced it all. Trust me, many things will happen in championship games that have never happened to you or to your team before. (Actually, my experience has been that the most unusual things happen in semi-final games, but many of these unexpected things happen in the final game as well.)

In the last State Final game, one might have assumed that since we were playing the game on a professional field with a full-size tarp, that the rain we had the night before the game would not significantly impact the playing conditions.

That would have been a very bad assumption. The grounds crew did not tarp the field and it was a muddy mess.

6. **No lead is safe in a playoff or championship game.**

Never forget this. This may be your one shot at winning a championship. Do not take anything for granted.

The "Bill Belichick Rule" applies. You keep your foot on their throat and the "pedal to the metal" until the final out is made, the final whistle blows, the final horn or gun sounds, or whatever. Do not go into a defensive shell or get conservative. That's how great comebacks get started.

Keep doing what you did to get the big lead to begin with.

Do not take unnecessary chances, but stick to your original game plan the entire game. The time for kindness and compassion is during the handshake line after you have won.

7. **Do not let the other team's key players beat you.**

Prepare a defense and a game plan to take them out of the game (figuratively, of course). One of the things that a coach almost always knows is who the key players are on the opponent's team. And yet, more often than not, those same players do key things to help their team win.

It is true that great players make great plays in big games. That is why they are great players. However, most of the time, only the great players on the *winning* team make great plays in championship games because winning coaches make sure that the other team's key players are not given a chance to beat them, particularly with the game on the line or in key situations.

This can be done in subtle ways as well as in obvious ways. In baseball, if the other team has a great pitcher, our hitters are patient at the plate making their pitcher throw as many pitches as possible so he might get fatigued and need to eventually be taken out of the game or, at a minimum, make a mistake that we can take advantage of later in the game. On defense, we will "pitch around" their best hitter(s) with weaker hitters to follow by teasing them with pitches close to, but not in the strike zone. We have a general pitching philosophy of "get ahead with strikes, get outs with balls".

Early in the game, we even do this with bases loaded where a walk will give up a run. We will simply not "give in". You will be surprised how often this strategy will work because the good hitters are, many times, not patient hitters. (If they were also patient hitters they would not be good hitters – they would be great hitters.)

They do not want to walk. They want to hit a grand slam home run and will, therefore, chase after balls close to, but out of the strike zone particularly in big games. You know who the great players are.

Do not give them the opportunity to beat you.

8. **Know the rulebook inside and out.**

Know it better than the other team's coaches and better than the persons officiating the game. I have read the high school baseball rulebook many, many times. The fact that I have read it many times does not matter. Prior to every season, I read it again – word-for-word, cover-to-cover.

I not only read it, I highlight it and make a quick-reference outline of it. And I do the whole process all over again every year before the playoffs start.

There's a famous story about the time when major league umpire Babe Pinelli called out Babe Ruth on strikes and Ruth said, " There are 40,000 people here who know that last pitch was a ball". To which Pinelli replied, "Maybe so, but mine is the only opinion that counts".

Officials are human and will make mistakes. Some of those mistakes will cost your team dearly, maybe even the game-winning run, points or goal.

But as I always tell my team, if we make as few errors as the officials, we will win every time. On the other hand, officials do make errors applying the rulebook to game situations that a knowledgeable coach can get changed to help his team.

One of my friends has umpired high school and college baseball games for many years. We talk after almost every game he umpires and after every game I coach. I ask him questions about how an umpire views the game and about rule interpretations.

More importantly, we talk about how and when to approach an umpire to question a call. Many coaches do irreparable damage, both in that game and in the future, to their team by constantly "chipping" at the umpires about judgment calls. "Choose your battles carefully" is great advice when questioning officials as well as in life in general.

Specifically, question only rule application calls, not judgment calls. The process by which you question the call is critical, as well. First, wait until the play stops and call time out. Have the time out call acknowledged by the home plate umpire. Talk first to the umpire who made the erroneous call. Keep your voice calm and respectful.

> **TIP** - Here's the most critical step that almost all coaches skip. First, ask the official who made the call, "What did you see?"

Most coaches just go running out on to the field arguing the alleged error before they even know for sure what all of the facts are that were the basis for the umpire's call.

This causes the umpire to be upset first that the coach is making an unprofessional public scene about a call that could have been handled calmly and professionally.

Second, the umpire now realizes that he better change what he thinks he saw to match the call or he will be embarrassed to have to admit he made a mistake. While the coach is rambling on and on about what the call should have been, the umpire is having time to "get his facts straight".

In many instances, a smart umpire will consult with his partner before he even talks to the coach who is challenging the call. Then they are sure to match what they saw with the call and the coach will have lost his chance to get the call changed.

Coaching Champions for Life

If you ask the umpire first, "What did you see?" you will get him to commit to the facts before he has time to think about it or to consult with his partner. Once he has committed to the facts, now you can get the call changed by pointing out the correct rule in the rulebook.

This, of course, assumes that you know what the correct rule is and can locate the rule in the book quickly to show it to the umpires. In most leagues, you have only a couple of minutes to locate the rule in the rulebook before the umpires have the right to restart the game and you have lost your right to have the call changed.

In attempting to get a call changed, the key is to approach the umpire calmly and ask, "What did you see?"

Here's a great story from my friend the umpire that actually happened to him early in his career. It was late in the game of an important playoff contest between two long-time rivals. The team at bat was down by one run. With one out, a full count on the batter and a runner on third base, the batter was fooled by a curveball and made a "half-swing". After the "half-swing", the ball got by the catcher and it come to rest at the backstop. The runner at third base scored and the batter-runner reached first base safely.

The coach of the team on defense came running out yelling, "The batter swung, the batter swung, he should be out".

The umpires conferred before they talked to the coach. They certainly were not going to talk to him while he was so upset. After the conference, the home plate umpire explained to the coach that yes, the batter swung, but the ball getting by the catcher with two strikes, less than two outs and first base "open" allowed the runners to advance.

The coach, barking angrily, merely went back to the dugout.

If the coach had used the correct approach and had calmly and professionally asked during a time out what the umpires saw, he would have been told that not only did the batter swing, but the ball also hit the batter. And if the coach had known his rulebook well, he would have been able to get the call reversed because when a batter swings at strike three, but the ball hits him, the ball is dead immediately, the batter is out and the runner at third base cannot advance.

As it turned out, the *tying run* scored from third base on the play at issue and the batter-runner eventually scored the winning run! Know your rulebook and follow the correct procedure when challenging a call. It will win you games.

9. **During the game, trust your instincts about what you should do to be successful in a certain situation.**

   Trust your instincts before what the "book" (not the rulebook, the traditional "book" of the way to do things in certain situations) says to do. (See also rule #1 above.)

   Being second-guessed by parents, fans, the media, etc. is just a part of coaching. Everyone thinks they know what the right thing to do is. The truth is, the only one who knows what's best for your team is you. Coaches work with their players day-to-day. Good coaches are in tune with their players mentally and physically. At any point in time, a particular player's confidence, mental focus and physical ability may dictate a play or a course of action far different than what would usually be done in a given situation. The "book" may say to bunt with runners on first and second and no one out late in a one-run game, but if your hitter has popped up his last two bunt attempts in prior games and is "seeing the ball really well" as a hitter right then, you probably should let him hit away.

As I always tell my pitchers, your best pitch at any given point in time is the one you believe in your heart you can throw at that moment and hit the spot you want. It does not matter what the "book" says about what you should do with a two-strike count on the hitter. Trust your heart and your instincts.

Good things will happen when you do.

10. Model composure and staying positive at all times for your players.

If your players like and respect you, they will want to model your behavior. You cannot expect them to do what you cannot do. If you want your players to be poised in the face of adversity, you will need to model it for them at all times.

If you want your players to not get down on themselves when they make a mistake, you need to stay positive with them when they make a critical error too. We talked in a prior chapter about being pro-active in helping players learn to deal with mistakes and adversity.

The same thing applies to coaches. You need to have an approach and a system to handle situations when your team, the officials, your assistant coaches and yourself, make mistakes so that the atmosphere on your team remains positive and supportive at all times. The approach may vary somewhat based on the maturity and personality of the person who made the mistake, but you need to know how you are going to handle errors in a positive way *before* they happen.

By the time you reach the championship game, you will have invested thousands and thousands of hours into your players and into the program. Reaching the championship game may be the crowning moment in your long coaching career and you can be sure there will be an incomprehensible amount of pressure and emotion boiling deep inside you waiting to erupt.

Here's some advice on how to deal with it:

Ask people you trust like your wife and your assistant coaches to monitor your tone of voice and the intensity of your words and actions in the days leading up to the game, as well as, on game day. Ask them to tell you, in private, as soon as possible, if they think you are losing your poise and composure. If so, your team will soon follow.

Learn to listen to yourself carefully too. Learn to listen to what you say and the tone in which you say it.

Finally, on the day of the big game, take out a photograph of a player or the team from the Miracle League (children with disabilities) games. Take a good long look at them and into their eyes. It will keep you grounded and give you perspective on what is truly important.

I will admit, however, that I walk a fine line between poise and the "controlled aggression" characteristic that we coaches all want our players and our teams to play with.

I was lucky to have grown up with, even at a very early age, a lot of great athletes in my neighborhood. We became close friends and we played football, basketball and baseball every day, year around during almost all of our free time until darkness made it impossible to see the ball. Great players would come from all around to the schoolyard where we played to compete against us. Most of the time, my team either won or we fought.

Those were the only two options on most days. Thankfully, we won most of the time.

Therefore, I had a "fighter's mentality" ingrained in my competitive psyche from a very early age. I carry that same intensity into every game I coach to this day. I teach it to all of my teams. From the moment I arrive at the ballpark, until the game is over, I intensely dislike the other team, their coaches and everything about them.

Losing to them is not an option.

We either win or we die trying. I do not care what others think about my on-the-field personality. It is always professional and respectful, but it is clear why I am there and what we intend to do. We will win and you know we will win from the moment we arrive. As Coach Dedeaux taught his players, "They're going to hate us anyway. We might as well give them good reasons".

As Marc Antony said, "I have come to bury Caesar, not to praise him".

11. Give your pre-game pep talk and your post-game "I'm proud of you no matter what" speeches the day before the game.

I think most coaches would agree that their teams usually play their best when they are loose and relaxed. If you give your team a big emotional speech right before the championship game, the flood of emotion that it will generate may backfire on you. It will rarely have a calming effect on them.

I think there are definitely things that need to be said to your team before the game. Most of those things, in my opinion, can and should be said the day before the game.

Keep your game day speech short and to the point. If you have your team primed and ready for the championship game, they should need very little more than a look in the eye and a "Let's get it done!" The same is true for the "I love you guys and I am so proud of you" speech. If you win the championship game, very little needs to be said. What you have told them for so long has just been affirmed. If you lose, the emotions are so overwhelming, initially, that the players are not ready to hear anything from anyone.

In that case, you had better have said what you want them to remember the day before the game.

About the only thing they need from you after the loss is a hug, and that same look in the eye that says you care and you will always be there for them.

12. There is no such thing as luck, only God's will.

You may use your "free will" to do everything right in preparing yourself and your team for the game and in executing your game plan, but if it is God's will according to His plan for you to lose, you will lose.

> *Win or lose, handle it with class and dignified grace. Remember, there are only two types of people in this world, humble and about to be humbled.*
>
> *Furthermore, there is only one score that counts, His. One game does not define who you are as a coach, does not define a players' career and does not define who you are as a team or the team's season.*
>
> *How you handle winning or losing a game says everything about those things.*

We had won 23 consecutive games leading up to the last State Title game. We had not lost to a team in our division all year. As I said before, we had beaten the team we lost to in that game seven consecutive times and had not lost to them in almost three years. So, the moment after we lost that last game, the human part of me was so disappointed that for the second year in a row I failed to lead my team to victory. But as the moments after the game passed and I witnessed how my players handled themselves, I was lifted to heights higher than anything I could have imagined.

Heights higher than any victory could have taken me. It would have been much easier to be gracious and classy as victors. But my players held their heads high and handled themselves with true dignity and grace in the face of what, for most players, would have been a crushing defeat. It was then I was again reminded that God's plan is truly great – much greater than our own. I was so proud of my team and the journey we had traveled together for the past four years.

They learned that God cares much more about how and why things are accomplished than what is accomplished.

For four years, our team worked hard, played hard, and win or lose, they conducted themselves with class. We may have lost the last game, but they had proven to everyone, under the most difficult circumstances possible, that they were Champions.

Champions for Life.

EPILOGUE

CHAMPIONS FOR LIFE

In short, what I have tried to illustrate in this book is if you want to teach your athletes how to be *Champions for Life* you must teach them that Champions:

Raise the bar and seek to get better every day.

Are not afraid to compete with anyone at any time.

Know that strong bodies are built through proper daily nutrition, sleep and perfectly-performed, sport-specific exercises.

Strive to be extraordinary not ordinary in their preparation and their execution.

Practice fundamentals before flash.

Believe that teams must become families and teammates must become brothers and sisters.

Take accountability for the growth and development of their teammates because teams are only as strong as their weakest link.

Are aware of the needs of others in their home, community and around the world regardless of what is going on in their own lives.

Know that integrity and empathy are worth far more than any trophy.

Feed their faith by daily prayer and service to others.

Give thanks to Him every day no matter what cross they are asked to carry.

Know that God's plan involves me, but is not about me.

Persevere through positive thinking because adversity is an opportunity for growth and to be an inspiration to others.

Know that there is only one score that counts…His.

Go and teach them well, in His name….

Coaching Champions for Life

APPENDIX A

COACHING PHILOSOPHY

1. We are role models for our players in every way:

   A. Energy - run everywhere, never sit on the bench or a bucket

   B. Toughness

   C. Resiliency

   D. Poise

   E. Intensity

   F. Competitiveness

   G. Positive attitude

   H. Work ethic

   I. Pride in the appearance of our facility and ourselves

   J. Passion for the game

   K. Listening skills

   L. Compassion and forgiveness

   M. Perseverance

   N. Timeliness - first ones to arrive, last ones to leave

2. We believe that the word *coach* is a VERB. We will challenge the players to get better every day in every way. We don't just preach it. We demonstrate it and make the player(s) do it over and over again until they can do it perfectly.

3. We will strive to develop each of our players to be Christian leaders and student-athletes, not just baseball players.

4. We are supportive of each other and the program philosophy. Stay true to the program's principles at all times regarding the fundamentals of the game, work ethic and code of conduct.

5. We will represent our program, school and community well by displaying sportsmanship and class at all times.

6. We will have high expectation levels for our program, our players and ourselves. Excellence is not our goal. It is our standard. Insist on excellence in executing fundamentals, running, ab/core work, stretching, etc. - in everything!

7. We will speak in positive terms. We will seek out opportunities to give praise and positive feedback to the players.

    We will give individual praise publicly, and individual constructive improvement comments privately.

8. Our "get better every day" standard applies to the coaches first.

9. We will strive to build a *community* of baseball in our program and our town.

10. If it is not acceptable at the college level, it is not acceptable in our high school program. Do not be afraid to discipline a player when you hear/see him disrespect another coach or player or the program's philosophy.

APPENDIX B

TOP 10 THINGS WE NEED TO DO TO
HAVE A CHAMPIONSHIP SEASON

10. Get better every day - "It's not about the result, it's about the commitment to the effort". Daley Thompson, Olympic Decathlon Champion '80 & "84. We need to prepare to play the #1 rated team every day by practicing perfectly, at game speed and with game intensity.

9. Remain accountable as individuals and as a team - our destiny is in our own hands. We can succeed in spite of the umpires, the weather, the field conditions, etc., etc.

8. Attitude = Input: Stay positive every thought of every day.

> *"Expectations handled in a negative way become pressure.*
> *Expectations handled in a positive way become support".*
> *~ Olympic Champion swimmer Ian Thorpe*

7. Accept your role - Ask not what you need to do to receive more playing time - ask what you need to do to help the team win.

6. Do not compare yourself to others on our team and do not compare our team with other teams. Be the best you can be and be the best we can be.

5. No one is perfect. Love them anyway, including yourself.

4. Communicate your needs in an appropriate time, place and manner. We can't help what we do not know about.

3. Be Student-Athletes. Student comes first.

2. Stay healthy and eligible. Proper rest. Proper nutrition. Avoid the "Three Biggest Thinking Errors of a Teenager" which are:

    a. I'm "bulletproof" - no serious injury or consequences will happen to me no matter what physical or behavioral risk I take.

    b. I can "have my cake and eat it too"

    -Good grades/get into college/be successful in business without good study and organization habits

    -Superior success in sports and life without superior commitment and discipline

    c. Any mistakes I make in (1) and (2) above, I will be rescued by the money and/or power of mom and/or dad.

1. **Win or lose, give all the glory to Him by remembering our purpose and our mission.**

APPENDIX C

TEAM RULES

1. Coaches and players will listen carefully to one another and will not make each other repeat themselves.

2. Coaches and players will ask thoughtful, respectful questions. *See also Rule 1.*

3. Coaches and players, when conversing, shall track along with the thought process, as well as, the content of the speaker's words. (e.g., the purpose of a drill or sequence of drills.) *See also rules 1 and 2.*

4. Coaches and players shall at all times seek to make the whole team better and will not spend disproportionate amounts of time by actions or words on the best players or the players in need of the most discipline.

5. Coaches and players will praise effort, proper execution and unselfish behavior.

6. Coaches and players will tactfully and respectfully ask "slackers" to pick it up.

7. Coaches and players will hold everyone accountable for excellence in attitude, effort, commitment, discipline and execution.

8. Coaches and players will, at all times, be models of integrity, hustle and hard work.

9. Coaches and players will always remain positive, and have a "can do" attitude. We will leave our excuses in the locker room.

10. Coaches and players will be flexible and open to change.

APPENDIX D

RUNNING FORM WARM-UP

❖ High Knees

❖ Dynamic "A Steps"

❖ Kick Butt

❖ Dynamic "B Steps"

❖ Backward skip

❖ Backward sprint

❖ Knee highs

❖ Quicks (linear run with short, rapid feet pick up)

❖ Side-to-side

❖ Carioca (switch which way you face at ½ way point)

❖ Zig Zag

❖ 80% Sprint

❖ Lateral Lunges (10 each direction)

❖ Rapid Responses

       a. linear with "Go"

       b. lateral with "Go"

       c. swivels with "Go"

APPENDIX E

RUNNING AND STRETCHING WARM-UP
(All running exercises are done for 40'-50')

1. High Knees

2. Kick Butt

3. Dynamic "A Steps"

4. Dynamic "B Steps"

5. Backward Skip

6. Backward Sprint

7. Side-to-side - low arm swing

8. Side-to-side - full arm swing

9. Jumping Jacks (5)

10. Seal Jacks (5)

11. Cross-Over Jacks (5)

12. Side Squat Groin Stretch - 2 each side for 5 seconds

13. Straight Leg, Toe Up Groin Stretch - 2 each side for 5 seconds

14. Standing Quad Stretch 2 each side for 10 seconds

15. Seated Butterfly Stretch - push down knees with elbows, then grab toes with hands - 10 seconds

16. Seated "V" Stretch - 10 seconds

17. Hurdlers Stretch - 2 each side - 10 seconds

18. Lying Lower Back, Hip Flexor Stretch - 2 each side - 10 seconds

19. Push Up Position Calve Stretch - 2 each side - 10 seconds

20. Kneeling Lat Pulls - 2 sets - 10 seconds each

21. Three side steps, groin stretch right & left (5)

22. Two Steps, Knee hug and Spiderman Stretch (5 each leg)

23. Throwing motion, back knee down, two side twists (5)

24. Three steps, standing quad stretch one leg, 3 steps, standing quad
     stretch other leg (5 each leg)

25. Three steps, alternating heel-to-hip stretches (5 each leg)

26. Three steps, alternate leg "Frankensteins" (5 each leg)

27. Arm Circles (shoulders pinched, arms extended, but slightly flexed in
     front of shoulders. 5 each, small, medium & large)
     A. Palms down, forward
     B. Palms up, backward
     C. Thumbs Up, forward
     D. Thumbs up, backward
     E. Thumbs down, forward
     F. Thumbs down, backward

28. Arm Stretch Across Chest & Then Over Head (10 seconds each arm)

29. Forearm Circle Warm-Up

30. Forearm Stretch (5 seconds each)
     A. Fingers pointing up, palm away
     B. Fingers pointing down, palm toward you
     C. Fingers pointing down, palm away

31. Carioca, no knee lift

32. Carioca with knee lift

33. Rapid Responses
      A. Linear with "GO"
      B. Lateral with "GO"
      C. Swivel with "GO"

APPENDIX F

RULES WHEN TALKING TO THE MEDIA

*These apply to questions asked by media people of all types, both inside and outside of the school.

1. Remember the job of the interviewer – sales! Most of the time they are trying to get you to say something controversial, inflammatory and/or outrageous.

2. Think before you speak.   What would Jesus say?

3. Players do not speak for the school, the principal does.

4. Players do not speak for the Athletic Department, the Athletic Director does.

5. Players do not speak for the baseball program, the head baseball coach does.

6. Every team we will play and every team we beat is a good team who is well-coached and whom we respect.

7. Each player's success in a particular game and/or for the season is a result of the support of this teammates and coaches. Without them, he would not be successful.

8. No one player or play is responsible for a victory or a loss.

9. The officials are NEVER responsible for a loss.

10. The weather and field conditions are the same for both teams and are NEVER responsible for a loss.

11. There is no such thing as luck, only God's will.

12. All outcomes, win or lose, are good.   Our job is to learn from the journey and the experience how to better serve others in His name.

APPENDIX G

PLAYER AND FAMILY CONTRACT

❖ I will not miss a baseball practice or a game as a result of my participation in another sport or elective activity.

Absences will only be excused for serious illness, extraordinary unanticipated schoolwork or attending a special family event (wedding, religious event, etc.).

A player may not miss school as a result of an illness and participate in a baseball practice or a game.

An absence of any kind is only "excused" if notice is given to a coach *prior to* the practice or game on the day in question. Unexcused absences shall result in loss of playing time, demotion to a lower team or, in the case of repeated offenses, expulsion from the program with no fee refund.

❖ I will always strive to be the best I can be as a student as well as on the baseball field.

❖ I will conduct myself with class as a person as well as a player. I will show respect and courtesy toward all coaches, teammates, parents, umpires and opponents.

❖ I will be on time every day for practice and for game days wearing my full uniform.

❖ I will always wear my baseball hat in the traditional manner -- bill forward and completely on.

❖ I will never use inappropriate language or throw a piece of equipment, my glove or my bat.

❖ I will strive to be a complete player by taking the necessary repetitions needed to improve my baseball skills on a daily basis.

❖ I will accept constructive coaching to make myself a better player.

❖ I believe if I study the game, there is always something I can learn to improve my game.

❖ There is always at least one part of my game and the game of my teammates that can be improved.

Therefore, sitting down at practice is not acceptable and will not be tolerated.

❖ I will avoid being over-confident. A great disservice that I can do to myself and to my teammates is not to respect my opponent.

❖ I am willing to work every day to improve our baseball complex and to help with any maintenance thereto.

❖ I will avoid the comfort zone. The comfort zone is the place where I become satisfied with my individual and/or our team performances. If I enter the comfort zone, I will prevent myself and our team from reaching our potential.

Great players and championship teams do not enter the comfort zone.

❖ I will play every game like it's the last game I am ever going to play so I will not have any regrets.

❖ I will practice positive thinking and mental imagery to make myself a better player and us a better team.

Mental imagery is where I see myself doing something successfully, before I do it... and then doing it.

❖ Since baseball is a team sport, I believe that whatever is best for the team is of the highest priority. It must be, "we" before "me", to help our team reach its potential.

In other words, as a T E A M -- Together Everyone Achieves More and "TEAM/me".

❖ Each team will have more players than the nine that can start and play at the same time. Also we will play the "best nine", not the "nine best" players.

Therefore, I will accept my role with a positive attitude whether I am a starter or a role-player.

❖ If I feel I have been treated unfairly or I am unhappy with my role on the team, I will discuss my feelings as soon as possible and at an appropriate time with my head coach.

If I am unable to accept my role on the team and to conduct myself as a team player according to the rules set forth in this contract, I will jeopardize the opportunity to be a member of this baseball program.

Player _____ Date _____

Parent _____ Date _____

APPENDIX H

SAMPLE TEAM INVENTORY

Write answers to these questions:

1. What is my role on this team?

2. What good things have I done so far this year and in my career to fulfill that role? What will be my "legacy"?

3. What things do I need to do better to fulfill that role?

4. What are our "team" strengths?

5. What things "physical, mental, attitude, work ethic, coachability) can we improve to be a better team?

6. Who are the three best defensive players on the team?

7. Who are the three best hitters on the team?

8. Who are the three best bunters on the team?

9. Who are the three best base runners on the team?

10. Who are the three best pitchers on the team?

11. What pitcher would you want on the mound with the State Championship on the line?

12. Who are our "best nine"?

13. What three players have the best and worst attitudes and work ethic?

14. What three players are the most inspirational to you and to others?

15. What three players have the best and worst baseball leadership skills?

16. If the coaches were not present for practice, which three players would most and least likely to step forward to take charge to be sure a productive practice was held?

17. Which three players have the best and worst social leadership skills?

18. Which three players are the toughest and most tenacious competitors?

19. Which players would you listen to first if the team needed a boost during a big game?

20. Which three players are the most and least committed to the baseball program?

APPENDIX I

INFORMED CONSENT FORM

I hereby give my permission for _____ to participate in _____during the athletic season beginning on _____.

Further, I authorize the school to provide emergency treatment of any injury or illness my child may experience if qualified medical personnel consider the treatment necessary and perform the treatment. This authorization is granted only if I cannot be reached after a reasonable effort has been made to do so.

Date_____

Parent or Guardian _____

Address _____

Home Phone (   ) _____

Cell phone (   ) _____

Family physician _____

Phone (   ) _____

Medical conditions (e.g., allergies or chronic illnesses)

_____
_____
_____

Other person to contact in case of emergency

_____

Relationship with person _____
Phone (   )_____

My child and I are aware that participating in _____ is a potentially hazardous activity.

We assume all risks associated with participation in this sport, including, but not limited to, falls, contact with other participants, being hit by a ball, the effects of the weather, traffic and other reasonable risk conditions associated with the sport.

All such risks to my child are known and appreciated by my child and me.

Player's signature_____

Date_____

Parent/Guardian signature_____

Date_____

APPENDIX J

INHERENT RISKS AND PARTICIPATION AGREEMENT

<u>(Name of sport)</u> is an exciting sport that often involves forceful contact with the ground or another player. The sport is also frequently played during hot, humid seasons. Because of these conditions inherent to the sport, participating in _____ exposes an athlete to many risks of injury. Those injuries include, but are not limited to, death, paralysis due to serious neck and back injuries, brain damage, damage to internal organs and serious injuries to the bones, ligaments, joints and tendons. Such injuries can result not only in temporary loss of function, but also in serious impairment of future physical, psychological and social abilities including the ability to earn a living.

In an effort to make the sport of _____ as safe as it can be, the coaching staff will instruct players concerning the rules of _____ and the correct mechanics of all skills. It is vital that athletes follow the coach's skill instructions, training rules and team policies to decrease the possibility of serious injury. Team rules and policies are listed in the team handbook each athlete receives at the pre-season meeting.

We have read the information above concerning the risk of playing _____. We understand and assume all risks associated with trying out, practicing and playing _____. We further agree to hold (School District/Club)

_____ and

(school)_____ its employees, representatives, coaches, volunteers and agents harmless in any and all liability actions, claims or additional legal action in connection with participation in any activities related to participation on the:(club/school)_____ _____ team.

In signing this form, we assume the inherent risks of _____ and waive future legal action by our heirs, estate, executor, administrator, assignees, family members and ourselves.

Note: The athlete and both parents or legal guardians (if living) must sign this form before any athlete may participate in the sport's practices or games. If one parent or guardian is deceased, please indicate so on the appropriate line.

Date:_____

Signature of athlete: _____

Signature of Parent/Guardian: _____

Signature of Parent/Guardian: _____

APPENDIX K

CONSENT FOR MEDICAL TREATMENT & USE OF OAK TREE HITTING/PITCHING FACILITY

As the parent/guardian of_____,

I hereby give my consent for emergency medical care prescribed by a duly licensed physician that is a result of the player's use of the Oak Tree hitting/pitching facility. This care may be given under whatever conditions are necessary to preserve the life, limb or well-being of the above-named participant. I know that a player's use of this facility may result in serious injuries and that protective equipment does not prevent all injuries.

I hereby waive, absolve, indemnify and agree to hold harmless Pacer Junior Baseball, its volunteers and participants from any and all claims arising out of any injury to the above-named participant which occurs by any cause except to the extent and in the amount covered by accident or liability insurance of Pacer Junior Baseball and/or of the participant. **The undersigned acknowledges that the above-named participant should be covered under a primary insurance policy and that any policy obtained by Pacer Junior Baseball is secondary.**

Date:_____
Parent/Guardian Signature_____

Telephone numbers:
Home: _____
Work: _____
Cell: _____

NOTE:

Parents will be notified in case of serious illness or injury as quickly as they can be reached. The intent of this consent is to facilitate prompt treatment. In the event we are unable to reach a parent/guardian indicated above, please contact the following:

Print Name: _____

Home/Work Numbers

_____

_____

Relationship: _____

Cell Phone: _____

If your child suffers from any health conditions, allergies, diabetes, etc. knowledge of which by our supervisors may be beneficial to the child's welfare, please describe the condition or symptoms and any special instructions in the space below.

Use the back of this form if necessary.

APPENDIX L

SAMPLE PRACTICE PLAN

"As you begin a new task or assignment, it is your attitude more than anything else that will determine your success". Get Better Today!

I. Announcements/Prayer/Practice Preview/Cheer:
3:15 - 3:25

II. Running Form Warm Up: **3:25 - 3:30**

III. Stretch/Daily Tutorial - Positive Thinking Drill:
poor weather & field conditions: **3:30 - 3:45**

IV. Conditioning - Part I: **3:45 - 4:00**

   A. Pitchers, Band Circuit -Mental Imagery Drill
   B. Non-pitchers - Ab/Core
      1. Crunches w/ legs @ 90 degrees 2 sets, 30 reps
      2. Scissor kicks - 2 sets - 45 sec. ea. set
      3. Jack knives - 2 sets - 15 reps
      4. Side bridge pushups - 2 sets - 15 reps
      5. Front Bridge w/ baseballs - 2 sets - 60 sec.
      6. "Supermans" - 2 sets - 20 reps

V. Base Running - leads, extensions & reads on sac bunts: **4:00 - 4:10**

"The right things must be done over and over again. They must become habits."

VI. Throwing and Receiving Progression: **4:10 - 4:25**

VII. Position Fundamentals - Bunt Coverages & Communication:
4:25 - 4:40

   A. Infielders, Pitchers & Catchers
      1. Non-verbal communication re bunt coverage
      2. "L-routes" and "exchanges" on bunt coverage
      3. Pitch selection and sequences in bunt situations

   B. Outfielders
      1. Non-verbal communication re bunt coverage
      2. "L- routes" and back up duties

Coaching Champions for Life

VIII. Hitting - Bunt Mechanics: **4:40 - 5:30**
       Stations (groups of 3):
           a. Dry Mechanics
           b. "Shot gun" bunting
           c. Top hand bunting
           d. Sac, drag, push & squeeze bunts off of machine
           e. Sac, drag, push & squeeze bunts w/ signs off of live pitching

IX. Team Defense - 3-in-1 Bunt Defense Drill: **5:30 - 5:45**

X. Game Simulation - Bunt Coverages/w Runners
    off of Live Pitching   **5:45 - 6:00**

XI. Conditioning - Part II - SAQ –
    Baseball Shuffle Toss   **6:00 - 6:15**

XII. Dress Down Field/Pitchers Ab-Core/
      Heartfelt Handshake: **6:15 - 6:30**

XIII. Announcements/Homework - Great lead-off hitters in baseball history
and what made them great.

*"The happiness of my life depends on the quality of my thoughts.
90% of the things that happen to me are good and only 10% are not.
To be happy, I just need to focus on the 90%".*

APPENDIX M

MULTI-TASKING OPTIONS

*Leadership skills can always be added to any part of practice.

<u>Pre-Practice</u>

>   Rapport Building
>   Prayer
>   Position Fundamentals

<u>Running Form & Cardio Warm-Up</u>

>   Base running mechanics
>   Signs
>   "Pass-Patterns"

<u>Stretching</u>

>   Signs
>   Game Review
>   Daily Tutorial
>   Mental Imagery Drills

<u>Physical Conditioning - Part I</u>

>   Signs
>   Mental Imagery Drills
>   Pitch Sequence Drills
>   Game Management Drills
>   Mental Conditioning and Visualization Exercises
>   Pick Move Footwork

Base Running

    Signs
    Pitchers picks to bases
    Catchers throws to bases
    Ground balls to infielders
    Fly balls to outfielders
    Tag Mechanics
    Relays
    Run Down Mechanics

Throwing & Receiving Progression

    Run-Downs
    Tag Mechanics
    Grips
    Footwork
    Bag Mechanics
    Hand Transfer skills
    Playing balls in the sun
    Short hops
    Digs
    Throws after strike-outs and ground ball outs with no runners on
        base and less than two outs routines
    Sliding Mechanics

Position Fundamentals

    Pitchers
      Base running
      Catcher's throws to bases
      Hitter's "broad focus", "fine focus", tracking drills
    Catchers
      Base running
      Signs
      Game management drills
      Pitch sequence drills
      Umpire rapport

Infielders
  Base running
  Picks to bases
  Run downs
  Triangle Pop-Up Drills with Outfielders/Catchers
  Relays

Outfielders
  Base running
  Triangle Pop-Up Drills with Infielders
  Relays

* Verbal and non-verbal communication can be added to any of the position fundamental sessions

Hitting

  Signs
  Base running
  Sliding
  Team Scrimmage
  Position Fundamentals
  Base coaching

APPENDIX N

CONTINUOUS FIRST AND THIRDS GAME

1   Start with a normal infield 1st and 3rd defensive alignment and a line of runners at 1B and at 3B.   (The extra runners wait in foul territory.)

2   The pitcher starts from the stretch position, as usual, checks the runners, picks 1B or 3B, or throws home. The runner at 1B steals, the catcher reads the runner at 3B and throws through the cut man at 2B. The cut man reads the runner at 3B and either cuts off the ball to throw back to HP or to get the runner from 1B in a run down or lets the ball go through to the fielder covering the bag. The runner at 3B must attempt to steal at some point. The player receiving the ball at 2B or the cut man must throw the ball to either HP, 3B or to 1B. The next runner at 1B cannot leave until the ball is received by the 3B or by the catcher.

3   If the catcher back picks to 3B, a new runner at 1B must attempt to steal 2B. After the third baseman makes his tag at 3B, he throws to 2B to attempt to throw out the new runner attempting to steal 2B. When the throw is made to 2B, a new runner at 3B attempts to steal HP.

4   Runners after attempting to steal, hustle to get in line in foul territory at the next base, i.e., at first or third base.

5   Runners continuously attempt to steal bases after each throw until a runner is picked off of a base or a runner is out in a run down. The half-inning is over when consecutive outs are made at 2B and HP or a pre-determined # of outs are made or if the pitcher picks off a runner at either 1B or 3B.

6   After delivering the pitch to home plate, the pitcher stays crouched at the mound in case a ball gets by the catcher in which case he must cover HP to tag the runner from 3B trying to score.   A new runner at 1B tries to steal 2B at this time, but cannot leave until the catcher throws the ball to the pitcher covering HP.

7.   When overthrows occur at a base, new runners advance on the base paths until an out is made.   However, a new runner may not leave his base until the other runner has touched 2B or HP.

8.   The team with the most runs after a pre-determined # of innings wins.

APPENDIX O

THROWING & RECEIVING PROGRESSION

(Catchers Gear Up)

1. Dart throws (10 stationary) / Run downs (3 @ 90')

2. Square offs (2 color balls) (10) - feet parallel and staggered. Back of glove reception on first five throws.

3. Stride outs/ 2x4 throws (10 @ 45')

4. Step behinds (10), power leg throws (3), front leg balance throws(3)

5. Crow hops / bicycle step, long toss - regular straight-on foot work, not step behind; continue to increase distance beyond 90'as long as the player can maintain good form and proper arc on the ball (10)

6. Relay Mechanics - infielders/Long hop throws - outfielders (5)

7. Rapid fire - infielders, catchers (2 sets of 20)

   "Do or die" mechanics (2 color balls) - outfielders (5)

8. Short hops - infielders - pairs facing each other or high throws-players charge (10 stationary, 5 charging)

   Blocking drill - catchers

   > a. 3 or 5 ball - pre-set stationary - 1 set
   > b. Basic blocking - glove in "5 hole" (10)
   > c. Live plus recover ready to throw or tag (6)

   Digs - 1B's and outfielders (5 balls from three directions)

Drills:

1. Have C's throw to infielders covering bases. Inf. throw to C from 15'. Hitter in box.   Hitter to switch sides every 2 throws.   8 throws total.

2. Have P's throw on flat ground to OF's CU's and CB's (10 CU, 5 CB) from 60'

3. Four corners

4. Strike out drill - quick hands, good footwork, snap throws

5. After ground out with no runners on base and less than two outs drill

The specific number of throws in a given day for a given type of throw may vary. The player should always pay more attention to how his arm feels than on doing a particular number of throws.

APPENDIX P

GENERAL PITCHING STRATEGY

1. This pitch. This moment. Flush the past.

2. Think positive and "half full" at all times. Something good is about to happen.

3. Trust your mechanics. Visualize, but don't aim.

4. Get ahead with strikes, get outs with balls.

5. DON'T BE PREDICTABLE! Keep changing eye level, working on inner and outer thirds of the plate and changing speeds. Example: curveball down followed by a fastball up at shoulder level.

6. Have as much command out of the strike zone as in the strike zone.

7. Show your off-speed stuff early in the game and early in the count.

8. Be able to throw an off-speed pitch that looks like a strike on any count.

9. Attack aggressively in the first inning and after your team scores. "Throw up a zero". Don't get cute. Throw strikes.

10. Re-focus with 2 outs, close out the inning.

11. Re-focus and bear down the second time through the heart of the opposing team's lineup.

12. Make the inside half of the plate yours. Always attack inside to a good hitter in his first at bat with no runners in scoring position to see if he can handle your fastball on his hands.

APPENDIX Q

PITCH SEQUENCE RULES AND DRILLS

A. Decide what pitch you want to get the hitter out with and work to set it up. It's like a chess game.

B. Generally, no two consecutive pitches in a given at bat should be the same speed in the same location to a good hitter unless the hitter has looked over-matched on a particular pitch. Even vary the speed of the fast ball by throwing 4-seam and 2-seam fastballs or by taking a little off of the 4-seam fastball and "spotting" it. Being unpredictable will require throwing consecutive curveballs or breaking pitches on occasion, however.

C. Pitchers should throw fastballs off the outside corner, fastballs shoulder high or curveballs for strikes to a 7-9 hitter with an 0-2 or 1-2 count. They should not risk a passed ball/wild pitch with their best curveball in the dirt especially with runners on base.

D. With a 2-2 count, a pitcher should shake off three signs and throw something hard.

E. Treat the 1-1 count like the 0-0 count. Throw a strike!

F. Use the 0-2 pitch to set up the 1-2 pitch.

G. Never throw a pitch on a 2-2 count that you won't on a 3-2.

H. Double up (throw 2 in a row) on curveballs on 0-1, 1-2, or 2-2 counts.

I. On fastball counts (2-0, 2-1, 3-1, or 3-2) or on the first pitch, be able to throw your best off-speed pitch for a strike to a good hitter. Throw a fastball for a strike to everyone else.

J. Know when to throw your best curveball and when to throw your "get me over" curveball. A 0-0 curveball is a "get me over" curveball. Statistically, when it is put in play by the hitter, his average is <.100. The 0-2, 1-2 curveball is your best curveball, but is thrown to break on the black, off the plate outside or in the dirt behind the tip of home plate (except to a 7-9 hitter).

Drills:

1. *Countdowns*

Pitcher throws the first pitch of a pre-determined sequence.

If the pitcher throws the pitch in the designated spot, he scores a "1". If not, he throws the pitch again and again up to four pitches until he hits the spot. The pitcher's score for that round is the number of pitches it took him to hit the spot.

The pitcher with the lowest total number of pitches at the end of the sequence wins.

2. *Set Sequence Drills*

Sample Sequence 1: 4-seam FB strike, down in zone; curveball for strike, 2-seam FB, inner third; 4-seam FB, outer third; change-up that is or looks like a strike; pitch-out to RHB; best curveball for low strike or in dirt between HP and catcher; letter-high 4-seam FB; best curveball for a high strike; 4-seam FB on outside corner or off edge.

Sample Sequence 2: 6 best-control pitch, 5 low outer third; 4 low inner third; 3 curveballs for strikes; 2 high inside; 1 change-up

APPENDIX R

3 'N 1 Drills

I. Session 1

    P's - picks to 1B, comebackers to HP & 1B

    C's - calling "Pre-set" pick to 1B, back pick to 1B, 1-2-3 DP

    1B's - picks from P, back pick from C, 1-2-3 DP

    2B's - 5-4-3, 6-4-3 & 4-6-3 DP's and 6-4-5 "backdoor" play; 5-4 & 6-4
        force plays

    SS's - 6-4-3 & 4-6-3 DP's and 4-6-5 "backdoor" play; 4-6 force play

    3B's - 5-4-3 DP's; 6-4-5 & 4-6-5 "backdoor" plays

        * All DP throws are to a first baseman in front of 7x7 screen
        short of 1B

    OF's - Ground Balls

        Hard at OF

        In gap

II. Session II

    P1 - bunts to 1B, covering 1B on GB to 1B

    P2 - bunts and comebackers to 2B (pre-pitch communication!)

    P3 - bunts and comebackers to 3B, squeeze bunts to HP

    C1 - bunts to 1B

    C2 - bunts to 2B

    C3 - bunts to 3B, squeeze bunts from P

    1B's - bunts from P1 & C1; GB's to P covering 1B

    2B's - force plays (bunts) and DP's (comebackers) from P2 and C2 (pre-
        pitch communication!)

    SS's - same as 2B's

    3B's - bunts and comebackers from P3 and C3

    OF's - Fly balls and ground balls at wall

III. Session III

    P's - picks to 2B

    C's - relays and tags from OF's

    1B's - relays from OF's to HP and 3B

    2B's - picks from P

    SS's - picks from P

    3B's - relays from OF's to HP and to 1B

    OF's - relays to HP after fielding "do or die" GB's and fly balls

IV. Session IV

        P's - picks to 3B

        C's - back picks to 3B (1st & 3rd defense)

        1B's - 3-6-3 DP' s throws & tag base at 1B and tag runner at 2B; 3-4
                bunt coverage

        2B's - covering 1B on bunt to 1B

        SS's - 3-6-3 DP throws and tags

        3B's - picks from P's, back picks from C's

        OF's - fly balls - coming in (dive rules - ball must be coming straight
                down or he must have back-up; high/low rule with infielder)

V. Session V

        P's - covering HP after PB's and WP's

        C's - blocking, throws to P's covering HP after PB's & WP's

        1B's - triangle pop-ups with 2B's and RF's

        2B's - triangle pop-ups with 1B's & RF's and SS's and CF's

        SS's - triangle pop-ups with 2B's & CF's and 3B's and LF's

        3B's - triangle pop-ups with SS and LF's

        OF's - triangle pop-ups with INF's ("late inning" rule and fence
                technique)

VI. Session VI

        P's - use machine to throw fastballs and curve balls in dirt to C

        C's - blocking, tags on hitter after strike 3, throws to 1B after strike 3

        1B's - receiving throws from C's after 3rd strike ball-in-dirt

        2B's - tandcm rclays to 3B

        SS's - tandem relays to 3B

        3B's - receiving tandem relays to 3B from 2B's and SS's

        OF's - tandem relays to 3B

VII. Session VII

        P's - pick footwork (done in foul territory)

        C's - throws to 2B on regular steal and 1st & 3rd steals

        1B's - receiving throws from 3B's after slow rollers; throws to 3B after
                hard bunt

        2B's - receiving throws from C at 2B on steals; throws to HP after cut
                (1st & 3rd defense)

        SS's - receiving throws from C's at 2B on steals

        3B's - throws to 1B after fielding slow rollers

        OF's - fly balls in gap (communication/shadowing)

VIII. Session VIII

P1 - step off after early steal, run down mechanics with 1B's and SS's

P2 - "inside move" pick to 2B, run down mechanics with 2B's and 3B's

P3 - pitch out to C, run down mechanics with 3B's and C's - squeeze bunt defense

C's - run down mechanics after pitch outs from P's with 3B's

1B's - run down mechanics with SS's after picks from P's

2B's - run down mechanics with 3B's after "inside move pick" from P's

SS's - run down mechanics with 1B's after P's pick of runner at 1B

3B's - run down mechanics with C's after pitch out from P's on attempted squeeze bunt

OF's - runners for run downs

IX. Session IX

P's - HP to C for tags and 1-2-3 DP's to 1B

C's - tags at HP and DP's to 1B from P's and INF's

INF's - throws to C's for "cut defense" tags and DP's to 1B

OF's - fly balls - going back - regular drop step and "wrong way turns"

X. Session X

P's - triangle pop ups with C's, 1B's and 3B's

C's - triangle pop-ups with P's, 1B's and 3B's

1B's - triangle pop-ups with P's and C's ("catch and carry" rule)

2B's - relays to 2B from OF's

SS's - relays to 2B from OF's

3B's - triangle pop-ups with P's and C's ("catch and carry" rule)

OF's - relays and back-ups on doubles

APPENDIX S

WALL BALL ROUTINE

1. Basic Receiving Stance (3 sets, hold for 30-60 seconds)

2. Set, Ready, Creep Technique (5)

3. Self-Toss ("soft hands", fingers of glove to ground), Capture, No Bare Hand (10)

4. Partner Toss ("soft hands", fingers of glove to ground), Capture, No Bare Hand, Glove Flip Ball to partner over shoulder without raising up (10)

5. Self-Toss ("soft hands"), get to throwing side of the ball, Capture with Bare and Glove Hand (5)

6. Self-Toss ("soft hands"), Capture with Bare Hand and Footwork - do not funnel ball into belly, take directly to throwing side ear. Tap finger tips of glove on ground before receiving every ground ball. (5)

7. Partner Toss, Creep, Capture with Bare and Glove Hand w/Footwork

8. Short Hops/Digs/Muffs

   a. Self (10)
   b. Partner (10 each)
      1. Two-hand
      2. Backhand - with & without rocker step ("Paint the ground" w/glove at an angle)
      3. Glove-hand

9. Throws
   a. 1B to P covering 1B (5)
   b. SS/2B - DP's (3 each)

      1. Underhand
      2. Dart - from knee
      3. Regular - 180 degree pivot
      4. Backhand
      5. Glove Hand Behind 2B
      6. Jump Throw

c. 3B slow rollers (5 each)

    1. Two-hand inside of left foot-throw off of right foot, i.e., first step

    2. One-hand outside of left foot-take step w/right foot & throw off of left foot

    3. Stopped ball, bare hand-scoop w/ full grip with bare hand on outside of right foot & then throw ball as left foot lands

10. Rapid Fire Exchange Drill (3 sets of 10-20)

    a. Use glove as hand pad

    b. Exchange is done out front, not behind head

    c. Receive ball with weight on back "power" leg

APPENDIX T

SAMPLE ON-FIELD BATTING PRACTICE ROUTINE

ROUND ONE: Bunts (SAC 1st, SAC 3rd, Drag, Push, Squeeze)
ROUND TWO: 5" no pop, no pull"
ROUND THREE: 2 hit and run, 5 on your own
ROUND FOUR: 2 hit and run, 1 SAC fly, 5 on your own

1st Rotation: 4 OF's hit, INF's ground balls (straight, backhand, forehand) and pop ups

2nd Rotation: 4 INF's hit, OF's fly balls, 1B ground balls

3rd Rotation: Catchers, 1B hit, IF double plays, OF ground balls

4th Rotation: Remaining players hit. All players play live off the bat on every other pitch

- ❖ This is a comprehensive batting practice designed to have all players working hard.
- ❖ Two fungo hitters going for 1st three rounds
- ❖ We will work hard on base running at this time
- ❖ 150 baseballs, minimal time spent getting balls to bucket man
- ❖ Base runners are expected to work on leads, extensions, jumps and routes. Defensive players play balls live when they are not receiving a fungo. Game intensity!

Coaching Champions for Life

APPENDIX U

SAQ/CONDITIONING DRILLS

1. Lateral Ball Pick-Up

❖ Place 2 cones 20 feet apart and 1 cone in the center between them.

❖ The player starts in front of the center cone with his partner on one knee 15 feet in front of him.

❖ Partner rolls the ball to the player's left or right, the player fields it with proper mechanics in his glove hand, tosses the ball back to his partner while staying in proper athletic position at all times and returns to the center cone.

2. Front and Back Ball Pick-Up

❖ Player starts next to a cone with his partner on one knee 25 feet in front of him.

❖ The partner either throws a slow roller in front of the player for the player to field and throw to a third person or throws a pop-up over one of the player's shoulders.

Note: *This drill may be combined with the lateral ball pick-up drill so that the player may have to field a ball to his right or left as well.*

3. Jump-Rope (see attached routine)

4. Agility Ladder (see attached guidelines and routines)

5. Agility Cones (see attached drills)

6. Agility Gauntlet (see attached)

7. T-Drill

❖ Set up 4 cones in the form of a "T" with cone 1, 10 yards from cone 2 and cones 3 and 4, 5 yards to the side of cone 2.

❖ Player sprints from cone 1 to cone 2, side shuffles or cariocas to the right to cone 3 touching the top of it and then side shuffles or cariocas to the left to cone 4 and touching it, side shuffles or cariocas back to the center to cone 2 and finally sprints backward past cone 1.

8. Pro-Agility Drill

❖ 3 cones are set up in a horizontal line 5 yards apart.

❖ Player starts in front of the middle cone with his right hand touching the top of the cone, sprints to his left to touch the top of cone 2, then sprints to his right to touch the top of cone 3 and then reverses his direction to sprint past the finish at middle cone 1.

9. Square Drill

❖ Set up 4 cones in the shape of a square with the cones 10 yards apart.

❖ Player starts at the lower right corner just outside cone 1 and sprints forward to just past cone 2, then shuffles to the left to cone 3, sprints backward to cone 4 and shuffles to the right to cone 1, then reverses his direction and cariocas to cone 4, sprints forward to cone 3, cariocas to his right to cone 2 and sprints backward to the finish past cone 1.

10. Ball Drop Drill

❖ Player's partner stands 8-10 feet in front of player with a ball in each hand held straight out to the side at shoulder height.

❖ Partner drops one of the balls and the player must react to catch the ball in his bare glove hand before the ball bounces a second time.

11. Reaction Wall Drill

❖ Player lines up in front of a wall at a distance consistent with the type of drill being practiced, e.g., 5 feet for short hops, 10 feet for catcher's blocks and 15-20 feet for ground balls.

❖ Player's partner stands behind the player and throws a ball over the player's shoulder, the player fields the ball and tosses it over his shoulder to his partner without looking back or without standing up from his proper fielding position.

❖ Note: the wall may also be used by the player himself to work on things like hand-transfer and relay mechanics.

Coaching Champions for Life

12. Lateral Shuffle Ball Toss

❖ Place 2 cones 20 feet apart in a horizontal line.

❖ Player shuffles from cone-to-cone as fast as he can while partner standing 10 feet in front of him tosses the ball underhand to him. Player catches ball in glove hand at each cone, a rope is held by two players on either side of the cones so that the player doing the shuffle must maintain the height he would be in a game fielding a ground ball.

13. Fartlek Run (jog-sprint-jog)

❖ Run a pre-determined distance varying speed at pre-determined intervals.

14. Native American Run

❖ Players run in a closely spaced single file line with the last player in the line continuously running to the front of the line

15. Shuttle Run

❖ Set up 4 cones in a vertical line 10 yards apart.

❖ Player starts at cone 1 and sprints to cone 2 touching the top of it and then either sprints forward or backward to cone 1 and then repeats this pattern for cones 3 and 4. Player does not stop at cone 1 after returning from cone 4, but sprints past it.

16. Base Running Drill

❖ Run a pre-determined sequence of base running routes using proper running form and correct angles continuously without stopping. Player does not stop at end of each route, but jogs to next base.

❖ For example: Double, squeeze bunt from 3B to HP, 1B to 3B, triple, single and 2B to HP

17. Two Ball Drill

❖ Two players stand 10' - 12' apart with one player holding two baseballs in one hand. That player throws the two balls "backhand" within an arm's length of the other player between his knees and his shoulders and the player tries to catch one ball in each hand.

Sample Jump Rope Routine

Instructions: Working with a partner, complete each of the following routines. Alternate with your partner jumping rope and resting. One player should begin his turn immediately after his partner completes his turn.

	# of Jumps	**Total Points**

1. Speed jump for 2 minutes. 1 point for every 2 jumps.

    _____ x ½ _____

2. Both feet side-to-side over a line for 1 min. 1 pt. each jump.

    _____ x 1_____

3. Both feet front-to-back over a line for 1 min. 1 pt. each jump.

    _____ x 1_____

4. Left foot side-to-side for 30 seconds. 2 points per jump

    _____ x 2_____

5. Right foot side-to-side for 30 seconds. 2 points per jump.

    _____ x 2 _____

6. Left foot front-to-back for 30 seconds. 2 points per jump.

    _____ x 2 _____

7. Right foot front- to-back for 30 seconds. 2 points per jump.

    _____ x 2 _____

Coaching Champions for Life

8. Both feet, four corners for one minute landing in a different corner each jump. 1 pt. each jump.

_____ x 1 _____

9. Alternate single jump, double jump for 1 min. 1 pt. each jump.

_____ x 1_____

10. Double right, double left for one minute.

_____ x 1 _____

TOTAL POINTS:_____

Agility Ladder

I. General Tips

    a. Keep body weight over your feet

    b. Stay on balls of your feet, never touch your heels

    c. Use arms aggressively, always bent at 90 degrees and in sync with your footwork

    d. Get a rhythm, then try and pick up your tempo. You want to develop quickness **and** control.

    e. Do not stop at end of ladder or slow down with last step. Rather, use a series of explosive steps when exiting the ladder (straight ahead when doing linear, cross-over when doing lateral.)

    f. Use rope held over ladder by two players to keep player low while doing drill.

    g. Be sure to take turns leading with each foot.

II. Drills

    a. Linear

        1. Ones - one foot in each square

        2. Twos - two feet in each square

        3. Hopscotch - alternate, two feet in, two feet straddle

        4. Diagonal ones - "ski jumps"

        5. Diagonal twos - both feet in and out

        6. Diagonal cross-over

    b. Lateral

        1. Ones

        2. Twos

        3. One in, one out - alternate feet

        4. Two in, two out

        5. Swivels

        6. Carioca

    c. Hybrid - add baseball toss in air on or on ground when player is exiting ladder.

Agility Cones

1. Lateral - one up, two down, backward to start (2 sets)

2. Lateral - one up, two down, after last one, explode forward five yards (2 sets)

3. Lateral - hop with two feet over cones, cross-over step then explode forward five yards

4. Zig-Zag diagonal - two-footed plant around each cone (2 sets)

5. Forward and back (2 sets)

6. Quick shuffles between cones, Cones 20 feet apart catching ball thrown by coach/partner with glove hand. Use rope at four feet high to keep player low and in good fielding position.

7. Same as #6 except two players on one knee just inside each cone throw ground balls (glove side and back hand) to player between cones.

8. Continuous cross-over -- 2 Discs/Cones 10 to 12 feet apart

9. 4 Cones in 20' square - random agility (front, back, side-to-side, carioca)

The Agility Gauntlet

Lateral Ladder	Cones (Lateral Step-Over Footwork)

Cones (Front & Back Footwork)	8 DISC PATTERN RUN

Side-to-Side Shuffle & Baseball Toss

4 Cone/Disc Random Agility

Linear Ladder	Cones (Zig-Zag Footwork)

*Option 1 - each player does all 8 stations consecutively and moves to next station with no rest when drill is done and his partner stays at station to assist the next player

*Option 2 - one player does station while partner assists him and then they switch roles after a given time lapse. The two players move from station-to-station together

*Ladder & Cone stations are done twice

*Two players at a station - one doing - one helping

APPENDIX V

CAMP/TRYOUT/SHOWCASE GUIDELINES

1. Smile. Be enthusiastic. Act as though you're having the best time of your life regardless of your performance.

2. Dress the part. Look your best. If you stand out from the rest, in a professional way, even better.

3. Be prepared. Double check your equipment for quantity and quality. Remember first aid supplies--tape, ice packs, sun glasses, Advil, Tums, etc. Pack more food and drink than you think you'll need. Always expect extreme weather. Dress in layers.

4. Introduce yourself by name and school to the people in charge and to the other players. Confident voice, eye contact, firm handshake, good posture, smile.

5. This is a competition. Be first in everything--first in line, closest to the person giving instructions, first from station-to-station, first in hustle, first in enthusiasm, first in energy, first in compliments to other players, etc.

6. You're trying out for a TEAM! Do the things that a TEAM needs:

   a. Be a leader - volunteer to lead running and stretching or to demonstrate how to do something.

   b. Ask the people in charge if there is anything you can do to help. Look for opportunities to help.

   c. Compliment and support the other athletes.

   d. Confidence and composure at all times.

   e. Listen carefully, follow instructions and do not be afraid to ask clarifying questions if they are intelligent and necessary. *(Think before you speak.)*

7. Fundamentals before flash.

8. Ask for feedback. Be coachable.

9. At the end, repeat the handshake routine and ask again if there is anything you can do to help.

10. Send the coaches an email telling them how much you enjoyed the experience, how much you learned and how you are looking forward to staying in touch. Send them a copy of your current season's game schedule and coach's contact info.

APPENDIX W

SAMPLE RECOMMENDATION LETTER TO COLLEGE COACH

Date:

Dear Coach _____:

Thank you for your inquiry regarding John Brown. John is an outstanding athlete who is definitely working hard toward his goal of playing major league baseball. Currently, he is lifting weights with me three times per week and is doing SAQ training at Velocity twice per week. John is about 6'2" tall and 188 lbs. now, but expects to be much bigger after his final two years of high school.

Attached are Johns' pitching stats from last year. Do not think his stats are suspect because of the level we play at.

I've coached at 6A High Schools and John would excel at that level as well. John proved this during the Baseball Northwest Prospect Series this Summer where he impressed both coaches and scouts with his performance against elite players from all levels.

In reviewing the attached stat sheet, I know you will be pleased with his strike-to-ball and strikeouts-to-walks ratios. John definitely knows the value of first pitch strikes. He pitched a six-inning perfect game in only 63 pitches this past season. (51 strikes, 12 balls and 15 strikeouts) He is able to throw three pitches for strikes (fastball, curveball, change-up) at any time and in any situation.

For example, he threw a 3/2, two out, seventh inning curveball to close out our league playoff semi-final victory last year.

During the next two years, he will continue to develop his two-seam fastball and will learn to vary speeds with his curveball as well. I expect the 3's and 3+'s on the rating card to be 4's by the end of his Senior year. For example, his fastball, which was as high as 85 mph last Summer after his Sophomore year, should be 90+ by the end of his Senior year.

John knows the value of being a complete student-athlete.

His current cumulative GPA is 3.4. Furthermore, I expect his teammates to vote him Captain in each of the next two years. He also has the blessing of having the love and support of a great family (Father- James, Mother- Patricia and Sister- Amanda).

You are welcome to contact the Browns through Mr. Brown's e-mail, jbrown@hotmail.com. Please feel free to contact me at any time to learn the changes to our game schedule (also attached), when John will pitch next or to answer any other questions you may have. My contact telephone numbers are 503-666-0600 (home) and 503-222-3333 (cell phone).

I look forward to staying in touch.

Best wishes to you and your team for another successful season.

Very truly yours,

Adam Sarancik
Head Baseball Coach
Westside Christian High School

APPENDIX X

QUESTIONS COLLEGE COACHES ASK YOU WHEN THEY ARE RECRUITING YOUR ATHLETES

1. In your experience, when you ask him to jump, does he ask "How High?" or "Why?"

2. Is he self-motivated to get better every day in every way (as a player, a teammate, in school, nutrition, etc.)?

3. If he were not a baseball player, would our college still be the best fit for him? How thorough was his research of colleges and academic majors?

4. Does the player put others and his team first or is he motivated primarily by his own personal glory?

5. Can he handle the intense pressure and expectations of college coaches, games and school without mom and dad there to rescue him?

6. Is he disciplined enough to do his best in school and his sport despite the many distractions and temptations of college?

7. Has the player demonstrated consistently the ability to play major college baseball without being micro-managed in a game?

8. Is he athletic enough and motivated enough to learn to play another position if the primary position he played in high school is not the position for him that best serves our team needs?

9. Is he thick-skinned enough and is his personality flexible enough to get along well with all types of players on a team?

10. Is the player intelligent enough and are his study habits good enough to handle the academics of our school and the rigor of our program?

11. How high is the player's baseball IQ?

12. Is he a student of the game and does he love the game?

BIBLIOGRAPHY

Author's Note: When I have recommended books that discuss the mechanics and fundamentals of baseball, it does not mean that I agree with 100% of the material in the book nor is all of the information in the books appropriate for every player or for every team in every situation.

All of the books, however, contain very valuable and worthwhile information and are great resources for coaches.

Coaching-General

Life Is Yours To Win: Lessons Forged From The Purpose, Passion, and Magic of Baseball by Augie Garrido (2011)

Successful Coaching by Rainer Martens (2004)

The Baseball Coaching Bible by Jerry Kindall & John Winkin (2000)

Practice Perfect Baseball by American Baseball Coaches Assn. (2010)

They Call Me Coach by John Wooden with Jack Tobin (1998)

Why We Win by Billy Packer with Roland Lazenby (1998)

The Man Watching by Tim Crothers (2006)

When Pride Still Mattered by David Maraniss (1999)

Baseball - Pitching

The Art & Science of Pitching by Tom House, Gary Heil & Steve Johnson (2006)

The Picture Perfect Pitcher by Tom House and Paul Reddick (2003)

Coaching Pitchers by Joe "Spanky" McFarland (2003)

The Mental ABC's of Pitching by H.A. Dorfman (2000)

www.biokinetics3D.com

Baseball - Defense

Drills for Winning Baseball by Cliff Ainsworth (2001)

The Baseball Drill Book by Bob Bennett (2004)

Baseball - Offense

Offensive Baseball Drills by Rod Delmonico (1996)

Baseball - Hitting

The Science of Hitting by Ted Williams and John Underwood (1986)
The Louisville Slugger Complete Book of Hitting Faults & Fixes by Mark Gola &
John Monteleone (2001)
www.biokinetics3D.com

Baseball - Mental Conditioning

The Mental Game of Baseball by H.A. Dorfman & Karl Kuehl (2002)
Heads Up Baseball by Tom Hanson & Ken Ravizza (1998)
Getting Focused, Staying Focused by Alan Jaeger (2000)

Baseball - Spiritual

Champions of Faith - Baseball Edition (2007) by The Catholic Exchange
www.championsoffaith.com
Champions of Faith - The Bases of Life (2008) by The Catholic Exchange
www.championsoffaith.com

Conditioning & Nutrition

Eat to Win for the 21st Century by Robert Haas (2005)
Complete Conditioning for Baseball by Steve Tamborra (2008)
Baseball Training - For The Athlete By The Athlete by Stack Media (2010)
www.sparqtraining.com (in general and their "Baseball & Fastpitch"
DVD)
www.stacktv.stack.com

Just for Fun

Baseball - A Film By Ken Burns (DVD set -PBS Home Video) (1994)

Odd Man Out by Matt McCarthy (2009)

Men At Work by George F. Will (1990)

Chicken Soup for the Baseball Fan's Soul by Jack Canfield & Mark Victor Hansen (2001)

You're Out and You're Ugly Too! by Durwood Merrill (1998)

The Miracle of Castel Di Sangro by Joe McGinniss (1999)

In These Girls, Hope is a Muscle by Madeleine Blais (1995)

The Quotable Baseball Fanatic by Louis D. Rubin, Jr. *(2004)*

Coach - A Treasury of Inspiration and Laughter by Jess Brallier & Sally Chabert (2000)

INDEX

A

ab/core work, 84 , 116 , 179 , 234

abdominal strains, 34

academic grant, 187

academic performance, 186

ACL, 47

Action, Repetitions and Competitions, "ARC", 93

adversity, v, 12 , 49 , 50 , 51 , 52 , 54 , 63 , 67 , 68 , 75 , 79 , 83 , 90 , 101 , 161 , 163 , 209 , 217 , 225 , 231

aerobic, 39 , 46 , 180

aerobic activity, 39

agility cones, 268 , 274

agility gauntlet, 268 , 275

agility ladder, 151, 268 , 273

Albert Pujols, 173 , 174

aluminum bats, 170 , 174

anaerobic, 46 , 180

announcements, 109 , 180 , 254, 255

annual plan, 184

Anson Dorrance, 18

anterior shoulder, 32

arm speed, 127 , 139

assistant coach, ix, 61 , 82 , 83, 87, 96 , 97 , 98 , 99 , 100 , 109 , 110, 159, 186, 194, 219 , 225

asymmetrical muscle flexibility and elasticity, 30

asymmetry, 33

athletic fit when choosing a college, 188

athletic scholarship, 26 , 183 , 184 , 185 , 189 , 193 , 203

Augie Garrido, 83

auditory learner, 95

B

Babe Pinelli, 221

back up meals, 37

backside drive, 173, 174

balance point, 95 , 122

Ball Drop Drill, 269

ball in hand drills, 92 , 160

Base Running Drill, 270

base running routes, 112

Baseball IQ, 180

basics to the mental part of defense, 150

basketball, 5 , 6 , 13 , 15 , 21 , 22 , 47 , 82 , 87 , 91 , 92 , 101 , 107 , 226 , 292

batting practice, 267

Batting Practice Pitchers, 175

B complex, 42

Benjamin Franklin, 160 , 161

best nine, 246

bicycle step, 128 , 260

bigger, stronger and faster, 22 , 25 , 26 , 37 , 189

Bill Belichick Rule, 220

Bill Self, 107

block booking, 200

blocking drills, 133 , 134 , 135

body clock, 44

breathe properly, 34

breathing, 29

broad focus, 122

brothers and sisters, 76 , 111 , 231

building block, 14 , 28 , 30 , 85 , 91 , 92, 118 , 120 , 163 , 209

bullpen, 94 , 95 , 142 , 143

bulletproof, 236

burn out, 26

C

caffeine, 38

Cal Ripken, Jr., 150

calcium intake, 40

calorie and nutrition guide, 38

calories, 36 , 38 , 39 , 41 , 42

camps, 147 , 194 , 195 , 196 , 197 , 202 , 275

carbohydrates, 38

carbonated drinks, 37

cardio exercise, 28 , 40

catchers, 103 , 125 , 133 , 143 , 147 , 150 , 200 , 254 , 256 , 257 , 260 , 267

catcher's bullpen, 94

Champions for Life, iii, v, ix, 7 , 14 , 56 , 62 , 75 , 81 , 163 , 228 , 231

championship games, 9 , 64 , 215 , 217 , 220 , 221

change up, 138 , 139 , 140 , 173

character, v, x, xi, 11 , 81 , 93 , 109 , 198 , 199 , 200 , 201

chipping, 222

choosing a college, 187

chronological age, 31

clarity of mind, 34 , 68

class, 28 , 31 , 74 , 116 , 141 , 186 , 187 , 191 , 205 , 227 , 228 , 234 , 245

coaching philosophy, 233

coaching style, 22, 94

coffee, 41

college scholarship, 65 , 184

comfort zone, 49 , 65 , 66 , 100, 101 , 131 , 246

community, 7 , 53 , 205

community college, 205

community service, 21 , 53 , 73

complete protein, 38

complex carbohydrates, 38 , 39

composure, 138 , 143 , 198 , 201 , 210 , 225 , 276

confidence, 9 , 20 , 66 , 68 , 96, 139 , 164 , 198 , 224, 276

consequences, 52 , 53 , 58 , 59 , 60 , 64 , 162 , 164 , 171 , 236

constructive criticism, 3 , 15 , 57

contact rule, 177

continuous first and thirds, 133, 259

core body temperature, 28 , 30 , 111 , 114

core muscles, 33

countdown Drill, 141, 264

creatine, 43

crow hop, 128

culture of winning, 9

curveball, 136, 138 , 139 , 140, 164 , 223 , 262, 263 , 264 , 278

D

daily calorie intake, 38

daily tutorial, 114 , 254 , 256

Daley Thompson, 235

dart throws, 123

decelerator muscles, 32
Dedeaux, Rod, 14, 66 , 121 ,
  162, 226
default routines, 96
defensive players, 122 , 150 , 177
designing a drill, 159
DI College, 197 , 199 , 204 ,
  205 , 206
diet, 39
differential, 139
dignified grace, 227
digs, 133 , 134 , 152
DII College, 199 , 205
DIIICcollege, 205
discipline, 57, 58, 59 , 62 , 68 ,
  71 , 74 , 79 , 82 , 98 , 99 ,
  115 , 164 , 175 , 189 , 234 ,
  236 , 237
dissension, 5 , 52
do or die, 132 , 157
Don Mattingly, 167
Dr. James Andrews, 26
dress down field, 179 , 255
drugs, 43
dry mechanics, 92 , 95 , 138,
  160, 167 , 170
dry swing mechanics, 104 , 167,
  170
dynamic stretching, 28, 239

E

eating enough good food, 36
effective practices, 5
efficient practices, 5
Eligibility Center ID number, 199
elite athletes, 26 , 41 , 59 , 66 ,
  197 , 205
empathy, 54
encouragement, 94 , 210
energy drinks, 37 , 38
entitlement, 19 , 59

entrance exam scores, 65 , 186 ,
  187
exchange, 131 , 146 , 194
executionoriented, 65
execution -oriented thinking, 65
expectations, 52 , 53 , 54 , 63 ,
  64 , 85 , 185 , 189
external controls, 65
extraordinary commitment, 2 , 4

F

failure, 50 , 83 , 101 , 159 , 160
Fartlek Run, 270
fast twitch muscles, 47
Fat, 39
feedback, 3 , 61 , 62 , 96 , 143 ,
  171 , 234 , 276
feeder program, 5, 6
field conditions, 100 , 219 , 235 ,
  242 , 254
field prep, 86 , 89 , 92 , 109
fifteen minute rule, 87
fighter's mentality, 226
financial aid, 203
fine focus, 122
flat ground throwing, 138
flip, 90 , 104
focus, 15 , 17 , 21 , 68 , 110 ,
  121 , 122 , 139 , 142 , 161 ,
  163 , 173 , 202 , 212 , 224 ,
  255 , 257 , 262
footwork, 28 , 103 , 111 , 118 ,
  120 , 121 , 127 , 130 , 131 ,
  132 , 143 , 144 , 149 , 151 ,
  152 , 156 , 157 , 160 , 174 ,
  175 , 261 , 273
four corners, 131 , 152 , 272
fresh food, 42
Front and Back Ball Pick Up Drill,
  268
front leg balances, 127

full length repetitions, 33
functional strength, 28 , 32
fundamentals of hitting, 164
fundraising, 8 , 85 , 196

G

game review, 114 , 256
game simulation, 178 , 255
game speed, 9 , 20 , 64 , 75 ,
    93, 120 , 124 , 133 , 134 ,
    153 , 176 , 177 , 217 , 235
Geno Auriemma, 87
get me over curveball, 138
gimmick plays, 216 , 217
glass halffull, 50 , 79 , 137 , 212
Glove Only Drill, 141 , 142
glucosamine sulfate, 43
gluten, 40
glycogen, 39
goals, 41 , 62 , 82 , 188 , 191
good coaches, 5 , 49 , 209 , 224
good cop, bad cop, 99
good posture, 34 , 47
good teachers, 209
Governing Body Websites, 195
GPA, 186 , 187 , 199 , 279
grades, 26 , 73 , 110 , 185 , 186,
    187 , 196 , 236
greedy, 204
grips, 138 , 139
ground ball rule, 177

H

handpads, 125
Hank Aaron, 173
Heart-felt Handshake, 76 , 180 ,
    255
hard focus, 122 , 142
healthy eating, 41
helicopter parents, 52
hitting fundamentals, 164

hitting machines, 175
hitting tee, 171
holding runners, 144
homework, 53 , 74 , 150 , 180
honey before vinegar approach,
    57
hot boxes, 120
human growth hormone, 43
hydration, 37
hydration, 37

I

Ian Thorpe, 235
individual skills, 17 , 19 , 20 ,
    21, 22
indoor alternative, 91
informed consent, 248
inherent risks, iii, 99 , 250
injury, 26 , 29 , 30 , 31 , 32 ,
    34, 36 , 40 , 43 , 44 , 47 ,
    91, 99 , 128 , 193 , 198 ,
    236, 248 , 250 , 252
integrity, v, ix, xi, 53 , 59 , 81 ,
    93 , 98 , 115 , 199 , 231 , 237
intensity, 20 , 64 , 156 , 217 ,
    225 , 226 , 235 , 267
internal controls, 65
isolate the muscle group, 33

J

Jacoby Ellsbury, 198
Jim Calhoun, 82
Joe DiMaggio, 173
Joe Paterno, 98
John Scolinos, 97
Josè Mourinho, 15
journal, 35 , 38
JUCO's, 205
Jump rope, 151
Jump Rope, 271
JumpRope, 268

Junior Colleges, 205
junk food, 36

K

Ken Griffey Jr, 173
key players, 220 , 221
kidney problems, 39
kinesthetic learner, 95
knee injuries, 47

L

lactosefree milk, 40
Lateral Ball PickUp, 268
Lateral Shuffle Ball Toss, 270
leaders, v, xi, 5 , 9 , 62 , 71 , 72,
    73 , 75 , 78 , 79 , 94 , 233
leadership, 5 , 71 , 72 , 73 , 74 ,
    76 , 79 , 93 , 96 , 112 , 147 ,
    198
leadership skills, 71 , 72 , 96
lean, 38 , 39 , 127 , 128 , 172
learning styles, 94 , 96 , 168
Leo Durocher, 149
let champions play, 210, 212
letter of intent, 205
Letter Writing Campaign, 199
life skills, 13 , 17 , 21 , 62 , 73 ,
    89 , 209 , 210
live pitching, 20 , 167 , 175 ,
    255
loft tosses, 172
Lombardi Rule, 88
Longoria, Evan, 205
long toss throws, 128
losing weight, 39
Lou Piniella, 17

M

machine batting practice, 167
Madeline Levine, 52 , 59

main meals, 37 , 39
manage risk, 99
Marc Antony, 226
max bench, 31 , 45
max squat, 31
maximum development, 36
mechanics drills, 138
Media Rules, 242
media relations, 51
medical release form, 99
meeting expectations, 51
mental approach, 65 , 118 , 120 ,
    138
mental aspects, 50
mental concentration, 29 , 34
mental conditioning, 52 , 62 ,
    115 , 117
mental errors, 63 , 162 , 217
mental imagery drills, 92 , 103
mental toughness, 12
mentality, 206
mentally tough, 63 , 65
metabolism, 37 , 41 , 44
micro tears, 29
micro-managing, 210
microtears, 29 , 114
Miracle Baseball League, 53
Mirror Drill, 152
mirror parts, 32
modeling, v, 89 , 209 , 210
moderation, 44
motivate, 7 , 9 , 18 , 35 , 57 ,
    93 , 167
multi-mineral, 42
multi-sport athletes, 26
multi-tasking, 96 , 97 , 99 , 103 ,
    120 , 133 , 143 , 147 , 160
multi-vitamin, 42
Murphy's Law, 100 , 102
muscle development, 32 , 35 , 41
muscle fatigue, 34

muscle group, 29 , 30 , 32 , 34

muscle growth, 36 , 44

muscle relaxation, 29 , 34

muscle soreness, 44

muscle strength, 32

N

NAIA, 205

Native American Run, 270

natural growth hormone, 44

NCAA, 60 , 189 , 191 , 193 , 195 , 198 , 199 , 201 , 219

negative, 3 , 4 , 34 , 35 , 57 , 58, 62 , 68 , 79 , 110 , 162 , 166 , 173 , 202 , 210 , 212 , 235

negotiating your scholarship, 203

nine best, 246

non-verbal communication, 61 , 254 , 255

nutrition, 36 , 115 , 282

nutritional requirements, 37

O

off-season training, 189

Omaha, Nebraska, 66, 92

Omega-3 fatty acid, 43

one inger curveballs, 140

oral communication drills, 86 , 92 , 158

osteoporosis, 39

out and backs, 157

outfielders, 103 , 134 , 135 , 156, 159 , 255 , 257 , 258

over training, 44 , 47

overstressing, 44

overweight, 40

oxygenated blood, 29

P

partial rep crunches, 34

partnerships, 79

pass pattern drill, 157

pass patterns, 103

pep talk, 226

perfect practice, 4 , 12 , 18 , 28 , 64 , 65, 96 , 111 , 121 , 151 , 164

perfect practice, 6 , 151

performing under pressure, 8

permanent change, 20 , 93

personal coaches, 16 , 17

perspective, 3 , 12 , 28 , 45 , 50, 51 , 53 , 62 , 63 , 189 , 195 , 226

perspective, 50

physical conditioning, iii, 116 , 179 , 256

physical ability component, 185

picks to bases, 120 , 135 , 144 , 256

pitch counts, 143

pitch sequence, 103 , 117 , 136 , 139 , 141, 163, 256, 263

pitchers covering home plate, 146

pitching strategy, 141, 262

player and family contract, 245

playing balls at or off the wall., 158

playing multiple sports, 22 , 25 , 188

points, 75 , 93 , 108 , 118 , 122, 131 , 175 , 217 , 222 , 271 , 272

poles, 59

poor posture, 34

pop times, 197 , 200

pop-up drills, 155

positive reinforcement, 210

Post Camp/Showcase Letter, 203
power leg throw, 127
practice plan, iii, 86 , 89 , 107 ,
   254
prayer, 56 , 79 , 109 , 110 , 181,
   231, 254, 256
Pre-Camp/Showcase Letter, 201
predictability, 96
pre-pitch mental routine, 51
pre-season meeting, 52 , 53 , 58 ,
   85 , 87 , 250
pressure, 5 , 9 , 12 , 20 , 34 ,
   38 , 40 , 54 , 64 , 73 , 93 ,
   120 , 121 , 134 , 150 , 162 ,
   163 , 180 , 212 , 217 , 218 ,
   225 , 235
pre-swing routine, 169
primary modalities, 94
proactive, 50, 177 , 225
Pro Agility Drill, 269
process, 65 , 184 , 194 , 203
process-oriented thinking, 65
progression, 20 , 28 , 30 , 85 ,
   86, 89 , 96, 97 , 99, 110 , 111 ,
   114 , 120, 121 , 123 , 124 ,
   125 , 126 , 127 , 129 , 131 ,
   132 , 133 , 134 , 135 , 152 ,
   159 , 160 , 167 , 169 , 178
   254 , 257
proper equipment, 100
protein, 38
protein shakes, 38

Q

qualified praise, 57
quotes, 14 , 89 , 108

R

"Rainy Day" practice list, 103
range of motion, 29
rapid fire, 123 , 129 , 131 , 132

reaction tosses, 157
Reaction Wall Drill, 269
reasonable goals, 54
receiving mechanics, 121 , 122 ,
   123 , 129 , 147 , 160 , 162
receiving progression, 134
recovery cycle, 36
recruiting class, 190
red-shirted, 189
registration, 199
relationship, 16 , 17 , 170 , 174
 relaxation, 68
relay mechanics, 129 , 269
relays, 129 , 257 , 258
rep, 35
rest, 12 , 22 , 26 , 27 , 36 , 43 ,
   44 , 46 , 47 , 74 , 82 , 116 ,
   117 , 179 , 183 , 185 , 223 ,
   236 , 276
rest intervals, 35
retooling, 20
reward, 62 , 74 , 90
rewards, 62 , 93 , 212
Ricky Williams, 94
right person, 16
right time, 15
right way, 17
role model, 27, 49, 63 , 68 , 71 ,
   72 , 73 , 89, 98, 189, 233
roleplaying, 50
rulebook, 221 , 222 , 223 , 224
run downs, 120 , 257 , 260
running form, 45 , 46 , 103 ,
   111 , 112 , 114 , 117 , 118 ,
   270
Running Form Warm Up, 111 ,
   238
Ruth, Babe 173 , 221

S

salt, 39 , 41

Coaching Champions for Life

Sandy Koufax, 136
SAQ, 41 , 45 , 46 , 47 , 125 ,
   151 , 179 , 180 , 255 , 266 ,
   278
SAQ Drills, 45, 268
SAQ ladders, 45
SAT/ACT scores, 199
scout, college, 19, 186 , 196 ,
   197, 198 , 200 , 201 , 202 ,
   203
scrimmage, 60 , 86 , 108 , 177 ,
   178
self confidence, 66 , 78 , 212
self esteem, 58 , 62 , 141 , 209 ,
   210 , 212
self toss, 174
serious recruiting interest, 194
Set Sequence Drill, 141, 264
set, ready, creep step, 150
short hops, 133 , 134 , 152 , 269
short toss, 20 , 101 , 167 , 172,
   173 , 174
showcases, 186, 195 , 196 , 198,
   201
Shuttle Run, 270
signs, 114 , 115 , 256 , 257 ,
   258
simulation drill, 86 , 97 , 124
skills tape, 201
sleep, 40 , 43 , 44 , 115 , 140 ,
   189 , 217 , 231
slump buster routine, 166
small ball, 218
snacks, 37 , 39
soccer, 15 , 18 , 19 , 47 , 92 ,
   217 , 218 , 219 , 250 , 292
social personality, 83
soda pop, 36
soft focus, 122
soft toss, 20 , 167 , 172
SPARQ, 45 , 198

special teams, 219
Speed, Agility & Quickness, 41
splitting the plate, 143
sport drinks, 37
sport-specific, 36 , 62 , 231
Square Drill, 269
square offs, 124
standard of excellence, 4
starvation mode, 40
static stretching, 28, 239
staying current, 14
staying on time, 108
step behind, 126 , 128 , 175 ,
   260
steroids, 43
strain, muscle 34
strength training, 29 , 30 , 32 ,
   34 , 35 , 36 , 39 , 41 , 140 ,
   143 , 189
stress personality, 83
stretching, 27 , 114 , 256
stride outs, 125 , 260
strike out curveball, 138
structure, 96
student athlete, 27 , 185, 187 ,
   190, 191 , 192, 193 , 205 , 233,
   279
students of the game, 180
study habits, 26 , 74 , 187
sun mechanics, 158
supplements, 38 , 42 , 43
surgeries, 26
symmetrical development, 29
symmetry, 33

T

tablet, 42 , 43
tablets, 42
tag up rules, 177
T Drill, 268
team captains, 79

team chemistry, 12 , 79 , 161 , 162 , 163

team competition, 79

team defense, 163 , 178 , 255

Team Inventory, 243, 83

team rules, 237

tear, 34 , 135

Ted Williams, 15 , 173 , 282

tee, 20 , 104 , 154 , 167 , 171 , 172 , 174

thinking errors, 236

this pitch, this moment, 68

Throwing & Receiving Progression, 260

throwing mechanics, 65 , 68 , 99 , 121 , 123 , 138 , 139 , 140 , 153 , 160 , 163

Tic the tee Drills, 104, 171

Timed Segments, 86

Tom House, 167 , 281

Tommy John, 26

Tony Gwynn, 167 , 173

toxicity, 43

tracking skills, 142

tradition, 9 , 13 , 91

trainer, 32 , 34 , 35 , 39 , 46, 47 147

training, 9 , 22 , 26 , 28 , 30 , 32 , 33 , 34 , 35 , 36 , 37 , 39, 41 , 43 , 44 , 45 , 46 , 47, 66 , 68 , 95 , 96 , 115 , 116 , 122 , 138 , 142 , 147 , 151 , 171 , 179 , 180 , 184 , 188 , 189 , 216 , 250 , 278

training partner, 35

treats, 41

triangle pop-up drills, 103

trick plays, 216 , 217

trophy hunting, 19

trust your instincts, 224

tuition assistance, 186 , 187 , 203

Two Ball Drill, 270

two color ball, 124

U

uniform, 90 , 245

V

verbals, 147

video, 95 , 96 , 139 , 167 , 168

Vince Lombardi, 5 , 18 , 66 , 88

visual learner, 95

visualization, 67 , 68 , 256

visualization drills, 62 , 68 , 139

vitamin D, 40

vitamins, 42 , 43

vocal leaders, 78

W

walkon situations, 190

wall ball, 103 , 151

Wall Ball Routine, 265

warm up, 29 , 32 , 33 , 96 , 103, 111 , 114 , 160

water, 22 , 37 , 40 , 95 , 111

weakest link, 79 , 154 , 180 , 231

weather, 50 , 64 , 65 , 66 , 67 , 79 , 85 , 87 , 91 , 100 , 110 , 138 , 143 , 188 , 195 , 198 , 202 , 220 , 235 , 242 , 249 , 254 , 276

weight lifting, 31

Wooden, John, 5 , 15 , 218 , 281

women athletes, 47

work ethic, 2 , 4 , 5 , 13 , 17 , 108 , 163 , 194 , 234

wrong way turn, 157

Y

yoga, 29
Yogi Berra, 11 , 166

ABOUT THE AUTHOR

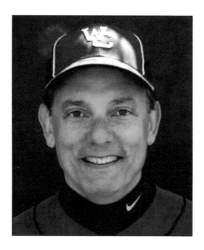

Adam Sarancik has spent most of his adult life coaching youth ages 8-18 in baseball, soccer and basketball. He is a favorite speaker at and director of coaches' and players' clinics. He has also developed several youth baseball leagues.

Adam is known for his comprehensive and innovative practice plans, and for consistently developing championship teams and players who excel at the next level. He earned his Bachelor of Science degree from San Diego State University, his J.D. degree from the University of San Diego School of Law and he is currently pursuing a Masters of Arts in Teaching from Western Oregon University.

He lives with his wife of 36 years, Karen, in Portland, Oregon. They have two daughters, Corinne and Lauren and granddaughters, Amayah and Leiyah.

Coaching Champions
for Life

Coaching the whole person, not just the athlete.

Book Order Form

To order a copy of this book, please call 503-327-9323
or send postal orders to:

Coach Adam Sarancik
25884 SW Canyon Creek Rd. #J201
Wilsonville, Or 97070

Your Name: _____

Address: _____

City: _____ State: _____ Zip Code: _____

Telephone: _____ Date of Order: _____

Signature: _____

# of Books _____ **x $25.00 + $5.00 per book shipping and handling**

Total of check or money order: _____

Coach Adam is available for coaches and players clinics,
personal training and motivational speaking. Please contact
Coach Adam at asarancik@gmail.com or 503-327-9323.

Made in the USA
Charleston, SC
15 May 2012